Praise for
Going Overboard

"Often funny and always humane, an unexpected voice in a world long defined by ironclad rules and abhorrence of emotion. It is that wry take on the life of a military spouse . . . one that questions the rules and regulations of the shadow military she embodies, that Smiley does best." —*The New York Times Magazine*

"Laugh-out-loud humor and poignant honesty set this memoir apart." —*The Florida Times-Union*

"Smiley is so painfully honest that readers who've been there are likely to feel that old familiar hot flush of hysteria." —*The Virginian-Pilot*

"An Erma Bombeck for the military-wife set. . . . [Smiley's] prose is simple and straightforward, and her humor is clever." —*Publishers Weekly*

"Smiley's not afraid to question the tight-lipped culture she inhabits, nor the government's decisions about Iraq. Her new book is sure to make Rummy sweat." —*Philadelphia City Paper*

"[Smiley] writes about her problems (real and imagined) and successes with disarming candor." —Bookreporter.com

"You will find yourself smiling and chuckling to yourself as you read." —DesMoinesRegister.com

GOING
OVERBARD

*the misadventures of a
military wife*

Sarah Smiley

NAL New American Library

New American Library
Published by New American Library, a division of
Penguin Group (USA) Inc., 375 Hudson Street, New York, New York 10014, USA
Penguin Group (Canada), 90 Eglinton Avenue East, Suite 700, Toronto, Ontario,
M4P 2Y3, Canada (a division of Pearson Penguin Canada Inc.)
Penguin Books Ltd., 80 Strand, London WC2R 0RL, England
Penguin Ireland, 25 St. Stephen's Green, Dublin 2,
Ireland (a division of Penguin Books Ltd.)
Penguin Group (Australia), 250 Camberwell Road, Camberwell, Victoria 3124,
Australia (a division of Pearson Australia Group Pty. Ltd.)
Penguin Books India Pvt. Ltd., 11 Community Centre, Panchsheel Park,
New Delhi - 110 017, India
Penguin Group (NZ), cnr Airborne and Rosedale Roads, Albany,
Auckland 1310, New Zealand (a division of Pearson New Zealand Ltd.)
Penguin Books (South Africa) (Pty.) Ltd., 24 Sturdee Avenue,
Rosebank, Johannesburg 2196, South Africa

Penguin Books Ltd., Registered Offices: 80 Strand, London WC2R 0RL, England

Published by New American Library, a division of Penguin Group (USA) Inc.
Previously published in an New American Library hardcover edition.

First New American Library Trade Paperback Printing, July 2006

REGISTERED TRADEMARK—MARCA REGISTRADA

New American Library Trade Paperback ISBN: 0-451-21851-5
The Library of Congress has cataloged the hardcover edition of this title as follows::
Smiley, Sarah.
Going overboard: the misadventures of a military wife/Sarah Smiley.
p. cm.
ISBN 0-451-21667-9
1. Smiley, Sarah. 2. United States. Navy—Biography. 3. Navy spouses—United States—
Biography. 4. Wives—United States—Biography. 5. United States—Social life and
customs. 6. Iraq War, 2003. I. Title.
V736.S65 2005
359'.0092—dc22   2005011559

Set in Requiem
Designed by Elke Sigal

Printed in the United States of America

146122990

For Big Jack,
who always had a trunk full of old books
and a writing file with my name on it

This memoir is based on my real-life
experiences as a military wife.
However, some names have been changed
and details rearranged because, well,
because people made me.

CONTENTS

GOING OVERBOARD

Prologue

DECEMBER 2002

Courtney was the only one I could call at a time like this, mainly because she was the only one likely to be up at midnight, but also because she has a wonderful way of putting my life into perspective.

I grabbed the cordless phone and snuck into the room where I conduct my most important business: the closet.

Courtney answered on the first ring.

"Courtney, I'm so glad you're awake." I glanced over my shoulder and closed the door behind me.

"Sarah? What's wrong? Is anyone hurt?"

And then—exactly then—the tears began to flow, reminding me of the way, when I was a child, I could maintain my composure until the moment I heard my mother's voice.

"Sarah? Is anyone hurt?" Courtney asked again.

"Just my panty hose," I said, sucking in clumps of air.

"Did you say 'panty hose'? Sarah, what's going on?"

I talked between sniffles and sobs. "I threw . . . my panty hose . . . out the front . . . door . . . and my neighbors saw it all!"

Theoretically, this is the part where a best friend is supposed to laugh or remind you that you really are a beautiful person . . . on the inside. This is when it might have been helpful for someone—someone named Courtney—to tell me I wasn't crazy, but passionate—clever, even!

But no, Courtney was silent.

I bit my lip and picked at a loose piece of rubber on the bottom of my pink bunny slippers.

Then finally Courtney said, "Was it—*control top?*"

At first I lied, because, well, no one wants to admit to heavily stitched undergarments. "I really can't remember," I said, wiping away tears with the sleeve of my flannel pajamas, and then added, "Oh, all right! Yes, it was control top—and all the neighbors saw!"

Courtney was as calm as ever. That's because (1) I've surprised her too many times before, and (2) Courtney is always polite. But eventually she had to ask: "Sarah, why did you throw your panty hose out the front door?"

"Well, it wasn't just the panty hose," I said. "I—ah—I kind of threw the entire basket of laundry."

This was difficult to say aloud, especially to someone like Courtney, who keeps copies of *Miss Manners* on her bedside table.

"I see," Courtney said. She was tapping her nails on a counter.

It occurred to me that Dustin might be standing on the other side of the closet door, so I crawled farther into the dark curtain of shirttails and dresses and settled behind a white terry cloth robe, hugging my knees to my chest.

There was a thin, feathery wad of Kleenex in the pocket of my flannel pajamas. I took it out to blow my nose, and when I did, a piece of white prescription paper came out with it.

"Oh, honey, listen to you!" Courtney cried, but I was already distracted. I unfolded the prescription and looked at the signature: Dr. D. Ashley.

"Wait a minute!" she said. "I know what this is about."

I jammed the paper back into my pocket, afraid I'd been caught. But Courtney said, "You saw that helicopter crash on TV tonight, didn't you?"

"What helicopter crash?"

"Oh, you didn't see it? Never mind then."

"Courtney—"

"So!" she said in a phony upbeat voice. "What time is the Spouse Club meeting tomorrow night?"

"Courtney, you can't say 'helicopter crash' and then change the subject!"

"I don't want to worry you, Sarah. I mean, you're not in the best mental state right now."

I held the ball of tissue to my nose. "Just tell me, was it anyone we knew?"

"No, they were from a different squadron," she said. "Look, you can't focus on these types of things right before the guys leave. You know as well as anyone that accidents happen. It's part of the job, and you knew that the day you married a Navy pilot, right?" She laughed. "My gosh, Sarah, *you* of all people should understand that!"

Pshaw! So just because my dad was career Navy, I'm supposed to be prepared for anything the military might dish out? I don't think so!

I made a mental note to check the newspaper in the morning for the crash.

"Anyway," Courtney said, a little too eager now, "the meeting is at Kate's house, right?"

"Yeah . . . No, wait a minute," I said, shaking my head. She was trying to get me off track. "Are you just going to pretend I didn't throw my clothes out the front door tonight?"

Courtney sighed. "Sarah, is your mother-in-law involved in any way?"

"What? Why would you . . . ?"

"There are only three things I know of that could make you throw laundry out the front door: Dustin leaving, your mother-in-law, or a bug in the kitchen you'll swear is five inches long. Am I right?"

How quickly Courtney had turned my crisis into a joke! I gasped out loud and put a hand to my chest. "Well, I never! What makes you think you know every little thing about me, anyway?"

Courtney laughed and then sighed again. "Have you been reading medical stuff online?"

"No!"

"Have you been talking to that doctor of yours?"

Gulp!

I shot upright, knocking my head into wire hangers, which clanked together and fell in a noisy heap.

"Well!" I said sharply. "It's been nice chatting with you, Courtney. Got to go now. Good night."

Dustin was already asleep when I crept out of the closet. That's because he has the maddening habit of being able to fall asleep anywhere—on a bus, at the movies, during dinner. He once took a nap on a bench at Disney World. I, on the other hand, have the unfortunate ability to do just the opposite: I can stay awake for indefinite amounts of time, staring at the ceiling, and working myself up into quite a state over the strange lump on my earlobe, the reason one fingernail grows lopsided, or something very serious like that.

In the middle of the room, a wicker laundry basket was upside down next to two piles of clothes. Dustin must have brought them in from the front yard while I was on the phone, and he'd probably heard me crying through the closet door.

Yet—and this is *so* like him—he'd gone to bed anyway.

Hmpf!

But, on second thought, wasn't it just like *me* to cry in the

4

closet? And in that case, did Dustin have any choice but to ignore my behavior and go to bed? I might as well post a DO NOT DISTURB sign on the closet door for all the times I've held telephone conferences in there.

I hung up the phone on its base and the charger beeped, startling Tanner, my sable-and-white Shetland sheepdog curled up next to the pile of darks. When she heard my feet padding across the room, she jerked her head upright, a mass of fluffy white fur sticking out in all directions from her Lassie-like ears, and sniffed at the air.

"It's all right, Tanner," I said. "Go back to sleep. Everything will be better in the morning."

She huffed noisily and laid her head back on the floor.

I slid under the covers next to—but not touching—Dustin. He stirred in his sleep and I turned my head to look at him. Tucked in a swath of blue floral blankets, he was lying on his side, with his arms crossed over his chest. Such an aloof posture, I thought, especially for sleeping. But was he really asleep, or just pretending in order to avoid another argument?

"I'll miss you," I whispered and turned to go to sleep.

1

I THINK MELANIE
IS TRYING TO SAVE ME

The next night I left my husband. I kissed the tops of our sons' heads—their wispy baby hair sticking to my lipstick—squared my shoulders, and walked out the front door, only stopping to collect my keys from the bead-board telephone stand in the kitchen.

Well, OK, so I wasn't really abandoning them, but it must have felt that way to Dustin when I waved over my shoulder and left him with a hungry newborn and a two-year-old wearing a silver colander on his head like his favorite cartoon character.

I was headed to a Spouse Club meeting, which is the Navy's answer to keeping military dependents occupied and informed. Navy pilots like my husband are organized into "squadrons," and their significant others are lumped into "Spouse Clubs." Membership isn't required, although thirty years ago, when my mom became a Navy wife, service members were "graded" on their spouses' participation. Back then, it was also called the "Wives' Club," but that's considered politically incorrect today, in case female members of the squadron have husbands who'd like to be occupied and informed.

Besides the name, however, not much else has changed since—well, since never. The Spouse Club is and always has been a cross between a sorority and Habitat for Humanity. On the one hand, there is the group's notable contributions to the community—raising money for underprivileged families, doing volunteer work, providing meals for single sailors at Thanksgiving—but one cannot ignore the Club's other side, which is kind of like a Parent-Teacher Association gone horribly wrong.

It doesn't help that our husbands, in their professional lives, are segregated by rank, a notion that is supposed to be overlooked in the Spouse Club but never ceases to be an irritant. Every so often an argument breaks out about "seniority," which none of us spouses are supposed to have anyhow.

In fact, there's an urban legend in military-spouse culture about an Admiral telling a group of wives to arrange themselves according to rank. The women shuffle around murmuring things like "I think my husband is senior to yours" and "My husband is a Commander. Isn't yours just an Ensign?" but once they are lined up from the "most important" to the "least important," the Admiral says angrily, "Wrong! None of you have rank! Only your spouses are in the military."

Alas, this story, admonishing as it may be, hasn't stopped the constant bickering among some wives about whose husband bosses around whose. It'll take someone higher than an Admiral to change the natural instincts of women.

Basically, imagine drinking wine and playing truth or dare—while planning a bake sale—with your husband's boss's wife, but having to pretend she is "just another friend," and that her husband doesn't have any influence over yours. That's what the Spouse Club is like.

Of course, the Spouse Club's primary function is to be a support system for family members left behind when the troops are deployed. In this way, friendships formed within the Club are truly indispensable and border on the familial.

But the Spouse Club is also an excellent source of information for questions ranging from "Can I call my husband while he's on the ship?" (No) to "Why do the other guys call my husband 'Dancing Bear'?" (You don't want to know).

Love it or hate it, the Spouse Club is one of Uncle Sam's necessary evils. When your husband is leaving for six months and he's just penned his social security number on the elastic of his last pair of clean white briefs, there's nothing like a bickering Spouse Club to cheer you up and make you feel ordinary.

It makes sense, then, that on this night, three months before the men were to leave for a six-month deployment, attendance at the meeting was expected to be phenomenal. Wives would flock together with lists of questions about the upcoming assignment. They would gather for support and encouragement and, of course, to see who had gained (or lost) the most weight during the holidays.

Oh, all right, we were also flocking to see if Rhonda showed up or if she truly did ask her husband for a divorce the day after Christmas.

The point is, with the clock counting down the days until our husbands' departure, it was important for us to be together to commiserate and swap stories. In the interest of bonding, of course.

Melanie would be the only exception.

Opposed to any form of gossip, Melanie was truly going to "help out" and "get information." And she was my ride to Kate's house that night, because she had the directions. Melanie always had the directions.

I waited for her on our short concrete driveway, trying to make O's with my breath and wishing I had taken down the Christmas decorations because now they just looked drab. The red front door, once so cheery and festive with a green holiday wreath, looked dirty and dusty. The wreath, in fact, had turned brown and most of its needles were on the stoop below, where they'd probably stay until they disintegrated and became dust, which I'd never sweep up.

Our house wasn't large by any means. I think our builder affectionately called it a "starter home," but it suited us just fine. Our children, Ford and Owen, shared a room, we had a bed next to the computer for guests, and if we parked carefully enough and climbed through the rear hatches of our automobiles, we could fit both our pickup truck and Explorer in the garage.

What sold me on the place, however, was the large picture window in front. Staring at it now from the driveway, I admired, once again, the perfect way the rectangular panes framed our one bold red wall (my idea) and my grandmother Doris's baby grand piano (my mom's idea). Warm light coming from a metal lamp on the piano's ledge reminded me of something out of a Dickens novel.

Who would think such a horrible fight had happened in there the night before? Who would picture "Dustin and Sarah: the world's cutest couple who had known each other since birth" standing inside that very doorway shouting? Who would imagine me throwing laundry out onto the grass and then dusting my hands in good riddance? Who would know that I spun around on my heel and ran into Dustin's chest like an animal flailing against the steel bars of its cage? And who could guess that Dustin grabbed me by the forearms and said flatly, "I can't wait to get out of here"?

I groaned, blowing more frosty air out of my mouth. "The neighbors, that's who." Many of them were standing in the cul-de-sac when our front door flew open and bits of laundry wafted to the ground like clumsy parachutes.

"Oh, well," I sighed, taking in the sight of the living room once more, my chest filling with pride; Mom was going to be so proud of that red wall next time she visited!

Melanie's Suburban rounded the corner and pulled into the driveway. I waved at her and went to gather my purse from the front steps. I was nearly running down the sidewalk, excited about a night out—even if it was for a Spouse Club meeting. (One's standards are so low after two children.)

Then, as soon as I hoisted myself into the passenger seat and saw Melanie's ironed khaki pants and white button-up shirt, I was reminded again that she was probably the only spouse who saw the night for what it was: a meeting.

"How are you?" she said and patted my knee. Her eyes sparkled, but I knew she wasn't wearing any makeup. Melanie never wore makeup.

I rubbed my hands together in the warm air blowing from the vents. "Freezing. How about you?"

"It is unseasonably cold, isn't it?" she said, looking over her shoulder and easing out of the driveway. Then she reached for the radio and adjusted the volume. "Oh, I love this song," she said.

I paused to listen but didn't recognize the lyrics. The music was mostly violins and an organ. "I don't think I've ever heard this before," I said.

Melanie smiled distractedly, then hummed along.

As we drove out of the neighborhood, her boxy SUV eclipsed patio homes sitting so close together you could spit out the kitchen window and hit the neighbor's stucco. Melanie lived in the same part of town, but in a different, more sophisticated subdivision, where her large vehicle looked a little less out of place.

At the first intersection, Melanie carefully turned the corner and merged onto a busier road, singing in a breathy voice, "Thy word is a lamp unto—"

Her hands were set steadfast at "ten and two," and she looked ridiculously petite behind the wheel. I smiled to myself when I thought what she must look like to someone on the street: a small head with wispy hair the color of sand, all but swallowed up by the brown Suburban.

"Thy word is a lamp unto—" she sang.

Christian music! I fidgeted in my seat, suddenly feeling like I took up too much space. Maybe it was the irony of listening to religious music less than twenty-four hours after throwing my panties out the front door and watching them land willy-nilly across the lawn. Maybe it was the fact that as I slammed the bedroom door the night before I screamed, "I hate you!" and Dustin's eyes welled with tears. Maybe it was the fact that I felt totally out of control, and secretly, I worried something was wrong with me—wrong with my marriage.

Did Melanie ever feel confused? I turned to look at her, and the way her profile stayed serene as she weaved in and out of traffic told me probably not.

I decided not to acknowledge the music and instead said, "I really appreciate the ride, Melanie."

She turned and smiled. Her skin was as milky and smooth as velour. "Sure thing!" she said. "I'm glad to have the company."

Melanie's daughter, Hannah, was only a few years older than Ford, but somehow Melanie seemed more like my mother than a mother of my generation. At times she was out of touch—like the way she dreamed of naming two girls Mary-Kate and Ashley, sincerely having no idea who the Olsen twins are—yet other times she shocked me with her hints of style (Ray-Ban sunglasses, chic jogging stroller, a stylish red Acura she only drove on special occasions). Melanie exuded some kind of parental quality, and although she never talked intimately about her relationship with her husband, on the rare occasion I saw them kiss or hold hands, I recoiled like a kid walking in on his parents.

Maybe it was Melanie's motherliness that attracted me to her, despite our differences. Maybe it was the doilies on her coffee table, or the painted wood church she used to cover a box of Kleenex. Whatever the reason, something about her frequently caused me to inappropriately announce my feelings in her presence.

"I really think this predeployment stuff is getting to me," I said suddenly, but Melanie didn't flinch. Perhaps she had already grown accustomed to my unfiltered bursts of emotion.

"I'm so on edge," I said. "I mean, on the one hand I want to spend as much 'quality time' with Dustin as possible before he goes, but on the other hand, he's driving me out of my mind and I can't wait for him to just leave already! Maybe it's knowing what might happen over there in Iraq. Somehow it feels different this time."

I was rambling, so I bit my lip and clutched my sacklike purse closer to my lap. I hadn't thought I was nervous about the meeting, but now I felt like a fake. There I was, the one who had grown up in the Navy, and I was terrified.

"Have you tried praying about it?" Melanie asked. "Maybe you should come to my Bible study group sometime. I'd love to have you come with me."

I pictured Melanie with her group, and an image of women with bows in their hair came to mind. Yet I was surprised by the lump of emotion that rose in my throat.

Kate's house was on the other side of town, or "across the river," as locals like to say, in a fancy planned community with concrete swans spitting water in graceful arcs at the entrance. She was older than I, although not by much, so I surmised this higher standard of living (hardwood floors, track lighting) was due to the fact that Kate was a career woman, and always had been. In other words, Kate had her own money, and probably more of it than our pilot husbands.

When Melanie and I came into the house, dozens of women

were already sitting on a sea grass rug in the open living room. They were chatting and throwing back their heads with laughter, while perfume blanketed the air like netting. I felt uncomfortable—and maybe a little responsible—for Melanie, who is sensitive to strong odors and isn't the chatty type.

Several women called out, "Hey, guys" and "Have a seat" when they saw us come in, but I just waved and scanned the room, looking for a spot where the least amount of small talk would be necessary. Social situations make me restless, and I would rather have banged my head against Kate's plaster walls (painted in shades of taupe, no less) than make small talk about the weather.

I followed Melanie to the kitchen, where she planned to do the adult thing: say hello and thank you to the hostess.

Kate was filling wineglasses with a deep red merlot when we came in. Her platinum hair and rings sparkled under the track lighting and her bright red lips spread into a toothy smile when she turned to see us.

"Oh, my gosh," she cried. "I'm so glad you guys could make it!" She squeezed my shoulder.

"Hi, Kate," I said. "Thanks for hosting this month."

"Oh, but of course!" she said. "I don't know about you, but I'm a wreck. I just can't believe my baby is leaving! Can you? I mean . . . our babies!"

With her manicured red nails and dangly earrings, Kate didn't look much like a "wreck." And what was it with all this "baby" talk? I had to move away before I started to hate her, which was unthinkable because I had admired Kate since the day we first met.

I excused myself to go to the restroom and found Jody in a candlelit sitting room just outside the kitchen. She might have been the only wife there with a healthy helping of appetizers piled on her plate, and she was definitely the only one with a can of beer. She had on blue jeans and a T-shirt with the name of some softball event from 1989 printed across the top. Her attitude toward these meetings was to simply survive the night unnoticed, like a kid who doesn't want to be called on in class. But this outfit and tennis shoes, tinted green from cutting the grass, actually made her stand out all the more.

"I'm glad you came," I said, coming up beside her.

She rolled her eyes. "I can't believe I'm here. Steve had to practically drag my ass out the door."

"Well, it will be a good experience for you, I'm sure," I said, laughing. "Take a good look around. These are the women who will become your family in the next few months."

We both peered around the corner into the living room, and Jody nearly choked on her chicken, because just then, the women—with their cackling laughs and flashy smiles—did seem like creepy Cub Scout moms in an Alfred Hitchcock movie.

This wasn't Jody's first deployment, but it was the first time she planned to "stick it out," as Navy wives often say. The last time our husbands left, Jody went home to her mother in Minnesota. Some spouses see this as "cheating," and Jody certainly felt her share of pressure to do it right this time. When she came back at the end of that last deployment, we wives treated her like the only person who had evacuated before a harmless storm, saying things like "Oh, you wouldn't remember so-and-so, because you weren't here then" and "That must have been when you were gone" or "Gosh, if only you had seen what it was really like, Jody."

I, for one, was proud of her for choosing to stay this time, but mostly for selfish reasons. Jody lived three houses away from me, and she was the only person I knew who allowed her two young boys to play putt-putt on the living room rug. Somehow that was a comfort to me.

"Where'd you get the beer?" I asked. From the smirk on Jody's freckled face, I knew I had walked into a trap.

"You want one?" she said. "Follow me."

We walked through the kitchen, beyond the track lighting, and out the front door with stained glass.

"Where are we going?" I said, doubling my step to keep up.

"We're going to get you a beer." Her hands were shoved in the back pockets of her jeans.

It wasn't hard to spot Jody's car. Even if it hadn't been parked diagonally in the driveway, with one tire dug into Kate's grass, the purple minivan (affectionately called "Barney") with a Harley-Davidson plaque where the front license plate should have been was hard to overlook.

I opened the passenger door and the smell of McDonald's chicken nuggets and dirty socks hit me at once. It was an aroma I had come to expect from Jody's car, and it was as comforting as knowing I'd have to throw baseball mitts and golf shoes to the floor before sitting down.

Jody fell into the driver's seat and released her thick brown hair from a ponytail. Strands of wavy, air-dried hair fell around her face, and the smell of Pantene rose in the air. She wore her hair up so often, she had a permanent bump in the back of it.

With the ponytail holder clasped between her teeth, she rummaged through partially melted ice in a cooler on the floor, then handed me a beer. I cracked open the wet can and shivered. Jody had hers clasped between her legs, and I watched with curiosity as she effortlessly looped her hair back through the band—now wet from her teeth. My hair is so slippery and straight, it takes a good amount of teasing and "goo" to get it into a ponytail. I could never just "flip it back" the way Jody often did.

I took another sip of beer and exhaled as the tingly liquid cooled my throat and chest, and then my stomach.

"I think Melanie's trying to save me," I said.

"What do you mean by 'save'?" Jody asked.

"You know, like she thinks I need saving . . . like I'm a bad person or something."

"Get out of here," Jody yelled. "You are way too sensitive. What on earth makes you think Melanie is trying to save you?"

"She was playing Christian music in the car."

"So?"

"So I think it was on purpose." I took a sip of beer and closed my eyes. Then I jerked upright again. "Hey, wait a minute. Why didn't you carpool with us?"

"Well, I would have, but Melanie didn't offer me a ride."

"You see! That's my point! She wanted to isolate me. That's what they always say about those 'saver' people. They try to get you away from your support network."

Jody laughed and smacked me over the head. "What's the matter with you? Maybe she tried to call and I wasn't home. We took the kids to play mini-golf today."

Jody's theory was entirely plausible. She and her husband, Steve, are the only people I know who still don't have an answering machine or call-waiting. Getting in touch with Jody is a complicated process consisting of dialing her number every ten minutes, then acting casual and a little less obsessive when she finally answers.

"Well, I don't know," I said, "but just imagine if she knew about Cute Doctor!"

Jody took a sip of beer. "Oh, she'd have you praying about that one for sure. And also for this." She held up the can and smiled.

"Speaking of," I said. "I found one of the doctor's prescriptions in my pajama pants last night."

Jody's eyes grew wide. "You never got it filled?"

"No. I mean, you know me—I was too afraid."

"Oh, well," she said, "at least you didn't keep the prescription to stare at his name all day. That would be—"

"Obsessive?"

"Exactly."

"Oh, yeah," I said. "It's not like I would just stare at his signature or anything."

I looked away and out the window just as headlights pierced the darkness and swept across the interior of the minivan. "That's probably Courtney," I said.

Jody looked at the clock. "Maybe we should get her a watch for her birthday."

"Wouldn't help," I said, knowing full well that not having a watch wasn't Courtney's problem. She is notoriously late to every event, which is ironic because she considers books like *Service Etiquette* something other than bathroom reading material.

A car door thumped closed in the distance and I peered through the dark window to see. There was the silhouette of a woman, backlit by the streetlight and burdened by a heavy bag, making her way up the driveway. "Yep, that's her," I said, turning toward Jody again. "What do you think she has in that big purse of hers?"

"Some vitamins? A hair dryer? Who knows?" Jody rolled her eyes, then pounded on the window.

Courtney jumped. "Who's there?" she called out and shaded her eyes with her hand.

I couldn't help but laugh; Courtney was so fragile.

Jody rolled down the window—a painfully slow process because it wasn't automatic—and said, "Hey, hey, hey."

"What are you guys doing in there?" Courtney said, coming closer to the car.

I hunched down to see across Jody and out her window. "Jody's afraid of the Stepford Wives inside."

Courtney frowned disapprovingly. "But you don't want to miss the meeting." She shifted her purse higher on her shoulder. Then she looked straight at me with her narrow blue eyes. "Especially not you, Sarah—not after last night."

"What happened last night?" Jody looked back and forth between the two of us, and I knew she was feeling left out.

"Oh, well!" Courtney said. "Sarah calls me at midnight, crying about some laundry she threw out the front door. I tried to calm her down, but you know how she gets." She smiled at Jody.

Jody turned in her seat to look at me again. Her expression changed from one of confusion and envy to one of concern. "What happened, Sarah?"

"Dustin was being a jerk, all right? I was having a mental breakdown about this deployment and he just sat there watching football." I finished my beer and put the can inside a Happy Meal box at my feet.

"Oh, well, he was watching football!" Courtney said. "You didn't tell me that part. You should know that men can't be disturbed during a game."

"Maybe zoning out with the game is Dustin's way of coping," Jody said, her knack for family counseling emerging. "Don't mistake watching a good game—it was the play-offs, after all—for not caring."

I got out of the car and walked toward Courtney. We hugged hello and exchanged the mandatory "you look nice" sentiments. Of all the women in the group, Courtney and I probably were the most alike. I understood things about her—such as her need to watch and comprehend *Oprah* on a deeper level than most—and I knew what she meant when she claimed to be "an inherently shy person who has trained herself to be outgoing." People even said we look alike. We're both short—or petite, as Courtney would say—with long, skinny fingers, short waists, and disproportionately large heads. (Well, actually, Courtney's fluffy Barbie doll hair accounts for much of the size of her head, so maybe it is just mine that is large.)

Jody got out of the car and came to stand beside us on the driveway.

"I think I've hit a new low," I said. "Growing up, I saw my mom do a lot of crazy stuff before my dad's deployments, but I can honestly say I never saw her throw laundry."

"You should have called me," Jody said, and I wondered then why I hadn't. There were times when I went straight to Courtney, and other times when only Jody would do. Courtney speculated that I chose who to call based on the answer I knew I would get or, more precisely, the answer I knew I wanted.

I took a deep breath and stared out across the lawn. "It's all Dustin's fault because he keeps hounding me about the checkbook."

"Geez! Would he cut it out about your finances, already!" Jody threw a hand up in the air. She knew Dustin well enough to say this; otherwise I might have been offended.

"What did y'all do last deployment?" Courtney asked. "Didn't you take care of everything while he was gone?"

I rubbed my forehead. A headache was beginning to form across my brow. "I really can't remember. It was all such a blur, with Ford being a newborn and all. Honestly, back then I never gave any of it much thought. I was merely surviving."

This was only partly true. Yes, the first deployment was a sleep-deprived blur—how well does anyone remember the weeks after their first baby was born?—but standing there on the driveway, I was positively sure I hadn't kept track of the checkbook. Me at the helm of our finances was like putting a knobby-kneed teenager in high heels. Dustin had never even considered leaving me in charge of the bills. So why was he taunting me with it now? Did he really have plans to hand over the reins this time? Or was it some kind of game?

"So what's changed?" Courtney said, raising a thin, plucked eyebrow. "Why is it such an issue now?"

"I wish I knew. But something is different this time."

The three of us stood in silence for a moment. I kicked the toe of my shoe against the ground and stared at white Christmas lights blinking on a house across the street. It was bad enough not to take the decorations down, but to turn them on a week past Christmas! Frankly, it was depressing, and the twinkling lights seemed to punctuate the heaviness gnawing inside me.

Finally, Jody broke the quiet: "Do you want Steve to talk to Dustin?"

"No, we'll be fine." I tucked my hair behind my ears and stared at my feet.

We were all staring off in different directions, presumably absorbed in deep thoughts. Then Jody burped and I laughed.

"You guys are so uncouth," Courtney clucked. "I swear!"

Jody looked at me and I shrugged.

The meeting was just getting started when the three of us walked through the front door. Kate had already cleared everyone's plates and was dishing up cheesecake for dessert.

"Here, let me help you," Courtney said, coming into the kitchen. She dropped her purse on the floor and went to Kate's side like a magnet. While she made herself useful distributing plates and forks, Jody and I went to the back of the room, carefully stepping between wineglasses sitting on the floor beside the women's laps. When I settled into a spot, I looked up and saw Melanie watching me. She smiled and I instantly regretted ditching my carpool buddy. It was guilt I vaguely recognized, like spotting your parents at a high school football game but being too embarrassed to sit with them. Melanie looked lost and small, and I felt a pang of sadness for her. But I just smiled apologetically, then looked away.

Kate made her way to the front of the room while Courtney finished serving the dessert. As the Spouse Club president, Kate had to officially begin the meeting. Years ago, groups might have rapped a gavel on a table to get everyone's attention, but seeing as how these meetings were now purely . . . I mean, somewhat . . . social, many formalities had fallen by the wayside.

Kate clapped her hands. "OK, ladies," she said, "can I have your attention up here please?" Everyone's eyes turned toward her in front of the thick white mantel of the fireplace. It was safe to address us as "ladies" because there was only one female pilot in the squadron and her husband had opted not to be a part of the Spouse Club. He'd said he wasn't interested in glossy magazines and gossip, but we hardly noticed the insult—we were all too busy lamenting the fact he was a professional cook and should have been making us dinner.

"As you all know," Kate said, "the men will begin the workup phase of their deployment next month, and of course, the six-month assignment will officially begin in April."

Moans rippled across the room. Some women—including Courtney—took tissues from their purses. A wife I didn't recognize, who looked all of nineteen years old and ninety pounds, raised her hand. "Um, what are workups?" she said. "I thought my husband was only going to be away for, like, six months? How come no one told us about this workup stuff?"

Kate nodded to Margo, the Commanding Officer's wife. Generally, technical questions about the squadron's schedule are best handled by the person married to, shall we say, the horse's mouth.

Margo stepped down from her place on a bar stool near the kitchen. Because of her husband's position of authority over ours, the CO's wife is an honorary member of the Spouse Club and only serves as the group's adviser. In this way, the CO's wife is an exception to "spouses carrying no rank," and we all moved our feet and glasses to the side as she passed through to the front of the room.

Margo was a petite woman with short, tousled hair. She was wearing a skort and a necklace with a tennis racket pendant. I leaned over and whispered in Jody's ear, "Gosh, she looks great for her age." Honestly, I didn't know what "her age" was. It just seemed like a good thing to say—like something my mom would have said at a Spouse Club meeting.

Looking sincerely—almost maternally—at the group, Margo began her spiel: "Workups are a necessary part of training," she said. "Before the crew leaves for the official deployment, they need these workups to prepare. The squadron will be going on several detachments, of two or three weeks, with maybe a week in between. However, it will feel like these separations are back-to-back, so you might as well keep your husband's seabag packed."

Margo laughed at herself, but no one took her lead, so she cleared her throat and said, "Anyway!" Then she took a deep breath and surveyed the room. She seemed to be choosing her words carefully now. "We've gotten word that the first workup will happen earlier than originally planned. The squadron will be leaving one week from tomorrow. They will be gone for two weeks."

The room was so quiet, you could hear Jody's fork noisily scraping her dessert plate. Courtney sniffled. If it weren't for the warm, soothing sensation the beer had made in my stomach, I might have started crying, too.

The fact that the men were leaving for a workup wasn't the alarming part; we all knew workups would begin sometime before the deployment. Rather, it was the suddenness of it, coupled with recent reports of tension rising in the Middle East. In the back of our minds, we all knew Margo's announcement was far from "routine," even though she tried her darnedest to make it appear that way.

"I know this is upsetting news," Margo said. "We all thought we had at least another month before it all began. But things like this happen sometimes. We, as spouses and our husbands' support system, need to remember to be flexible and patient."

Leslie, who was eight months pregnant, raised her hand. "I

don't understand!" Her voice was shaking but determined, almost angry. "What about my baby? I'm due in a few weeks! How can they just change the schedule like that?"

"I know. I know." Margo put her hands up defensively in front of her. "Keep in mind that neither your spouse nor mine has control over the Navy's schedule. Nobody could have seen this coming."

"I don't mean to sound selfish here," Leslie said. "It's just that, well . . . a baby! What will I do? Will they send my husband home?"

Margo shook her head slowly, yet seemed afraid or unwilling to say the word no aloud.

All at once women talked out of turn, speaking louder and faster than the person next to them. Margo, looking resigned, put her hands in the pockets of her denim skort. Her sculpted brown arms were set off by her maple hair, and although her cheeks were flushing with frustration—fear? anger? embarrassment?—she nodded sympathetically at everyone who was trying to ask questions. Her style was one of casual elegance, very East Coast. I imagined her, like myself, growing up on the Chesapeake Bay. But the first time I met Margo's husband (Dustin's boss), I was shocked by his coarse Texas accent and his tendency to say things like, "Well, Say-rah, your Dustin is a fine lad, Ah tell you." He and Margo were a complete mismatch and just then, as the room lost control and Margo struggled to speak, I found myself wondering what their sex life must be like.

"Wait a minute! Everyone calm down," Margo said. "Let me say one more thing." The room quieted to a few murmurs here and there and Margo continued, straining her feathery voice to be heard.

"I know many of you saw the news coverage of a helicopter crash last night. I got a lot of calls from anxious wives, so I want to reiterate here tonight that if, God forbid, there is an accident with one of our men, you all will be officially notified before you hear it on the news. I cannot stress this enough. If a plane goes down and it's one of ours, the wife of the downed pilot will be notified in person, and the rest of the Spouse Club will be notified via the phone tree. On that note, raise your hand if you need to update your emergency information."

We glanced around the room at one another, but no one raised a hand. We were too busy swallowing the words "downed pilot."

"Emergency forms" are a grim part of Spouse Club life. They go along with the general theme of so many aspects of the military: Necessary Evil. The questions seem nonthreatening enough—"Emergency contact not related to you," "Who has a key to your home?" "Who has permission to pick up your kids at school?"—but it is the obvious implication of the form that makes you want to go back out to the van for another beer.

"Anyway," Margo said, "I'm going to pass this sheet around and I want everyone to list their current information—address, phone number, e-mail—anything we might need to get in touch with you during an emergency. And if you need to update your emergency form, please pick one up before leaving tonight."

Kate stepped forward again, visibly shaken, with splotches of red creeping up the fair skin of her neck. Obviously Margo hadn't forewarned her about the news.

"For those of you who, like me, are feeling a little anxious about this upcoming deployment," she said, "I've invited Brenda Crawford from Fleet and Family Support to talk to us about what to expect. Mrs. Crawford will be able to answer your questions about dealing with stress and the different emotions we're all feeling."

Kate turned and nodded at a heavyset woman with short salt-and-pepper hair. There was a flutter of light applause as the woman rose from a chair and made her way through the maze of laps and wineglasses. Her polyester skirt and panty hose brushed against each other and made a terrible scratching sound.

At the fireplace, the two women shook hands; then Kate sat down on the arm of an overstuffed leather chair. There was an awkward moment as the woman riffled through a stack of hand-outs, her breath audible and strained; then she cleared her throat and began.

"First, I want to thank you for having me here tonight. I'm sure you all have questions, but before we get to that, I want to pass out a brochure with important phone numbers and informa-tion about Fleet and Family Support's counseling services—"

I couldn't help it—my mind began to wander. I thought about how weird it was to be sitting there in the role of "wife." Grow-ing up I had gone to countless Wives Club meetings with my mom. Each Club has its own set of rules, and Mom always lobbied that children be allowed at meetings. She was pretty adamant about that, mostly because of my unhealthy, yet unwavering, at-tachment to her. While the other kids ransacked the hostess's playroom and snuck forbidden sweets past the meeting room, snickering and giggling as they went, I stayed next to Mom, hid-ing my face behind her arm.

"Keep this information in a safe place," Mrs. Crawford was saying when Jody handed me a stack of papers. I took one and passed the rest to my right. When I looked up, I saw Courtney sitting at Kate's feet, a pen and a notebook poised in her hand. Her back was erect and she was nodding enthusiastically at the speaker. I was dying to see what she would write in that notebook.

Next to Courtney, sitting cross-legged on the floor, was Sasha. Although Sasha was much older than most of the group (who av-eraged approximately twenty-eight), she dressed like a teenager. Her flat chest and waiflike figure lent themselves nicely to the spaghetti-strap-shirt-and-capri-pants outfit that was her signa-ture style. Her pixie haircut was usually disheveled or spiked, and she carried a backpack instead of a purse. The thing that irritated me most about Sasha though was that she always walked into a room talking and didn't shut up until she left. Her silence at the meeting that night was like something "off" that everyone probably felt but couldn't put their finger on.

"Are you listening to this?" Jody whispered at me.

I looked back at Mrs. Crawford. She had her hands clasped in a triangle in front of her heavy bosom, reminding me of my old college professor who held his hands together like a tepee and pressed his lips to the tips of his fingers when he was thinking.

"Many of you are in stage one, or predeployment," Mrs. Crawford said. "This might explain your increased nerves and agitation. You are on the cusp of a typical emotional cycle, which mirrors patterns of grief. Right now you might feel distant from your spouse. You might even be fighting more than usual. This is all part of the process of separation. Subconsciously you know it will be easier for your spouse to leave if you are mad at him."

Hmmpf!

Mrs. Crawford clearly had it all wrong. I wondered if she was ever even in the military, because obviously she was missing a critical point: I wasn't mad at Dustin to protect myself emotionally. This wasn't some sort of psychological game. Oh, no, it was much worse than that. I was truly so mad I could spit! He was about to abandon me again—this time with *two* small children—and I worried I might never get over it. I knew when Dustin left, I would only have two options: either fall apart or grow up . . . possibly without him.

2

THAT'S ILLEGAL OR
SOMETHING, ISN'T IT?

Afew nights later, Dustin and I invited Jody and Steve and
Courtney and her husband, Derek, over for dinner. It
would be our last hurrah together before we separated into our
individual families, like bears hibernating before the first winter
storm. Typically, just before the squadron leaves, husbands and
wives become somewhat reclusive as they try to "make the most"
of the time they have left. It's not unusual for military wives to
take leave from work, stop taking phone calls, and put every other
aspect of their normal lives on hold while they wait for the big
good-bye. For instance, someone might use this time as an excuse
to quit doing laundry or making dinner . . . not that I would know
much about that or anything.

Usually, though, this sort of behavior comes right before the
deployment, not a detachment, and the fact that we were already
falling into predeployment mode further intensified everyone's
fears that something was different this time.

We had arranged for a babysitter at Jody's house and left all
the children there. Then the six of us gathered for fondue and

game night in my small living room, which seemed claustrophobic with more than two people in it. The three men, with their broad shoulders and long feet, awkwardly filled up the space and made me feel guilty for not having more furniture for everyone to sit on. Tanner skittered among the laps filled with plates of cheese fondue, sniffing at the air and whimpering. She begged not for pats on the head (she was never an overaffectionate dog), but for a scrap of pita bread or a bit of apple.

We were playing our favorite group game, which has no name because we totally made it up. Basically, someone asks another person a question, and once they answer, the asker must decide whether it is a "truth" or "lie." The person who detects the most lies wins.

It's a great game, but it should be played with caution, because without mentioning any names (Courtney), I know some people use it as an opportunity to find answers to their most bothersome queries: Which of my friends does my husband think is the most attractive? If I died, who would he date? Which part of my body does my husband like the least?

Why do women ask these questions? We want to know the answer about as badly as we want a nail through the eyeball. But more troublesome than that, why do our husbands actually answer them?

Courtney opened the first Pandora's box and threw it squarely at her husband: "Derek, if you could pick anyone besides me to be your wife, who would it be?"

Derek was too far into the gin and tonics to be tactful. He raised his eyebrows, wrinkling the pinkish skin just below his receding hairline, and said without hesitation, "Carmen Electra. Dude, she's hot!"

Courtney's mouth flew open. "But I don't look anything like Carmen Electra," she cried. She was sitting on the floor with her legs tucked beneath her.

Derek looked at Dustin and Steve and smiled. "Exactly!"

"So it's a truth then," Courtney said.

"Heck, yeah, absolutely," Derek said.

Like winged fairy godmothers, Jody and I fluttered to Courtney's aid: "He doesn't mean it," I said. And Jody added, "It wouldn't be a fantasy if it was someone just like you."

But Courtney recovered quickly and simply said with a wave of her hand, "You don't even understand the game, Derek!"

"What do you mean?" He smiled again at Dustin and Steve for backup. "You asked me a question, and I answered and then you guessed it was a truth."

"That *is* how we play the game," Dustin agreed, smirking at us women.

Courtney groaned. "Mental Lilliputians, I swear!"

Jody and I looked at each other; her eyebrows were creased and questioning. "It must mean something like cavemen," I said, shrugging.

Next it was Derek's turn to ask the question. He cleared his throat and puffed up his chest, drawing attention to the yellow-orange hair visible through the open top button of his Hawaiian-print shirt. "This one's for Sarah," he said.

He was grinning, and that made me nervous, so I grabbed a handful of pretzels from the plastic snack tray in front of me and stuffed them in my mouth.

"If you weren't married to Dustin, who would you be hot for?" Derek asked.

"You mean, 'in love with,'" Courtney corrected him.

Derek scratched at the bald spot on the back of his head. "Yeah, that's what I said: Who would she be hot for?"

Courtney rolled her eyes.

I thoroughly chewed and swallowed the mouthful of pretzels, trying to delay.

Gulp!

"Oh, come on," Derek shouted. "We don't have all night!"

I laughed anxiously. I was never good at bluffing in this game. The others could always tell by the smirk on my face or the way the corners of my mouth quivered that I was telling a lie, not a truth.

"But there's no one except Dustin," I said sheepishly.

"Answer the question," they all yelled.

I sighed. "OK, well, I guess it would be my . . . gynecologist."

Steve and Derek nearly fell over with laughter. "No way," Derek cried. "That's the best thing I've ever heard!"

But Dustin just stared at me. His honey-colored eyes never blinked.

"Now wait a minute," I said. "No one has guessed whether mine is a lie or a truth."

"Oh, that's got to be a truth," Steve said.

"Well, yeah, kind of." I put more pretzels in my mouth.

"Dr. Ashley?" Dustin said. "The one I know?"

I talked with my mouth full: "Yeah, he's really cute . . . and nice . . . and sensitive."

"That's because he's your doctor!" Derek said. "He's *supposed* to be nice and sensitive."

"It's like waitresses," Steve said. "They're always nice—even the hot ones—because they want a big tip. It's their job."

Jody put out a hand to hush everyone. "Hey, we didn't pick apart anyone else's answer. Remember the rules: no questions asked."

"But her doctor?" Derek said again. "I mean, that's like illegal or something, isn't it?"

"She didn't say she was having an affair with him," Courtney said. "She said he's cute, that's all. Trust me, we've all heard about Cute Doctor. Sarah's always had this, shall I say, *improvident* sort of crush on him."

I looked at Jody and said, "It means irresponsible. An irresponsible crush."

Dustin was still staring at me and not smiling or blinking. His bottom jaw was thrust outward, the way it always is when he's thinking, which made the square shape of his head seem even more rugged and hard. The lines that usually frame his mouth like parentheses were smoothed out and invisible.

I shrugged and tried not to look at him. "It's not a big deal."

Jody got up for another beer and called over her shoulder, "OK, Sarah's turn to ask now."

Steve had been quiet, and I don't know who elected me conversation police, but I always find myself worrying about anyone who isn't talking in a group.

"All right," I said, "this one's for Steve."

I felt pleased and somehow responsible for the way Steve unfolded his legs and leaned back on his wide hands. Generally, the men dreaded our questions because ours were more thought-provoking and potentially dangerous than theirs.

"Go for it," Steve said.

"OK, if Jody could be in any profession, what do you guess it would be?"

Steve rubbed his prickly chin, and looked thoughtfully at the ceiling. In this game, though, you can't stall too long or everyone will know you're constructing a lie, so very quickly afterward he said, "She's always wanted to be a policewoman, actually."

"Really?" Courtney and I said together. "Like with an actual gun?" Courtney added.

"That's got to be a lie," I said, then looking at Jody: "Isn't it?"

She was blushing and pulled at her taut ponytail. "No, he's telling a truth," she said. "It's something I've always thought about, once the kids are older, maybe."

Derek slapped his knee. "Dude, I think that's like the coolest thing I've ever heard . . . next to Sarah having the hots for her doctor."

Courtney threw a balled-up cocktail napkin at him and it hit him in the forehead.

Frankly, however, all this talk of Jody having a desire to carry a gun made me uncomfortable. It was as unsettling as looking at my mom's high school yearbook, or hearing stories about my dad's childhood girlfriend. These things simply aren't supposed to happen. Well, they can happen, of course, but I'm not supposed to know about them. Jody was always just— Well, she was just "Jody." The idea of her having a life outside of what I knew about her was shocking.

I stuffed more pretzels in my mouth.

"All right, Dustin," Steve said. "Your turn to answer: Did you know that your wife has the hots for her doctor?"

"Yes," Dustin said without hesitation, and Derek yelled, "No way, man! That's such a lie! Did you see the look on his face when she said it? There's no way he knew!"

"Yep, got to be a lie," they all said.

I didn't guess.

"Dude, I hope it's a lie," Derek said. "Or else, why do you let her go to him?"

"So is it true or not?" Steve said to Dustin. "Did you really know?"

Dustin looked straight at me. "No, it's a lie."

The next few days passed quickly, like the last days of summer vacation when you're a kid. Dustin and I had recovered from the fight about the checkbook and "the laundry incident" (as we were calling it now), but everything seemed raw and unstable, as if we could slip and begin fighting again at any minute. He never mentioned Dr. Ashley. And I didn't either.

It was as if we were in a slow march to the inevitable: the day he would leave. True, he was only leaving for two weeks at this point, but once the workup phase begins, it's a fast unraveling to deployment: The squadron is home two weeks, gone for three; home one weekend, gone for two.

In some ways, this home-again-gone-again schedule is even worse than the actual deployment. Just when you get into a routine and are comfortable with the idea of your husband being away, he comes back. But only for the week. The day when the ship leaves for good, not to return for at least six months, is awful, but the process beforehand—the training and workups—feels like pulling off a Band-Aid one agonizing millimeter at a time. Wives begin to think, "I wish he would just leave and get it over with." They're eager to rip the Band-Aid off in one daring pull. But these thoughts inevitably turn into guilt, in that ominous be-careful-what-you-wish-for sort of way.

Dustin and I had been avoiding the D word (deployment) all week. I guess our reasoning was "If we don't talk about it, it doesn't exist." Or maybe that was just Dustin's reasoning, because the real reason I never brought it up was simply that I expected Dustin to read my mind and bring it up first. This dangerous mental game of chicken is the only sport I play and excel at, which irritates Dustin endlessly. "You always beat me to the punch," he'll say. "First you tell me what you want for your birthday, and then you're sad I didn't buy something else. Why don't you just trust me to pick out something on my own?"

The day I finally spilled the D word, we were waiting in the lobby at the base legal clinic. Drawing up wills was something that needed to be done, and Dustin, being the responsible person he is, wanted to take care of it now, rather than later . . . just in case.

The waiting room was like most military facilities—fluorescent lights overhead (some functioning, some merely flickering greenish-yellow light), metal chairs covered with plastic that was cracking, and a large triangular sign glued to the beige cement that read FALLOUT SHELTER.

I was flipping through an outdated issue of *AARP* magazine while Dustin watched the news on a boxy television set hanging from the ceiling. Words like "Iraq" and "war" and "troops" echoed from the news anchor's tiresome voice and filled up the room like a fog. Owen was asleep in the baby carrier on the floor, and I was rocking him with my foot. Ford played with a red-and-yellow plastic toy kitchen, which, by the looks of its white-turned-gray pots and pans, seemed like it had been around since the Gulf War. Every child on base had probably played with that kitchen while their parents waited to make wills.

I looked up from my magazine, suddenly struck by our surroundings, and said, "Can you believe we're here doing this?"

"Huh?" Dustin's eyes were fixed on the television. A muscle in his jaw flinched as he leaned his ear closer to me.

"I mean, can you believe you're leaving for deployment so soon?" And just like that, the D word was out of my mouth and floating through the air like a hovering blanket of insects. I instantly regretted bringing it up first. How long would it have taken Dustin to address the situation without my prompting? I would never know.

"We've still got a few months," he said without looking at me.

"Well, not really. Now that the workups are starting, time will go by fast. You'll be leaving for the deployment before we know it."

Dustin turned in his seat and stared at me. "You're really worrying about this, aren't you?" His five o'clock shadow, which always seems to appear midmorning instead of late afternoon, was just beginning to soften the sharp lines of his jaw.

"Oh, I wouldn't say I'm *worried*, really." My voice became unnaturally breezy; I was aware of Ford listening to us as he pretended to cook a plastic hot dog in the toy microwave.

"Then what is it?" Dustin said, looking back at the television.

"I guess—I guess I just don't know what to expect."

"But you've grown up with this stuff, Sarah. It's nothing new."

At first I thought he was being sarcastic. I watched his profile, waiting for him to smirk and say, "I'm just kidding. What's on your mind, hon?" But he stared up at the television.

Nothing new? Apparently Dustin had failed to notice the demanding infant and toddler who had taken up residence in our house. I was indignant.

"You're kidding me, right?" I said. "Nothing new? I'm going to be the sole person responsible for two little children while you're away. We have no family nearby to help me, and you won't spend the money to hire a full-time babysitter!"

I paused for effect and Dustin turned to meet my stare. His face was blank and I realized he might not have heard anything I had said. I didn't want to fight—not today, not again, not here—but blood burned in the tips of my ears.

I laughed bitterly. "Oh, but that's right, honey. You don't even know what it's like to be responsible for a family. You're too busy packing your seabag every other month." This was an exaggeration, but, in fact, he had only been home for six months out of the two years since Ford was born.

Dustin glanced at me. His eyes seemed to be scanning my face for clues. I wondered if he felt just as angry but was too sad to start an argument.

"Well, you know," he said, looking up at the television again, "you might feel a little more confident if you'd let me teach you how to balance the checkbook—"

I rolled my eyes and groaned. "That's the least of my concerns, Dustin! I can learn how to balance the checkbook online! Geez!" I shook open the coffee-stained magazine again. "Why don't you just get over the whole bank account thing or take the damn checkbook with you, for all I care?"

Dustin sat back in his seat and put a bent arm behind his head. "OK, tell me what you're worrying about, then."

The fact that he wasn't looking at me made me anxious. I was reminded of a time when I was eleven and tried to start a conversation with my dad. We were standing on the back patio and Dad had just fired up the grill for hamburgers. He was whistling and standing with one hand in the pocket of his faded corduroy pants, a posture I always thought exaggerated his broad, rounded shoulders. A bird swooped down and landed several feet away from us on a bird feeder. "What kind of bird is that?" I asked. Dad turned over patties with a spatula and said distractedly, "Hmm?" I didn't repeat my question and he didn't seem to notice.

Conversations with my dad always went that way. He blamed it on "compartmentalization," which is a skill the military teaches people—to focus on one thing at a time, or to compartmentalize their emotions away from their intellect. It's an important skill for keeping pilots and soldiers safe in combat, but unfortunately, compartmentalizing sometimes rears its ugly head at home, too.

Now, as I sat next to Dustin, who was engrossed in the television, I had a familiar lump of emotion in my throat and my eyes stung.

"Well," I said, tossing the magazine onto a faux-wood coffee table, "I'm worried that I won't be able to handle the boys, that I won't be able to keep up with the grass and the home repairs, and that"—I paused and bit my lip—"and that, well—that you won't come home this time."

Dustin reached over and patted my knee. "That's my Sarah! Always borrowing trouble! I'll be gone less than a month and you'll be on to worrying about something else. Promise." He smiled and turned toward the television again.

I swallowed hard and stared at the side of his face. He had the same blank look as my dad, like their minds are elsewhere.

Then without looking at me, Dustin grinned and said, "Just promise me this: If you find a roach in the kitchen while I'm gone . . . don't sell the house."

"I'm trying to be serious, Dustin."

"So am I!" He crossed his arms over his chest. End of discussion.

I picked up another tattered magazine and flipped deliberately through the pages. I read nothing. Ford asked me to open a pretend milk jug for him and Owen sucked on his pacifier so hard it made a wet, squeaking sound. I pulled the plaid flannel blanket up under his chin.

A few moments later, the door opened and a man I didn't recognize walked in. He and Dustin looked like twins: same olive green flight suit, same red-and-black patches Velcroed to the chest, same clunky black boots. He was obviously from Dustin's squadron, but I didn't recognize the last name embroidered on his name badge. Must be a bachelor, I thought.

Dustin turned to look when he heard boots clomping on the cement floor. When he saw who it was, he stood up, stretching out his right hand. "Sean, man! What's up?" he said. The two of them shook hands and patted each other's backs. "This is my wife, Sarah. I don't think you've ever met."

I lifted from my seat only halfway and shook Sean's hand. We made some small talk about the circumstances ("Depressing place, huh?" "I know you must be getting lots of things ready for Dustin's deployment."). Then he sat down across from Dustin.

"Doing your will?" Dustin asked him.

"Yeah, man," he said. "Not much to leave anyone though—just my Corvette, I guess. I'm packing up all my stuff and putting it in storage while we're gone."

Sean's voice surprised me. He was so muscular, he had no neck to speak of, but when he talked, his voice was soft and almost feminine.

"Who's going to handle your mail? Your bills?" Dustin asked, sitting forward now, with his elbows on his knees and looking directly at Sean.

"My parents, I guess. I'll have everything forwarded to them." Sean paused to watch Ford stir imaginary pudding on the stove. "You sure are lucky, man. I know it must be hard to leave these guys, but you'll have a family to come home to. Nothing compares to that."

Dustin looked down at Owen in his carrier. He smiled thoughtfully and said, "Yeah, this one probably won't even know who I am when it's all over."

I reached down to fix Owen's blanket again. Not that it really needed fixing—Owen was too young to kick it off or pull it down—but I felt compelled to tuck it in at his sides, bundling him in like a sausage.

A man in a khaki uniform with several lines of red and green and gold ribbons on the breast stepped into the waiting room. "Smiley!" he called out. "Is there a Smiley here?" and I resented the sound of our cheerful name.

"That's us," Dustin said and stood up.

"You here to do your will?" the man asked.

"Yes, sir. I leave to begin workups in a few days."

The man motioned for Dustin to follow, so I gathered up our belongings. But Dustin turned around and said, "Why don't you wait here, Sarah? I'll be back in a few minutes." Then he turned to Sean and said, "See you on the boat," and the two of them shook hands.

I was too stunned—not to mention embarrassed and indignant—to say anything, so I sat back down in the hard metal chair with my mouth open. The man in khaki led Dustin through a swinging door that squeaked and thumped as it came to a close. Sean opened a copy of *Woman's Day* and pretended to be interested. I wondered if he knew it was upside down.

"Momma?" Ford said from beside my chair. He peered at me with big, round eyes the color of licorice. "Read book?" he said and handed me *The Three Little Pigs*. I pulled him into my lap for a story and was grateful for the distraction—or, the excuse not to talk to Sean.

By the time Sean was called back for his own appointment, he hadn't said much more to me than "Wow, kids, huh? They must keep you busy." I felt the muscles in my cheeks suddenly relax once he was gone. Small talk is always so painful.

Once I had the waiting room to myself again, I rummaged through my purse for the cell phone. Courtney's number was on speed dial.

"How did I know it would be you?" she said when she answered the phone. And then, "Where are you anyway?"

"We're on base at the legal clinic, making Dustin's will."

"Oh," she said sympathetically.

Then I corrected myself. "Actually, I guess I should say *Dustin* is making the will. I'm sitting in the lobby."

"You probably don't want to be back there anyway," she said. "Maybe if y'all had done this earlier, but not this close to the deploy—er, detachment. It's too hard to hear it all."

"I met Sean from the squadron," I said, changing the subject. "Do you know him? He's a bachelor."

I was surprised when Courtney said yes. "I know his girl-friend," she said. "She lives down the street from us. She wants to join the Spouse Club, but I'm not sure Margo will go for it since she isn't technically married to Sean yet."

We were both quiet for a moment, and then Courtney said, "Hey, I'm really sorry I said that about the doctor the other night."

"What do you mean? I'm the one who answered the question."

"Yeah, but I said you've always had a crush on him, and Dustin looked a little shocked."

"He'll get over it," I said. "What's the harm in a little crush?"

"So do you know what you're going to wear to the air terminal?" Courtney asked.

"I really haven't thought about it."

"Haven't thought about it?" she screamed. "Sarah! See, I knew something was wrong with you! What's going on?"

The swinging door squeaked and thumped. I looked up and saw Dustin walking toward me with quick, purposeful steps.

"Gotta go," I whispered into the receiver and threw the phone into my purse.

Dustin tried to smile as he came closer, but it looked more like a frown. He knelt down beside Owen and smoothed his fuzzy duck hair.

"So did you leave everything to me?" I said jokingly, but Dustin didn't laugh. He took my hand and covered it with his own and said, "That was possibly the hardest thing I've ever had to do. I'm glad you didn't come in."

He had made a will before his previous deployment and I didn't remember it being so traumatic. What was the matter with all of us? I wondered.

"Well, is there anything I should know about the decisions you've made?" I said. "Can I look at the will?"

Dustin pulled me close and kissed my forehead. "Let's not worry about that now," he said. Then he bent to pick up Owen's carrier and took Ford's hand. He didn't say another word as he led us out the heavy front doors and into the parking lot, but I noticed that the clomp of his boots was more subdued than before.

3

I SHOULD PROBABLY CALL MY PARENTS

The last night Dustin was home, we finally undressed the Christmas tree. Why? I don't know. There couldn't have been anything more depressing or symbolic. With each ornament I wrapped in tissue and packed in a box, I felt like I was tucking away more than tinseled decorations. The ornaments were so much like our lives: packed away, dragged back out again, put on display, then wrapped in tissue and stowed in a box for the next move.

There were so many ornaments—scattered on the floor, on the piano bench, on the tree waiting to be taken down—it was almost ridiculous. Most families collect ornaments from places they've visited; military families collect ornaments from all the places they've lived. It gets confusing to remember the significance of them, and that night Dustin and I found ourselves bickering over one ornament in particular: a wooden sailboat with SD marked in red ink on the bottom.

I thought the initials stood for "Sarah and Dustin," but Dustin insisted that it would say "DS" for "Dustin and Sarah" if it were our initials.

He thought the letters stood for "San Diego," where we had lived twice already, once together as husband and wife, and one time when we were children and our parents were neighbors. This began to trigger some vague memory, and I reluctantly admitted he might be right.

But then we were disagreeing over which year: Did the sailboat signify our childhood memories of San Diego? Or the year we lived there when we were first married?

"I think my mom gave it to us," Dustin said. "To remind us how we met as kids."

"No, no," I said. "She gave us the picture-frame ornament for that. The picture frame I've never found a one-inch photo for."

He crinkled his nose and laughed. "Gosh, my mom gives us some strange ornaments, doesn't she?"

I only raised an eyebrow at him, as I dangled the ornament by its red ribbon and watched it twirl. "I think Courtney and Derek might have given it to us," I said. "That first year we met them in San Diego. When you were still in flight training."

Dustin accepted that explanation, and I tossed the sailboat into a cardboard box.

"Whoa, wait a minute," he said. "Why did you put it in that box?"

"I don't know. Who cares?"

"Well, I think that box is mine."

"We have our own boxes?"

It was a sincere question, but I see now how it might have seemed baited.

I scratched at my hair and looked down at the side of the box. Sure enough, DUSTIN'S ORNAMENTS was written on the side . . . in my mother-in-law's curvy handwriting.

"She gave you your own box?" I said. "Even though you're married?"

Dustin looked flustered and embarrassed, but he spoke in a

practiced, easy voice. He obviously saw where this was headed. "I think those are just some ornaments from when I was a kid," he said. "She brought them down last time she was visiting. I don't know why. I thought you saw her give them to me."

I peered into "Dustin's" box. It was filled almost to the brim with ornaments fastidiously wrapped in tissue paper. There were dozens and dozens of little bundles. I wondered how I'd overlooked the box when we were decorating a month before, and how Dustin had snuck the ornaments onto the tree.

"My parents keep my childhood ornaments on *their* tree," I said. "What do your parents put on theirs if they've sent you these?"

Dustin massaged the back of his neck and knitted his brows. "I don't know, Sarah. Do we have to get into this tonight? I'll put the ornaments in the attic and we can give them back to my mom next time she's here."

"This is so typical," I started to say, but just then Ford padded into the room in his red footed pajamas. He squinted at the light and came to stand between us. "Water," he said, in a voice thick with sleep.

Dustin and I both rushed to the kitchen, relieved by the interruption, I suppose, but it was Dustin who got to the sippy cup cabinet first, and once Ford drank the entire cup—with us staring and smiling at him, but not speaking—Dustin volunteered to take him back to bed and read another bedtime story.

I finished with the ornaments, now highly annoyed by any that were supposed to go in "Dustin's" box. I could feel the anger building inside me and my ribs felt tight.

I was wrapping one of Ford's "Baby's First Christmas" ornaments (one of the twenty people had sent us) when I thought about my first major run-in with Dustin's mom.

I was pregnant with Ford, and Dustin and I were living at my parents' house in Virginia. (We were between orders and waiting for our house in Florida to be built.) Everyone was taking bets on when the baby would be born. November 17 was my guess (I had heard that first-time mothers go early), but Dustin said, "Duh, the baby will be born on the twenty-second, just like the doctor said."

"Sweet, naive Dustin," we all laughed. "Babies are never born on their due date!" *Ha, ha, ha, ha.*

It was just a few weeks before Thanksgiving and my mom had come up with a "brilliant" idea: "Let's invite all the Smileys down to celebrate!"

"No way, Mom," I said. "Either I will have just given birth or I'll be ready to, and I can guarantee you the last thing I'll want is a bunch of company!"

Clearly, though, whatever I wanted didn't matter (I was merely a vessel at this point for everyone's long-awaited grandchild), and ever the hostess with her hospitable Southern heart, Mom invited the Smileys anyway.

"Oh, goodness!" my mother-in-law squealed. "What on earth should we bring? We could bring the potatoes . . . and stuffing . . . and dessert . . . and rolls. . . ."

What was once my family's small, intimate Thanksgiving was now turning into a Smiley circus. As a general rule, when you gather more than two Smileys in any room, the food multiplies by twelve and the noise increases exponentially. In fact, the biggest difference between my family and Dustin's is the volume of our voices. While I sometimes have to ask my dad or brothers, "What was that? Could you speak up?" Dustin's family talks—or, rather, bickers—all at once, until the conversation becomes mere noise. Loud, annoying noise.

But besides all that, who ever heard of being invited to a dinner and bringing ALL of the food?

"Why don't you just bring a pie," I told my mother-in-law. "Except not pecan pie because I'm already making that for Dustin. It's his favorite."

45

She gasped with delight. "Pecan pie is Dustin's favorite? Well, I never knew! My goodness, let me make it for him if it's his favorite!"

"No, no," I said through clenched teeth. "It's sort of a tradition of mine: I always make one for him on special occasions."

"But, honey," she said, "you'll either be taking care of a newborn or getting ready to deliver—you don't need to be worried about making a pie! Let me. I'm his mother, after all."

For the next several days, our conversations were a pie-making tug-of-war: "No, I'll make the pie," I'd say, and she'd come right back with, "No, let me, let me!"

To my friends I said, "I'll be you-know-what if I don't make that damn pie! Even if I have to bake it between contractions, I'm making Dustin's pecan pie!"

My plan was to make it the day before Thanksgiving (my due date). I even had all the ingredients. But sure enough, Dustin had been right with his prediction, and in the wee hours of the morning on the twenty-second, I went into labor. I hadn't baked the pie yet.

At about four o'clock in the morning, as I gripped the bars of the metal hospital bed railing, Dustin said, "I think I should call my parents."

Mind you, I was not waiting to be admitted to the hospital, nor waiting for that magical dilation; I was in active labor, and minutes away from having a baby. This was no time for my husband to divide his attention. I needed him.

"Whatever!" I said, rolling my eyes. But Dustin mistook my emotion for predelivery husband hating and called his mom anyway.

"Sorry to wake you, Mom," he said, "but we're in the hospital and your first grandchild is going to be born soon."

Through the receiver came a loud squeal like a jumbo plane taking flight. Then I could hear my mother-in-law's voice squawking like a bird's. Dustin was listening closely and knitting his brows. "Hmm, I don't know, Mom," he said. "But I'll ask her."

He covered the phone with the palm of his hand and bent down toward me in the bed. Then, in all sincerity, and with the innocence of a child, he said to me, "Mom wants to know if you had a chance to make the pecan pie yet."

Sitting on the piano bench now, with ornaments in my lap, I laughed to myself, thinking about what my face must have looked like to Dustin that day. Because although I never answered him, he got back on the phone and said, "Uh, I'm going to guess she did not, Mom."

I wiped at my brow. Most of the ornaments were packed away, but a shiny silver wedding cake with our wedding date engraved on the bottom sat on the black piano top. I held the ornament in my hand and sighed. Dustin's mom came to Thanksgiving dinner that year with not one, but three varieties of pecan pie. "So typical," I said to myself and tossed the wedding cake ornament into a box.

But then I remembered something else: Dustin didn't eat a single bite of his mom's pies. In fact, I think he even told her, "I'm going to wait until Sarah can make me one of hers next time."

Yet when *was* the last time I had made Dustin a pecan pie? I wondered. Had I ever made him one since Ford was born?

I heard Dustin softly closing the door to Ford and Owen's room and then coming down the hallway in his socks. I taped up the last box of ornaments, trying to stall, and maybe hoping Dustin would come out and get me, before I gave up and went to our bedroom.

We met in the bathroom and both started getting undressed.

"I'm sorry about earlier," I said.

Dustin winked at me and threw his dirty clothes into the wicker laundry basket. "We're both on edge," he said.

Then I walked past him on my way to the dresser, and ran a hand across his bare back. "The counselor from Fleet and Family Support said we might argue more than usual," I said.

Dustin came up behind me and rubbed the sides of my arms. The white flag had officially been raised.

"I'm sorry, too," he whispered in my ear. "Now let's forget about all that."

"All right," I said and turned around to face him with a playful smile. "But we're sending that box back to your mother."

Dustin grinned and patted me on the rear.

We got in bed and I curled up behind him. Our legs fit into one another in a familiar way, just like a clasp. My nose was pressed against his back and the musky smell of his skin sent waves down to my stomach.

In that moment, as we were lying there in the dark together, all the emotions of the previous week seemed insignificant. I couldn't embrace him tight enough or long enough to suit me: I knew all too well how empty and cold his side of the bed would be tomorrow night.

Dustin turned to face me and we stared at each other until I saw green spots from the darkness. I was trying to memorize his face—his full eyebrows, the mole next to his lip, the scar beneath his nose where a mustache won't grow. I wanted to take it all in, to store the images like dots of light that stay on your retina after you've looked at the sun. But most of all, I wanted to believe, there in the silence, that he was memorizing my face, too.

And then he said, "I should probably call my parents."

I blinked. "What? What for? You're only going to be gone two weeks! It's not like this is the big good-bye. It's not the deployment."

But Dustin was already throwing back the covers and swinging his feet over the edge of the bed.

"Yeah, but things are so uncertain," he said over his shoulder. He put on a shirt and stepped down to the floor. "I mean, what if they send us straight to the Middle East after our training?"

"They'd really do that?" Now I was sitting up and my heart was pounding. From fear or anger, I wasn't sure.

"It's a possibility," he said and stepped into a pair of boxer shorts.

He lifted the phone off the charger and it beeped. Tanner woke up beneath the bed. Her dog tags jingled as she shook her head and groaned. I knew she was stretching, preparing to see what trouble was brewing in the house. Then she poked her nose out from under the dust ruffle and eased her body out to follow Dustin into the living room.

I threw myself back into the pillows. I should call my parents? My teeth were beginning to clench. Why does my mother-in-law have a way of sneaking up at the most inopportune times? Whether it was her fault or Dustin's, I wasn't sure. No one in their right mind would expect a phone call from a man on his last night home with his wife, and honestly, I didn't think she was an exception.

"Hello, Mom?" Dustin said, and I strained to hear his muffled voice through the wall.

"We're leaving tomorrow. . . . No, it's only a two-week workup. . . . We'll be doing some training for our upcoming deployment. . . . Yes, I did tell you I was leaving for deployment. I told you that several months ago. . . . Yes, I'll be careful. . . . No, I won't be able to call you. . . . No, I won't be able to use e-mail every day. . . . Yes, I'll try to send you a postcard."

The words were fading into one another, as if I had heard this same conversation over and over again, only in different forms.

But then my breath caught when I heard something different: "Mom, look after Sarah and the boys for me," Dustin said. "Call on them every now and then, OK? I'm worried about Sarah. She had such a rough time last deployment, and now with the two boys . . . Just promise me you'll take care of them for me—during these next two weeks and then during the deployment as well."

I hugged the blanket to my chest and waited for him to come back to bed.

The next morning, Dustin paced through the kitchen, visibly bothered. He has such a low tolerance for chaos. I was sitting on the floor of our bedroom, surrounded by piles of underwear, undershirts, and packing supplies. "Don't forget to pack a picture of me and the kids," I called out, and then, "Did you remember to pack a camera? And what about your razors? You always forget your razors. Oh, and did you pack floss? You do have a picture of me and the kids, right?"

Originally Dustin had packed for two weeks on board the ship, but a phone call from the squadron at eleven o'clock the night before informed him to "pack for six months . . . just in case." After Dustin had fumbled in the dark to hang up the phone, he jumped out of bed and rushed around in his underwear to gather more pairs of socks and undershirts for the seabag. I had sat up against my pillows and, with drooping, tired eyes, penned Dustin's social security number on the extra clothes. I felt like a mother marking her son's backpack and jacket before the first day of school. And with that thought, I was mad at my mother-in-law and her boxful of ornaments all over again.

After the harried assembly line in the middle of the night, Dustin and I should have been exhausted, but instead we were jittery, perhaps functioning on overdrive, as if we'd had too much caffeine or were high on adrenaline. I noticed my hands trembling when I put Ford's Pop-Tart into the toaster, and Owen arched his back and wailed when I tried to nurse him. Kids can be awfully perceptive, and I knew—mostly by the way Ford chewed on his thumb and ate a clump of Play-Doh when he thought I wasn't looking—that mine sensed something was wrong.

Even Tanner was turning circles in her bed, feverishly scratching the denim-covered pillow.

"Dustin, look," I said, leaning toward her. "Tanner's sad you're leaving. Poor thing." I stroked her head and smacked my lips, making kissing sounds at her.

Dustin smirked and continued searching through a drawer for his missing keys and wallet.

"What?" I said, looking up at him. "What are you smiling about?"

He shut the drawer, scratched his head, and said distractedly, "Oh, nothing. It's just that you're talking through Tanner again."

"What?"

"You're talking through Tanner," he said and wandered out of the room.

I knelt down and smoothed the fluffy hair between Tanner's ears. "I don't understand what you mean," I called out.

Dustin wandered back into the room, still in searching mode. "Sometimes when you get upset," he said, "you tell me your feelings through Tanner."

"What? I do not! That's absurd!" I cupped Tanner's muzzle in my hands and stared into her watery eyes. "Tell him, Tanner. I don't talk through you, do I?"

Dustin was pacing in and out of rooms now, seemingly half interested in our conversation. "Have you seen my keys, Sarah?" he yelled from the kitchen.

Tanner rolled onto her side and I patted the soft pink skin of her belly. "Tanner, say, 'No, Mommy hasn't seen your keys, Dustin.' Will you tell him that, Tanner? Say, 'If Mommy knew where your keys were she'd have found them for you by now.' "

Dustin was standing in the doorway again. "That's exactly what I'm talking about," he said. "Right there! You're talking through the damn dog."

The word "damn" struck me as unfair, but I tried not to cry. "Oh, Tanner," I said, "tell Dusty Wusty to calm down and relax a little bit. Maybe if he put his keys in the same place every night, he wouldn't lose them so much. Isn't that right, sweetie?"

Dustin stared at me for a moment, then threw up his hands and left the room.

It was five o'clock in the morning when we finally pulled out of the driveway. The exhaust blowing from the car, mixed with the cold winter air, made an impressive cloud of white frost as Dustin backed down the driveway. Houses all around the cul-de-sac were quiet and dark, with only a few dim lights coming from front porches and lamps on end tables inside. Our neighbors were either still sleeping curled up next to their spouses, or they were sipping coffee and reading the morning paper. When the garage door squeaked closed behind us, I worried we might wake up all those sleepy neighbors. And suddenly it occurred to me, by the time I drove back up the driveway alone later that afternoon, I would see all the houses filled with families and twinkling lights in a new and different way—the envious way.

We drove in silence to the Navy base. The boys were both sleeping in their car seats and Dustin and I were too cold and hunched over in our jackets to speak. I tried to remind myself, "It's only for two weeks," and repeated the words in my mind like a mantra. But I still felt distressed, and I wondered if this was how defendants feel when they are shackled and shuffling into the courtroom to hear a verdict.

At the terminal, Dustin parked in the farthest spot and removed the keys from the ignition. It was a familiar routine: kissing me in front of his peers is Dustin's idea of total humiliation. His training at the United States Naval Academy, where midshipmen are instructed not to show public displays of affection, only increased Dustin's natural inclination toward modesty. Most times, I was lucky to get a peck on the cheek when we were on base and he was in uniform.

Dustin unfastened his seat belt and turned to face me. He took my hand from my lap and placed it between his. "Sarah, I hope this is only for two weeks," he said. "But you know there's a chance—"

"I know. Don't say it aloud. Not right now." I stared at my lap and swallowed back tears.

Dustin looked down at our hands clasped together on the armrest. "You know I love you?" he asked. I nodded. "Promise me you'll show the boys my picture and talk about me often?"

I looked up. "Dustin! Don't talk like that. You'll be home in a few weeks."

"I know . . . I mean, I hope. But, Sarah, I need you to understand that we might be sent overseas without coming back first. Are you prepared for that?"

Tears spilled over my eyelids and onto my cheeks. The crying came so fast and with such force, it felt like my ribs were squeezing my lungs. Dustin put his hand behind my head and drew me to his chest. I sobbed into the olive green material of his flight suit and soaked his patches with tears.

"I don't want you to go," I cried. "Please don't go! I can't take this anymore. I just want you home . . . home all the time."

Dustin ran his hand through my hair and rubbed my back. "I know, Sarah. But you've done this before. You—"

"No!" I cried. "Please don't leave me. Not again. I can't take it anymore." I was beginning to feel tired and heavy.

"You're going to be fine," he said. "You've got Jody and Courtney and all the other wives to support you."

I sat up and looked at him. "That's the thing, Dustin. I shouldn't need other people to support me. Why can't I get it together myself? Maybe I'm not cut out for this. Maybe you should have married someone else." I buried my face in my hands.

"Hey," he said, touching my leg, "this is only temporary. Soon you'll have me home again to help you. Promise."

I cried harder. "I'm not cut out for this. Oh, my gosh, I'm not cut out for this."

Dustin pulled my hands away from my face. "This hurts me, too, Sarah. I realize you married me thinking I would be home to take care of you and our family. It kills me to know I can't do that right now. But I'll be home soon. And you're going to be fine." He put a hand to my cheek and grinned. "But seriously, Sarah, don't sell the house if you find a roach, OK? And try not to burn down the garage or anything."

I tilted my head back on the headrest and sighed in spite of myself. "Ha! Very funny," I said, drying my nose with the sleeve of my jacket. "But, Dustin—"

"I know," he said and squeezed my hand. "I know."

I flipped down the visor to look at myself in the mirror. My brown eyes were circled with red, and mascara was running down my drawn, pale cheeks. The tip of my nose was moist and red, and little blue veins (inherited from my mom) were beginning to appear between my eyes.

I flipped the visor shut with a thud. "I look like a wreck!"

"Nah, no one's going to look great in there," Dustin said, and then he turned to look at the boys sleeping in the backseat. "Are you sure you even want to come in, though? You could just go home if you want."

I thought about that. Avoiding a long, drawn-out good-bye seemed like a good idea. Besides, when Dustin leaves for a short detachment—and this *was* scheduled to be a short detachment— I simply drop him off at the curb, lean over the console, and surprise him with a peck on the cheek, then smile and wave as I drive away.

But no, somehow this felt different and I couldn't just turn and go.

"I think I need to come in," I said.

Dustin patted my knee. "OK."

We walked through the automatic sliding doors and the air terminal's greasy smell comforted me. It is an oddly familiar scent that can take me back to my youth in an instant, like the musty hooked rugs in my childhood bathroom. Was this how other children—children whose dads had offices and secretaries and never left home for weeks at a time—felt when they smelled coffee brewing or the odor of new office-grade carpeting?

The terminal's bare concrete walls were yellow—a desperate attempt at cheerfulness, I've always thought—but even paint could not mask garish plastic signs on the wall: HIGH VOLTAGE, FALLOUT SHELTER, AUTHORIZED PERSONNEL ONLY.

On the floor there were a few scattered pieces of red, white, and blue confetti left over from another squadron's recent homecoming. The bits of paper were stepped on and mashed into the stained gray carpet, like the dead pine needles from our Christmas tree at home.

Metal straight-back chairs were arranged in rows, and families sat in clusters, huddled together and not speaking to anyone outside their circle.

Dustin carried Owen in his portable seat, and Ford was asleep slumped across my shoulder. His head bumped and wobbled as we walked, and I could feel his breath on my neck. We went past the rows of families, and solemn faces looked up at us with wet eyes. Friends and squadron mates nodded ever so slightly but said nothing—the most sorrowful of hellos, like a congregation acknowledging a grieving widow as she walks up the aisle after her husband's funeral.

No, this definitely didn't feel a like a typical good-bye.

Dustin found a spot for us near the vending machines and a metal trash can. He set Owen's carrier on the floor, and I handed him Ford to hold in his lap. Dustin nestled him like an infant, cradling him close to his chest, and Ford sighed in his sleep.

I fell back into a metal chair. From across the room, I saw Courtney and Derek. Courtney was crying on his shoulder with a handkerchief pressed to her nose. Who besides Courtney actually carries a handkerchief? I wondered.

A few rows over, Jody and Steve and their two boys were huddled together. Steve was bouncing Michael on his knee and though the delighted three-year-old was giggling and smiling, Steve was not. Melanie and Paul were sitting quietly in another corner. Hannah was crying in her dad's lap and Melanie reached over to pat her back.

Dustin put his free arm around the back of my chair. "Sarah, try not to dwell on it," he said. "Remember what your mom always says: 'Plan for the worst and wait for the best.' Or is it: 'Wait for the worst and plan for the best?' Anyway . . ." He grew quiet and looked down at Ford. "I know that doesn't help, but . . ."

Near the double doors, I saw Kate, dressed in black slacks and a red boatneck sweater, kiss her husband and then walk out to the parking lot without looking back. I wondered if she had the right idea, to leave before the scene got worse.

Dustin glanced at his watch. "They'll be boarding soon. Take care of the boys for me, you hear? And remember that e-mail takes a while to get set up on board. You may not hear from me for a while."

I nodded, but stared straight ahead.

A man in a flight suit and heavy black boots walked briskly between the families. "One more minute, folks," he called out. "Say your good-byes and wrap it up!"

Dustin stood up with Ford still cradled in his arm. "I've got to go," he said and took my hand to help me stand.

"Just a few more minutes," I begged.

"Sarah, I can't. You know that. When it's time to go, it's time to go." He drew me close and kissed my forehead. "I love you," he whispered.

I heard Courtney break down across the room. Her sobbing was like a wounded animal: "Don't go! Please don't go," she cried.

Tears started running down my cheeks again. My eyes were beginning to sting. How many times had I done this—as a child and now as an adult? I wondered, growing more weary. How many times had I witnessed this same dramatic scene?

"It's only two weeks," Dustin whispered.

"Let's go, folks!" the man with the boots shouted again. "Time to get on the plane!"

Dustin hugged me with one arm, squishing Ford between us. "I've got to go now. Hopefully, I'll see you in a few weeks, OK?"

He transferred Ford still sleeping into my arms and kissed both of our heads before leaning down to kiss Owen. He lifted the bulky green seabag and threw it over his shoulder like a sack of flour, then straightened and gave me a thumbs-up sign, before smiling and turning to leave. I waved halfheartedly and smiled. He turned around and fell in line with the other men.

When a set of double doors opened, allowing the men to spill out onto the runway, the whistle of a waiting transport jet filled the lobby. I picked up the boys and moved closer to the door. Jody and Courtney came to stand next to me, but no one said anything.

Outside the large-paned window I saw clusters of men in green making their way across the tarmac to the jet. One figure turned around, stared back at the building, and waved. Was it Dustin? They all looked the same. But I raised my free hand and waved anyway. "Good-bye," I whispered.

The man turned back around and boarded the airplane.

And just like that my husband was gone.

4

A WOMAN
WITH JUMPER CABLES

The first day was easy. It always is. I could almost imagine Dustin was simply at work . . . then late for dinner . . . and then doing a night flight.

It wasn't until I woke up alone the next morning that things began to seem real. It wasn't until I rolled over in bed and snuggled up to a pile of clean laundry instead of my husband. It wasn't until then that the situation was undeniably not like those routine late-night shifts, when Dustin was required to fly by the light of a full moon with night-vision goggles and didn't come home until after I was asleep. All those times, I woke up with him next to me, despite going to bed alone.

So it was the second day—specifically the second morning—when I started to freak out.

Had it really happened? The day before seemed like a dream. I tried to remind myself that Dustin would be back "in two weeks." (So why was my stomach churning?)

Courtney called that afternoon to check on me.

"Do you want to come over for lunch?" she said.

"No, I think I'll just stay here." I didn't feel like getting out of my pajamas.

"How was your last night?"

"Terrible. We took down the Christmas decorations—don't ask me why—and then just when we were getting into bed, Dustin decided to call his parents."

"His parents?"

"Yeah, well, you know how he worries about whether or not he's doing enough for them and all that. Everything has to be fair, right?"

"But still!" Courtney said. "On the last night? Well, that was just churlish, now, wasn't it?"

What-ish?

"I make Derek call his parents after dinner," she continued. "Then we take the phone off the hook."

"Sounds like a good plan," I said. And then, "Hey, Courtney, do you think I talk through Tanner? You know, use her to express my feelings?"

She laughed. "Well, sometimes, yes. Why?"

"Yesterday morning, before we went to the terminal, Dustin accused me of talking through 'the damn dog.' "

"Oh no," she cried. "He actually said that? He called Tanner 'the damn dog'?"

"Yep."

"I can only imagine your face. I mean, I know how you are about Tanner."

"I know. It ripped my heart out."

"Well, I'm sure he didn't mean it," she said. "It was probably just stress."

"Sure, stress."

That night, after Ford went to sleep, I settled into the living room to feed Owen. The warmth of his tiny pink body bundled in blue footed pajamas, plus the sound of his delicate sucking, made me feel almost drunk with tiredness. I sank farther into the couch, hugging him against my chest and smoothing his unruly fuzzy hair.

Babies have it so easy, I thought. They don't know enough to feel alone or afraid, and they always have someone taking care of them. Oh, to be that oblivious!

Once Owen was asleep and soft purring noises came from his open mouth, I turned on the television and flipped through channels mindlessly. I was enjoying the way each blurb faded into the next, making funny sentences (*Colgate toothpaste for— fresher kitty litter—during tomorrow's storms*), until I came across the news.

Admittedly, I'm someone who should never watch the news— especially the evening news—because then I might contract all the terrible afflictions mentioned in the health segment. Yet while Dustin is away I feel more vigilant if I keep abreast of world events.

So I was half listening and softly patting Owen's back, when a reporter with a solemn face and dark suit came on the screen. He looked important, so I turned an ear to hear. There was a lot of political jargon and other nonsense, but what caught my attention was this: Representative Charles Rangel, a Democrat from New York, had introduced a bill in Congress to reinstate the draft.

And all at once . . . I knew.

I knew by the way my hands turned cold and my body froze. I knew by the way my cheeks tingled and my mouth became dry. I was breathing too fast or too slow (I wasn't sure).

I knew I should be worried about the greater implications of the news—about world peace and a war with Iraq—but in that moment . . . well, I just wasn't. I couldn't see beyond myself or beyond my family.

And then a few days later, CNN reported that the United

States had begun "psychological warfare" against Iraq. E-mail messages were sent to Iraqi servers with information about how to defect and appeals to the Iraqi people to turn over biological weapons.

Jody was the first one to call. "Did you see the latest?" she asked.

"Yeah, what do you make of it?"

Jody paused. "I'm finding it harder to believe they'll send our guys home."

"Have you gotten an e-mail from Steve yet?"

"No, nothing," she said, then quickly changed the subject: "Did you see our crazy neighbor has a pink flamingo in her yard now?"

It was as if we were treating the idea of war as "innocent until proven guilty." Until we had definitive information, we were going to believe the detachment was a short one.

Increasingly, however, all evidence indicated otherwise, and like a losing defense team, our spirits sank. We held our breath for the verdict.

It came soon after.

"Sarah? Are you busy?" Kate's voice came over the phone with a flatness that made my heart race.

I looked up from my spot at the kitchen table and watched Ford dump a box of sixty-four crayons on the vinyl floor. "No, not at all," I said, snapping my fingers and glaring at Ford. "What's up?"

"Well, it's nothing to get excited about yet," Kate said, "but there's been some—how should I say this?—there's been some . . . *developments.*"

She said "developments" in a slow, deliberate way, and I smelled a cover-up.

"Developments, Kate? Are we talking new-Super-Target-going-up-on-Tenth-Street developments, or our-husbands-aren't-coming-home developments?"

She laughed. "I can't say for sure just yet, but I'm hosting an emergency meeting at my house tonight. Can you make it?"

"What about the kids? Can I bring them? I don't have a regular babysitter."

Kate didn't have kids of her own, and her house was filled with beautiful, delicate things, so she hesitated, if only for a second, but her pleasant voice never faltered. "Oh, sure! Yes, bring them," she said. "We'll figure something out."

So at four o'clock, I bundled Ford in his jacket and Owen under a blanket in his baby carrier. The car was parked on the driveway instead of in the garage because the day before I'd found a frog sitting atop the lawn mower, and because frogs make me think of snakes, I was afraid to go back inside.

I shuttled the boys to the car one at a time in the cold, all the while cursing Dustin for not letting me spend money to hire a babysitter.

Across the driveway my neighbors Brent and Danielle pretended not to watch me. It's a typical civilian reaction; people don't know what to say, but they are curious, so they wind up making you feel like a spectacle.

Danielle, in blue jeans and a white cable-knit sweater, was kneeling in the flower bed pulling weeds. Brent wound red Christmas lights around his arm. When I looked up, they both quickly looked away. I glanced back down and felt their stare. I knew I'd have to be the one to speak up first.

"Hi, guys," I shouted across the yard. "How are you?"

Brent looked up from the tangled mess of lights and said, "Oh! Hi, Sarah. Didn't see you there."

"Where ya headed?" Danielle called out.

I snapped Owen's car seat into place and talked over my shoulder. "To a Spouse Club meeting across the river."

"I thought you went to one a few nights ago," Brent said. "How often do you gals meet?"

Brent was a car salesman, and he and Danielle had no concept of military life, so I guess I was their token connection to all things Navy.

"Usually we meet once a month," I said, "but there's, ah . . . stuff . . . going on."

Brent put down the lights, and he and Danielle walked across the yard. "Yeah, we've been watching the news. Have you heard from Dustin yet?"

"Their e-mail won't be up for a few more days," I said. "It takes a while. But he probably couldn't tell me anything anyway."

Danielle ducked her head into the car and waved at Ford. As a nurse and mother, she took particular interest—and possibly pity—in the fact I was raising two children virtually by myself.

"Say, do you want Brent to watch the boys while you're out tonight?" she said. "I'll be working late, but Brent and Blake will be home. Blake just got a new train table that I bet Ford would love."

"Ford does love trains," I said absently, reviewing Brent in my mind. Brent-the-Neighbor was someone I could call at two o'clock in the morning to kill a spider when Dustin was gone. (He would likely show up in his pajamas and mismatched shoes and wouldn't care that he forgot to take out the retainer in his mouth.) Brent-the-Dad encouraged his four-year-old son to watch professional wrestling. And Brent-the-Man pretended to leave the cul-de-sac for a "jog," but stopped and walked the rest of the way as soon as he was around the corner and out of Danielle's view.

I looked at him now, standing there next to Danielle in a gray sweat suit and a backward FSU hat, and smiled. Brent had a wonderful way with children and Ford loved the fact he let him ride Blake's go-kart (even though it was clearly marked for ages four and up), but for some reason I felt compelled to keep the boys with me. Maybe they were even a comfort to me.

"I really appreciate that," I said. "But I think I'll take them with me tonight."

"All right then," Danielle said. "I've got to go get ready for work, but you just let us know if you ever need anything, OK?"

"I will."

They waved and turned to walk away. Then at the grass, Brent stopped and turned around again. "Hey, you want me to fix that squeak in your garage door while you're gone?" he said.

Brent had been my resident handyman for some time. He mowed my lawn when Dustin was away. He chopped wood. He trimmed bushes. He killed fire ants on the sidewalk and treated my plants for fungus. He also once touched Ford's infant hand after setting a rodent trap in the garage, and I nearly fell to the concrete in horror before rushing inside for the disinfectant. I had never met anyone like Brent, and I had no point of reference for his character. Yet his presence next door gave me an odd sense of security.

"I do need to get that door fixed, don't I?" I said, turning to look at it. "How about this weekend though? I really should get going now."

I opened the car door and hoisted myself inside.

"All righty then," Brent said, waving. "You have a good time tonight."

I shut the door and put the key in the ignition. Brent was still waving on the driveway. I smiled and turned the key, but the engine wouldn't start. I turned the key again. Nothing. Brent looked concerned. I waved and smiled. "Engine must be cold," I said through the window, but he couldn't hear. I turned the key one more time. Still nothing.

Brent motioned for me to open the door.

"Looks like you've got a dead battery," he said. "Pop the hood."

I pulled a lever beneath the steering wheel, and when Ford heard it pop, he wiggled in his seat and whined, "Momma? What wrong? Let's go."

"The car won't start, honey. But it's going to be all right. Brent will fix it."

I looked at him in his car seat in the rearview mirror and saw Jody's purple minivan coming around the corner. "Oh, thank God," I said, reaching for the door handle.

Jody circled the cul-de-sac and pulled up to the end of my driveway, kicking up rocks and gravel with her worn tires.

"I thought you were coming to pick me up," she yelled out her window.

"I was, but my car won't start. It did this little whining thing and died."

"A whining thing? Dead batteries don't 'whine,' Sarah."

I threw my hands up in the air. "Well, how the hell should I know? Why do these things always happen when Dustin is gone?"

Brent came up beside me, wiping grease from his hands onto his sweatpants. "Hey there, Jody," he said. "Looks like Sarah has a dead battery."

"It isn't a loose hose or anything?" she said as she got out of the van.

"No, definitely a dead battery," Brent said. "I'll go get some cables." He turned to leave and Jody and I watched as he made his way across the grass again. Once he was out of sight, I stomped my foot and said, "I can't believe this!"

"Well, it's nothing to cry about," Jody said. "Get in your car. Where are your jumper cables?"

I looked at her and shrugged.

"You don't know where Dustin keeps the jumper cables? Do you even know what jumper cables are?"

I rolled my eyes.

"Oh, never mind," she said. "I have my own!"

She opened the back door of her van and rummaged through a pile of backpacks and softballs, then pulled out copper clamps attached to red and black wires. After pulling her car next to mine, she fixed the wires to each of our batteries. Or, whatever. Really, I had no earthly idea what she was doing.

"Go ahead and start the engine," she yelled.

"I'm afraid," I called back. "What if it blows up or something?"

Jody pulled her head out from under the hood. "Please tell me you aren't really this helpless."

"I mean, seriously, Jody! What if you have those things attached wrong and the car blows up!"

She shooed me out of the driver's seat, saying, "Give me a break," under her breath, and then started the car.

By the time Brent came back, with a toolbox in one hand and a beer in the other, Jody had both cars idling.

"Now that's what I like to see," Brent said. "A woman with jumper cables."

Thankfully, Jody didn't give him the finger.

I went straight to a mechanic for a new battery, and Jody went on to the meeting at Kate's house. I wasn't all that disappointed about not going. In some way I felt I had delayed my fate, and I knew Jody would update me later. But as I pulled into the gas station parking lot, her words ("Please tell me you aren't really this helpless") rang in my head.

The greasy lobby had a half dozen green plastic lawn chairs set out for customers, and I sat down to unload the diaper bag. I was prepared for a long wait and had crayons and coloring paper for Ford and a binkie for Owen. Things were popping out of the vinyl bag like fried rice from a Chinese take-out box.

A teenage girl with long burgundy hair sitting across from me put down her *People* magazine and chuckled.

"How old is the baby?" she asked, nodding at Owen asleep on my shoulder.

"Almost six weeks," I said, and suddenly I felt aware of my postpartum body and the loose pooch of skin hanging over the band of my elastic-waisted "transition" clothes. The teenager was wearing wind pants with a stripe down the leg. She had on a hooded sweatshirt, which was unzipped, exposing an intact navel and a tight white halter top. I couldn't remember the last time my belly button saw the light of day when I wasn't breastfeeding.

"I can't wait to have kids someday," she said, staring at Owen.

I laughed. "Oh, well, they're a lot of work, too, so don't rush."

I thought about the fact that I wasn't much older than a teenager when I had Ford. Because I got married at twenty-two and had Ford thirteen months later, I often felt I went straight from Daddy to sorority to Dustin without any time in between. While other friends had lived in apartments with groups of girl-friends, I was buying diapers and learning to make pot roast. When my friend Amy rented her first apartment in New York City and was going out for cosmopolitans with a slew of single men, I was waiting for the mailman and hoping desperately for a postcard from Dustin overseas.

At times it seemed I had grown up too fast. Or was it that I hadn't grown up at all?

"Your husband must be so proud," the girl said. "I can't wait to have a husband." She blew a bubble with her gum and the smell of strawberry momentarily masked the new-tire and popcorn odor of the lobby.

"My husband's in the Navy," I said, "so he's not around much."

The girl shook her head with pity, but I laughed and said, "Actually, sometimes it's the best kind of husband to have." Although I knew I didn't really believe it. Especially not then.

I noticed the girl watching Ford with interest. "What's your name, hon?" she asked him, and he giggled.

"Me Ford."

She misunderstood him—it was easy to do. "You're four years old?" she said. "What a big boy you are!"

"No, me Ford," he said again, and then he put a car-parts catalog with greasy fingerprints on it in her lap. "Read book?" he said.

"Oh, well, this isn't really a book," the girl said. "But I can tell you a story if you want. Do you like superheroes?"

Ford stared at her with eyes like saucers. He was mesmerized and nodding his head enthusiastically as he crawled into the teenager's lap.

By the time the mechanic called our name over the loud-speaker, the girl must have told Ford a dozen stories about Wonder Woman and Superman and Flash.

"Well, that's us," I said, gathering my belongings with one hand. The girl helped me with the diaper bag; then she followed us to the service counter.

"I'm just wondering," she said. "You mentioned your husband is in the Navy. By any chance, do you know a lady named Melanie?"

I stopped and turned to look at her. "You mean Melanie Davis?"

"Yeah, I think that's her name. She has a little daughter about four years old?"

"Yes, that's Melanie. Her husband flies with mine. Do you know her?"

"She goes to my church," the girl said. "I babysit her daughter, Hannah, in the nursery on Sunday mornings."

I thought this over. "You babysit at the church?" I said it mostly to myself, and then before she could answer: "Maybe this is strange because we just met here at the gas station, but I'm looking for someone to help me out while my husband is gone. Would you be interested in babysitting outside the church?"

"Oh, my gosh! I would *so* love to babysit!" she said. She was clapping her hands and jumping up and down so that her perky breasts bounced in her halter top and made me feel old and fat. "That would be totally cool!" she said. "Your boys are precious!"

She gave me her name—Lauren—and phone number on the back of a Victoria's Secret receipt from her purse, which was the size of a small wallet.

It occurred to me that Amy was probably exchanging business cards with an acquaintance at a hip restaurant at that very second . . . and I was picking up a babysitter at the gas station.

When I got home, the only light in the house was the red glow of the answering machine.

"You have ten messages," the computerized voice said.

Ten messages? Holy cow! But what were the chances one of them would be Dustin? Military wives hate missing calls from their husbands overseas.

I put the boys in bed, changed into flannel pajamas, and sat down in the kitchen to listen to my messages.

> **Message #1:** "Sarah, it's Mom. We're worried about you. But Dad says not to worry about the news yet. Call us when you get home."

This was, at its core, a hysterical message from Mom, covered up with an overcheery tone that said, "I'm your mother and I say not to worry!" Her choice of "we" and "us" tickled me most of all: Dad hadn't picked up the phone in probably twenty years. In fact, I'm not sure I had ever spoken to him over the phone.

> **Message #2:** "Sarah? . . . Sarah? . . . Pick up the phone, Sarah. . . . Well, I guess you're not there. . . . Sarah? . . . Are you there? . . . It's Doris. . . . Bye."

Message interpretation: Mom, in a state of panic, called her mother and enlisted my grandmother's help so she herself wouldn't look so neurotic. Her choice of ally was interesting, though, because Doris is just as irrational at times. This is the woman who, on the night I was born, believed Charles Manson was sitting on the back patio spying on her. And basically, that's all she recalls of the event.

> **Message #3:** "Hi, it's Jody. Just want to update you on the meeting. Call me when you can."

> **Message #4:** "It's just Mom again. Dad still says not to worry. Everything will be fine. Call us."

Her voice was noticeably more shaken than before.

> **Message #5:** "Sarah! It's Doris. . . . Are you there? I've got your momma callin' me all in an uproar. Pick up the phone . . . Sarah? . . ." (Her voice trailed off into a mumble as she struggled to get the phone back on the hook, but I'm pretty sure she said, "These cotton-pickin' machines. Who ever heard of such a thing, talking to a box!")

> **Message #6:** "Hi, Sarah, it's Dustin's mom. Just wondering if you've heard from Dustin yet. His dad and I haven't gotten anything. Do you think it's too soon for e-mail? I thought he would have sent a postcard by now. Anyway, just call us when you can."

> **Message #7:** "It's Mom again. Where are you? Well, I guess you could be at a Spouse Club meeting or something. Anyway, I'll let you know when Dad seems concerned about the media coverage. Call us."

> **Message #8:** "It's Dustin's mom again. Our phone just rang, but when I picked it up, no one was there. Just wondering if it was you trying to call . . . or do you think it could have been Dustin calling? Do you think he'll call back? Oh, dear!"

Message #9: "It's Courtney calling. Just wanted to check on you. Jody told me about the car. Only you, girl, only you. Anyway, has Jody called you about the news yet?"

I wondered what news everyone was talking about. I'd better call Jody back, I thought, or turn on the news. But then the last message started to play.

Message #10: There was static and a beeping sound. Then it was Dustin, his voice sounding like it was coming from a box. "Sarah, are you there? It's me. I was hoping to catch you at home. I guess you know there's stuff going on. I hope the Club is giving you updates. Are you there? I waited in line to talk to you. Everything's kinda crazy here. Well, I wanted to hear your voice. Maybe you could change the outgoing message on the machine to your voice? That way I can hear you even if you don't answer. OK . . . well, someone else needs the phone now. You're really not there? Guess not. OK, I love you. Bye."

I ran to the machine and hit rewind. Dustin's voice echoed off the kitchen walls again. I played the tape over and over until Dustin's voice sounded strange, like a word you repeat until it no longer seems like a word. Then I crumpled into a sitting position on the floor, and hugged the phone to my chest.

My eyes were heavy and I felt like I could drift to sleep as I tipped my head backward against the wall. Until I'd sat down—until I stopped moving—I didn't realize how tired I was.

The phone rang in my hand and I jumped. "Dustin?" I said. "Is it you?"

"Sorry, Sarah. It's me, Jody. You weren't asleep, were you?"

I held up my head with my hand. "No, I'm awake. What's up? How was the meeting?"

She paused a long time. Then finally she said, "They're not coming home, Sarah. Margo said they probably won't be home for another year."

5

I THINK PSYCHOLOGISTS CALL THAT TRANSFERENCE

"Mommy, wake up. Someone's at the door."

I opened one eye and saw Ford's cheeky face barely an inch away from my nose. He was tugging on my arm.

"Why'd you sleep on the couch, Mommy?" he said and crinkled his pink button nose.

I pulled myself up and looked down at my lap. I was still dressed in my clothes from the day before. I thought about my conversation with Jody and my stomach cramped.

"Oh, my gosh," I said, jumping to my feet. "What time is it? Where's Owen? Did you say someone's at the door?"

I ran to the boys' bedroom with Ford toddling behind. Their room glowed white, mostly from the whitewashed crib and toddler bed my mom had bought for us, but also because sidewise winter-morning light was already beginning to seep through the slats of the blinds. What time is it anyway? I wondered. Had I overslept, or did Ford wake up early?

Owen was asleep on his back in the middle of the crib, with his arms stretched above his head. The doorbell rang and I turned to leave the room, nearly falling over Ford. I ran through the carpeted living room, past Tanner still asleep next to the sofa (her hearing was so bad these days), and looked at the clock on the television. Seven o'clock. Who rings someone's door at seven in the morning?

My socked feet slid across the wood floor of the foyer as I clambered to the door and peeked out the side window. A bearded man in faded jeans and a flannel shirt stood on the stoop with a young girl, who looked to be about eight years old and had straight brownish-blond bangs hanging in her eyes.

"Can I help you?" I said, cracking open the door.

"Yes, ma'am," the man said. "My name is Trevor and I'm with Community Church up the road. This here is Rachel." He put his hand on the girl's shoulder and she looked up at me through her bangs. She wasn't smiling.

"We've noticed you're living alone most of the time," the man said, "and so on behalf of our church and its congregation, we'd like to invite you and your boys to come worship with us."

I stared at him a moment. How did he know I was alone? How did he know I have boys? And why hadn't I heard of this "Community Church" before?

"I'm sorry. We already have a church," I said, closing the door. It was a lie, but I was scared.

The man put his foot between the door and the frame. "If you'd just hear us out," he said. "We'd like to ask you—"

"I'm sorry," I said, looking down at my wrinkled clothes. "I just woke up and I'm a bit disoriented. Do you think you could come back later?"

Come back later? Dammit, Sarah, I said to myself. Just tell this guy to get the hell away!

"We won't be in your neighborhood later, ma'am, and we really would like to talk to you. You see, we just baptized Rachel down at the river. Have your boys been properly baptized?" He inched himself farther into the doorway.

My heart was beating in my throat. Ford peeked out from be-tween my legs.

"They have," I said, "and I really appreciate your asking, but I just got up, and I'm really—"

Tell him to leave, Sarah. Tell him to leave!

"And have you accepted Jesus Christ as your Lord and Savior?" the man asked.

I pushed harder on the door, hoping he couldn't open it all the way with his weight.

Owen woke up and his crying floated through the house to the foyer. It started as a soft whimper but quickly escalated to a frantic wail. If the man heard Owen's cries, he gave no clue. He was staring directly at me.

"Look," I said. "I really need to go get my baby and I don't have time. If you could just leave a card or something—"

No, Sarah! Just tell him to leave, dammit!

"Are you telling me this is an inconvenient time to accept Jesus into your heart?" the man said.

Tanner had woken up now, and she staggered into the foyer, stretching each of her hind legs before noticing something was amiss. When it occurred to her that the man at the door was a stranger, she leaped forward, her long nails clicking on the wood, and started barking. She would never go outside without my permission, so I didn't bother reaching down to grab her collar. She stood at the threshold and barked so excitedly her whole body shook.

Took you long enough, I thought.

But the man didn't seem frightened by Tanner's display. I guess twenty-five-pound, elderly dogs aren't that much of a threat.

"That's a purty dog you got there," the man said. He winked at Ford. "Is that your little puppy, son?"

My hands were trembling; muscles in my stomach tensed. Yet I was still smiling at the stranger and the girl with bangs, wasn't I?

What is wrong with you, Sarah? Just tell the man to leave!

Then suddenly, feeling a bit like a mother bear protecting her cubs, I pulled back my foot and kicked the man's shin. He doubled over and I slammed the door. I flipped the metal latch—*click!*—and pressed my back against the closed door.

"We only want to help you," the man called out. "May God bless you and your family."

That afternoon I met Jody and Courtney for lunch at a deli downtown.

"So you just kicked him?" Courtney said, unfolding a napkin and placing it in her lap. "Right in the shin?"

I nodded. "Yep, I actually feel kind of bad about it though."

Jody was still paying for her meal at the counter, so I cut Ford's grilled-cheese sandwich and gave half to Jody's son. "Here, Michael, eat this," I said. "Your mom's on her way."

He took a bite of the nine-grain bread and stuck out his tongue. "Yuck! What is this stuff?" he said.

I turned back to Courtney. "Isn't there a story in the Bible about Jesus knocking on a man's door, but the man doesn't recognize Jesus and turns Him away?"

"I can assure you, Sarah, the man at your house wasn't Jesus." She took the cap off her bottled water. "You did the right thing."

"No, no," I said, shaking my head and staring down at the table. "I just slammed the door on Jesus, didn't I? My gosh, what kind of person am I? What does that do to my karma? Or is it dharma?"

"You did not slam the door on Jesus!" Courtney was beginning to sound irritated. "And it's karma. K-a-r-m-a."

Jody walked up and dropped her tray on the table. A piece of bread fell off the top of her sandwich, exposing a pile of tomatoes and bacon.

"Who shut a door on Jesus?" she asked and looked back and forth between us. "Oh, wait, let me guess—Sarah?"

She sat down and got situated, divvying up French fries and

sodas between her boys, as I retold the story about the man and the girl. Jody nearly blew lemonade out her nose. "Only you, Sarah!" she said. "Remember that time some high school girl came to your door?"

"Yes, please don't remind me. Do we have to go over this again?"

Jody's round face was red with amusement. "She said she needed to practice her public speaking, right? Isn't that what it was? She said she was nervous talking to strangers, and you slammed the door in her face. That girl will probably be in therapy for the rest of her life."

"I thought she had a gun," I said.

"She did not have a gun!" Jody turned toward Courtney. "The girl came to my door, too. She was selling books to raise money for the band."

Courtney put a napkin to her mouth to hide her laughter. "Did she come to your door *before* or *after* Sarah's?" she asked.

Jody smiled. "Well, before, of course. I'm sure the girl went straight to therapy after Sarah was done with her."

"Very funny, guys," I said and leaned over the stroller to put Owen's pacifier back in his mouth. "The girl had her hand in the pocket of a long black trench coat and it looked like a gun. What was I supposed to do?"

Courtney groaned. "I don't know why you even open the door for these people. Don't you have a peephole? Why do you even give them a chance?"

"I just feel bad for them, I guess. I don't know."

We all focused on our meals for a moment. Ford threw a French fry on the floor and Jody's younger son, Brandon, giggled. Jody was watching them and smiling. Soft crow's-feet appeared at the sides of her eyes.

"A year is a long time," she said softly, and it seemed like the entire deli came to a halt.

In fact, didn't the world stop just then?

The three of us looked back and forth at one another. We knew Jody was saying what we all were thinking: The guys were gone and we could feel it in every part of our day, every inch of our being.

Then Courtney broke the silence. "Well, you know what I always say: just more closet space for me!" She chewed noisily on her salad and smiled at us.

The clattering of plates and utensils coming from behind the deli counter seemed to resume. Life resumed. And I knew then that I had already settled into a new state of existing.

It happens to military spouses at different times, but eventually everyone wears her new reality—the reality of being alone and afraid—like a cast. And as with a broken limb, you learn to function in spite of the crippling sense that you're just barely hanging on. It's only later that you look back and say, "How on earth did I get through that?"

I looked at Courtney and Jody. They were chewing their food and glancing around at the other diners—some of whom were with their spouses or whole family. And there we were, three lonely women trying to pretend everything was OK and that our lives were "normal." Whatever "normal" is.

I leaned in over the table and said to them in a whisper, "I have a doctor's appointment tomorrow."

Courtney gasped. "With the Cute Doctor?"

"Of course, who else?"

"I don't know how you do it," she said.

"Do what?"

"How you can go for an exam with this man who you claim is so incredibly attractive."

"Courtney's right," Jody said. "I could never go to a male doctor. I just wouldn't feel comfortable."

"Especially because all these military doctors know we're alone half the time," Courtney added.

I put down my sandwich and wiped my mouth. "It's not like

that, guys. The Cute Doctor wasn't always cute. He became that way—I'm not sure exactly when."

"I think psychologists call that transference," Jody said.

Courtney wasn't buying it either. "So you're telling me you never knew he was cute until Owen was born?"

"Exactly. I mean, obviously I knew he was good-looking, but I never got nervous around him, like I do now." I took a sip of tea and stared out across the restaurant. A man was helping his wife take a baby carrier out of the restaurant. "I don't know. It's hard to explain," I said. "Dr. Ashley is so sensitive, and attentive, and calm. He takes care of me."

"Well, just be careful," Jody said. "It's fine to have a crush—married people are allowed to notice attractive people, after all—but don't let it come between you and Dustin."

For someone who was normally unemotional and never revealed much about her own marriage, Jody surprised me with her insights into other people's relationships. Her ability to stay objective was something I admired.

"How very perceptive," Courtney said and smiled at Jody. "I didn't know you had it in you."

"What?" Jody said. "You think you're the only one who can be prosaic?"

Courtney stifled a laugh. We both stared at her.

"What?" Jody said again.

"Prosaic means 'mundane,' 'ordinary,' 'colorless,'" Courtney said. "I think you meant to say 'poetic.'"

I gazed at Jody. She didn't like to be called out like that.

"Thanks. I'll make a note of it," she said and sneered across the table.

But Courtney just smiled with satisfaction.

The next day, Owen and I were scheduled for back-to-back appointments with Dr. Ashley, aka Cute Doctor. Owen was having his six-week checkup, and I was having my six-week postpartum exam. Because military hospitals are often understaffed and Dr. Ashley was technically our "family physician," he scheduled the appointments one after the other to save me time.

I told you he was great.

I didn't think I was nervous about the appointments until that morning, when I found myself painting my toenails and feeling nauseous each time I thought of Dustin.

It was true what I had told Courtney and Jody: While I once saw Dr. Ashley—with his slightly rounded shoulders, gold-rimmed glasses, and receding hairline—as a bit geeky, at some point he miraculously morphed into the world's most incredible doctor and the sexiest, smartest man alive.

Once, when I was pregnant with Owen and obsessing over the possibility of having gestational diabetes, Dr. Ashley calmly said to me, "I know you worry about things, Sarah, but don't lose sleep over this. It's going to be OK, and I'll call you just as soon as I get the test results back. Promise."

Dustin, however, sat in the corner of the exam room, fed up with my hysteria. "You just need to chill out," he said angrily.

We fought the whole way home that day, and when I told Dustin that Dr. Ashley had been sensitive where he was, let's see . . . a *jerk*, Dustin said, "Yeah, it's real easy for him to put up with you for twenty minutes every two weeks, but I'm the one who has to live with you!"

From the very beginning, Dr. Ashley and I had a certain kind of chemistry. Even before he became so cute, I always knew if he weren't my doctor, we'd be friends. He was close to my age, single, and we shared the same sense of humor. Even the unpleasantries of being pregnant and going to prenatal exams were made easier with his lighthearted jokes and his radiant, toothpaste-commercial smile.

But that was before everything started to change. It was before Dustin, in predeployment mode, became distant; before I was facing another six months alone; and—most of all—before I was twentysomething years old with two kids and a house.

Ford, Owen, and I got to the hospital just after lunch and just in time to smell the aroma of heated meats and sauerkraut coming from the vendors on the sidewalk outside.

I have always said that going to a military hospital is a little like going to the store to buy Pepsi and coming home with the store brand "cola." They are stripped of everything but the essentials. There are no carpeted waiting rooms with aquariums and glossy-covered copies of *Child* magazine. No, military waiting rooms are more likely to be littered with public-service brochures with titles such as "How to Discipline Your Children When Your Spouse Is Away," and "Is It Postpartum Depression or Predeployment Blues?" And the brochures are never fanned out in a pretty way on the coffee table. Usually they're just scattered across the seats and floor, with boot marks across the places where they've been stepped on. And like the lobby they reside in, the brochures are also stripped down to the essentials: stick-figure illustrations in black-and-white.

I went to a civilian hospital once. It was like arriving at a Saks Fifth Avenue after shopping at Wal-Mart: The automatic doors slid open, cool air-conditioned air feathered my hair, and the mahogany receptionist's desk looked like a majestic ship surrounded by plump waiting chairs and sofas. I could swear I heard choirs singing and joyous bells ringing when I stepped onto the ceramic-tile floor and gazed at the wall filled with oil paintings and hanging greenery.

I had been admitted to the civilian hospital to deliver Ford because the military facility was full and could not accommodate me. The room I gave birth in was nicer than our living room. It had wood floors, an oak armoire for hanging up my clothes, and believe it or not, an actual remote control (with batteries and no duct tape holding it together!) for the large-screen television hanging across from the bed. The room was so cozy, I could almost forget I was there to give birth to an eight-pound baby and that my mother-in-law was bugging me about the pecan pie.

It was almost like a vacation. "But where are all the instruments?" I had asked the civilian nurse. "Where are the forceps and needles and speculums?"

At military hospitals, I was used to seeing these things—things a patient never should have to look at if she doesn't want to vomit.

The large redheaded nurse turned and looked at me as if I were crazy. "For Heaven's sake," she said, "why would you want to see those things? We tuck them away in that wooden dresser over yonder."

What a concept!

Yet, despite all my complaining about military hospitals, it felt like "coming home" when I stepped through the sliding double doors and walked the boys up the stairs to the family practice wing. After all, I was literally born and raised in military hospitals, and there was a certain amount of familiarity and safety in them for me.

Dr. Ashley had made my appointment near lunchtime, so there was no wait, and a nurse escorted me to one of his exam rooms as soon as I had checked in.

The barren room with fluorescent lights was frigid, so I bundled more blankets around Owen in his carrier and made Ford put on a jacket. Then I got out books and crayons from the diaper bag and handed them to Ford.

"Be good," I told him. "And remember, no touching the dirty hospital floors and walls! If you need waterless soap, Mommy's got it in her purse."

I fidgeted with my hair and tried to find the best, most slimming, way to sit when Dr. Ashley came in.

A few minutes later, he came into the exam room dressed in

blue scrubs and a white overcoat. He seemed to be moving in slow motion, like a Diet Coke commercial. I could almost imagine him with his shirt off and beads of sweat dripping down his back. My knees went weak at the thought. No, no, no, I told myself. I can control my feelings. . . . I can control my feelings.

Dr. Ashley smiled at me and the boys, then collapsed into a chair like an old friend falling onto his neighbor's sofa.

"Man, what a day!" he said and pulled off his glasses to rub his eyes. "How have you guys been?"

"Great," I said, "the weather's perfect." Then I immediately cursed myself for doing small talk. Dr. Ashley wasn't a small-talk kind of person—was he?

He pulled a pen out of the front pocket of his coat and flipped through Owen's records. "So any problems with this little guy?" he said. "How's his sleeping? And eating? Are you still nursing?"

I couldn't look at Dr. Ashley's deep blue eyes without feeling nervous, so I stared at a poster with a diagram of a uterus on it above his head.

"Yep. All good!" I said, purposefully avoiding the last question, lest I be forced to say "breast" or anything similar.

Why did I always feel like a teenager around him? I wondered. Why was I suddenly overly aware of my nose and my lipstick and my breath?

My foot tapped uncontrollably on the cement floor. I put a hand on my knee to steady it.

Dr. Ashley looked at me thoughtfully and put down his clipboard and pen. "Are you sure everything's OK? You look a little tense. What's up?"

"Nothing's up," I said. "Really! We're doing great. And, oh, it's a beautiful day out. Did I already say that?"

Damn!

Dr. Ashley smiled crookedly and pulled his spinning stool closer. Since when are crooked smiles sexy? I thought.

"You can talk to me about anything," he said. "You know that, right, Sarah?"

I nodded and looked away. My foot started tapping again. I knew Dr. Ashley was going to grill me until I gave him an answer; he knew me well enough to know I was nervous. I had to come up with something. Wasn't there anything that had been bothering me in the last few days? Anything that didn't involve fantasizing about Dr. Ashley's wispy blond hair?

Then, with a rush of adrenaline that reminded me of standing on the edge of the high dive when I was ten years old, I blurted out, "Well, so long as you're asking, there is this little thing with Owen. It's silly, really, but he . . . well, he sometimes smells like pancake syrup and . . . and . . . um . . . his pe . . . his pe . . . pe . . . ."

"Penis?" Dr. Ashley supplied.

"Yes, that. Well, it's . . . um . . . it's, you know, kind of purple."

Dr. Ashley cleared his throat. "I'm sorry. Did you say he smells like syrup and his penis is purple?"

Oh, my gosh! Is that what I just said?

He picked up the chart and started to make notes.

"Yes, and I think I read something on the Internet about that being a sign of some disease," I said.

"I've told you to quit reading that stuff on the Internet," he said, smiling.

"I know. I know." I covered my face with my hands.

"Well," he said, "there is a metabolic disease involving amino acids which can present itself with urine that smells like syrup, but Owen had a PKU test after birth." Dr. Ashley stood up and kicked away the rolling chair with his foot. "Nevertheless, let's get him undressed and do a little exam."

I took Owen out of his carrier and took off his footed pajamas and diaper. He wriggled and cried when the cold air hit his stomach, but Dr. Ashley was thoughtful as always and rubbed his hands together briskly before touching him. Then he was poking and probing around Owen's groin.

I had to look away.

"I think that purple tint you're seeing is normal," Dr. Ashley said. I heard the latex gloves snap as he took them off. It was safe to look again.

"He's still recovering from the circumcision and things will be irritated for a while," Dr. Ashley said. Then he turned around and searched through a drawer cluttered with tongue depressors, Band-Aids, and cotton balls.

Owen's chart was lying on the paper-covered exam table and I inched closer to peek at it. There, in all capital letters, it said: MOTHER EXTREMELY ANXIOUS. COMPLAINS OF SYRUP SMELL AND PURPLE PENIS.

Oh, no! That was going in his permanent record? Mother "extremely anxious"?

Dr. Ashley turned back around and I quickly looked up from the chart.

"As far as the smell goes," he said, "it may be a reaction to something he's sensitive to in the breast milk. But I'm not worried about it."

I blinked when he said "breast."

"Now," he said with a sudden loudness and clapped his hands together, "go ahead and get Owen dressed and back in his carrier. I'll give you a few moments to get yourself into one of the paper robes on the counter, and then I'll be back with an assistant to do your exam."

He winked and patted my shoulder before turning to leave and closing the door behind him.

My heart was pounding in my throat. I looked over at Ford sitting in a plastic waiting chair with a Superman book in his lap. His chubby shoulders were hunched over and his short legs stuck straight out across the seat. He was absorbed in the picture book and didn't notice me, but I felt my eyes moisten when he distractedly bounced the heel of one of his chunky white tennis shoes on the plastic edge of the seat. He looked so much like his dad, it was stunning, and I wondered why I had never noticed the resemblance until just then.

When Dr. Ashley returned a few minutes later, I was sitting on the exam table, completely naked—except for my watch—and wearing a mint green paper gown like a toga.

I chewed on my thumb and stared at my feet dangling from the table. My knees were purple from the cold, and that made me feel somewhat like a child sitting at the lunch table with a carton of milk. Plus I had red bumps up and down my shins from shaving.

Dr. Ashley sat down on the round twirling stool and looked at me with a thoughtful frown.

"I've decided to wait a moment before we do the exam," he said. "My assistant will be here shortly. But first I want to talk with you. You seem a little on edge, Sarah. Where's the peppy girl I know?" He playfully punched at my shoulder. "Where's that smile? Is there something on your mind?"

"What would be wrong?" I said with a little laugh. "Besides the purple . . . um . . . *thing,* and pancake smell, everything is great."

"Come on, Sarah," he said. "I know you better than that by now."

I instinctively ran my fingers through my hair.

"Tell me what's on your mind," he said again.

My eyes met his and suddenly I relaxed. "Well, Dustin left for deployment," I sighed. "They weren't supposed to leave for a few more months, but with everything that's going on . . . but I'm doing fine. Really."

A crease formed between Dr. Ashley's eyebrows. His head was tilted slightly back, and he seemed to be studying me from underneath the rim of his glasses. I knew by the way he turned the corners of his lips down that he saw right through me.

"And you're scared, aren't you?" he said.

I waved my hand. "Oh, gosh, no. Are you kidding me? I've done this before. . . ." My voice trailed off and started to crack.

Don't cry, I told myself. Whatever you do, don't cry.

I tried to smile but my lips were quivering.

Dr. Ashley stood and handed me a tissue just as tears spilled down my cheeks. "Thanks," I said and dabbed at my eyes. "Oh, God, I didn't mean to cry. How stupid."

He put a hand on my shoulder, and the paper gown crinkled. "This is an emotional time for you," he said. "You just had a baby and your husband's gone. No wonder you're a little on edge. But I have faith in you, Sarah." He was squeezing my shoulder. "I've seen you coming in and out of this office for ten months now, and I know that anyone who can break her elbow tripping over a baby gate and then refuse pain medicine in the ER is someone who can deal with anything."

I laughed and blew my nose. "I only refused the pain medicine because I was afraid it would make me loopy. Basically I was more afraid of the medicine than I was of the pain."

Dr. Ashley grinned. "I know," he said softly. "But trust me. You're going to be fine. And I'm here to help you."

I straightened my back, took a deep breath, and said, "I don't want to get upset right now. If I break down, I might never stop. Let's just go ahead with the exam."

He stared at me a moment while I sniffled and wiped away more tears. Then he said, "All right," and walked back to his clipboard.

"By the way," he said, looking up, "the nurse noted that your heart rate was a little fast today. That's unusual for you, so I think I want to follow up on it."

I put two fingers at my throat and felt my pulse.

"Are you nervous about something, Sarah?" Dr. Ashley said.

Yes, having your hands under this gown, I thought. But what I said was: "Well, I did walk up five flights of stairs to get here."

"What? Why didn't you take the elevator?"

I smiled. "I'm afraid of elevators. I thought you knew that. Didn't you know I walked eight flights to labor and delivery the day Owen was born?"

"Interesting," he said under his breath. He stared at me and his eyes seemed to be searching me in a reflective way that I had never experienced from a doctor before. "Well, anyway," he said, shaking his head as if coming out of a trance, "I'm going to write down the name of a counselor at Fleet and Family Support. If you think it might help to talk to someone, give them a call." He scribbled something in the chart and looked up at me again. Our eyes met for a second, but then I looked away.

"Right now, though, I think you should take care of that one over there." Dr. Ashley pointed with his pen at Ford and I turned to look at him. He had gotten into my purse and scattered lipstick and tampons and money across the floor.

"Oh, my gosh," I said, jumping down from the table. "Ford, I told you not to touch the hospital floor!"

"I'm sorry, Momma," he said. "Waterless soap?"

Dr. Ashley laughed.

I bent down to pick up my wallet and a box of baby wipes, and when I did, I felt a rush of air go up my backside. Clutching the edges of the gown closed behind me with one hand, I shrieked and spun around.

Dr. Ashley was covering his smile with a hand. He stepped forward and bent down to pick up a small blue rectangular book off the floor. He handed it to me and said, "Here, you don't want to forget this."

"The checkbook!" I whispered. "He left the checkbook." I meant to say this to myself, but Dr. Ashley heard and said, "You didn't want Dustin to leave you with the checkbook?"

I flipped through the pages filled with Dustin's minuscule markings and arithmetic. "I've barely even looked inside this thing except to write checks," I said.

When I looked back up, my eyes met Dr. Ashley's and he smiled. "You're something else," he said, patting my shoulder. "Dustin's a lucky man."

He gathered up my charts. "I'm going to go get the attendant so we can start your exam," he said. "But before I forget, I want to give you this." He handed me a small piece of paper with an advertisement for Viagra across the top and a phone number scribbled in the middle. I already had the appointment-line number, but this one looked different.

"Now listen," he said, "if you need anything—anything at all— just give me a call."

I tucked the paper into my purse and said, "Thanks."

"I'll be back in a minute."

Dr. Ashley's assistant played with Ford and cooed at Owen while I lay with my feet in the stirrups, chattering nonstop from nerves.

"I've always thought of you as more of a friend than a doctor," I said to Dr. Ashley.

"Uh-huh," he said distractedly. Metal instruments clinked together on a tray.

"The only difference," I said, "is that you see me naked ninety percent of the time."

Dr. Ashley peered up at me with a surprised look on his face.

I am such an idiot.

"So how about incontinence?" he asked.

"Inconti-what?"

"Your urination. Do you feel like you're going to the bathroom often?"

"Nope! All good!"

He slid across the room with the rolling chair and peeled off his rubber gloves before tossing them like a basketball into a trash can. "So everything looks great," he said.

Everything?

89

I pulled myself up on my elbows and Dr. Ashley lent his hand and helped me sit up.

"You're good for another year," he said and gathered up my chart.

"Hey, thanks for everything," I said. "I mean, you always know exactly—"

Dr. Ashley smiled. "Don't mention it," he said. "Anything for my favorite patient. And remember, call me anytime."

His favorite?

He walked to Ford and tousled the top of his fine hair. "Take care of your mom," he said. "She's a special lady."

Then Dr. Ashley closed the door behind himself and the assistant, and for a moment I felt like a piece of me had walked out with him.

I was alone again.

6

YOU'RE NOT SUPPOSED TO FEEL GOOD ABOUT YOURSELF

It was Friday afternoon and the weekend was ahead of me. Most military wives will tell you that weekends are the worst, because that's when other families—families that are intact—take trips to the zoo, attend birthday parties, and share a pan of lasagna over a loud, but lively, dinner table. That's when the reality of being a family separated by an entire ocean and a few continents becomes painfully obvious.

There is no easy way to get around the inevitable pain when you see your neighbor's husband come home and take his kids outside to play ball, but some wives fill the void by taking up a new hobby. They become interested in art, yoga, or learning a new language. Some even go back to school.

But these ventures all require money, so our Spouse Club came up with something entirely different and a lot less intellectual: BUNCO. I'm not even sure I liked BUNCO, but staying home alone and missing Dustin was not an option if I wanted to survive.

Jody was hosting the game at her house on this particular night, so I left the boys with Lauren and showed up early to help with the preparations: tossing baseball bats and Matchbox cars into random closets, and stowing away the stack of romance novels Jody kept on the back of her guest bathroom toilet.

I opened the front door and let myself in without knocking. "Jody?" My voice echoed off the bare walls and floors.

"Come in, Sarah," she yelled from a back room. "I'm giving the boys a bath."

I walked through the kitchen and smelled Lysol and Mop & Glo. That was encouraging. But then I rounded the corner and came into the living room, where Michael's bicycle was leaning against the purple-and-green-plaid sofa.

It was good that I had come early.

I looked around the cluttered room, wondering where to start first. Jody's house was so much like herself: simple, unrefined, and sporty. She is not at all interested in home decor. In fact, I think she once threatened me with eating canned ravioli if I ever brought a copy of *Martha Stewart Living* into her home again.

Whereas I consider painting the walls of my house various shades of red and brown just as necessary as unpacking and plugging in the toaster, Jody prefers to leave hers "the way they came." The three most decorative items in her house were a framed print of a moose, which hung above the couch, café curtains in the kitchen with lighthouses on them, and a fake (although very life-like) squirrel that sat atop the television and changed his attire with the seasons.

I passed Mr. Squirrel and felt compelled to pet him. I always imagined his eyes following me like those of the *Mona Lisa*. But on this night, he was still wearing a red Santa hat, and that disturbed me.

Michael and Brandon streaked through the living room, giggling and leaving a trail of wet carpet. Jody came after them with a handful of wet towels.

"You need to take down that Santa hat," I said. "It's depressing me."

"Not until Valentine's Day," she said, "when Mr. Squirrel can put on his red sweater." She ducked into the laundry room and called out over her shoulder, "If it bothers you, just don't look at it."

She was always so practical.

The rest of the wives arrived in spurts, until soon Jody's cavernous house was bustling with gaggles of women clustered in cliques and doing the mandatory party talk.

I watched the parade of high heels, painted nails, and blond highlights. Each woman was so different, yet fundamentally alike, and all of us were alone. Spending the evening with them was like visiting family. It was just as painful and tedious as talking to my husband's aunt's niece's boyfriend at Thanksgiving dinner, but also felt just as necessary. As much as I disliked some of the other wives, in that moment, with our husbands out at sea, we were bonded in a way I could feel, but couldn't necessarily define.

Besides playing BUNCO, we were also welcoming a new spouse to the Club (Lynette) and celebrating the recent engagement of Trish, whose fiancé hastily popped the question after receiving news of the sudden detachment-now-turned-deployment. In an unexpected gesture, Jody had made a congratulatory cake in the shape of a diamond ring. I didn't even know Jody could bake. She also pulled out decorations from her own wedding to use as centerpieces. In the center of each rickety folding table were light blue fabric flowers sticking up from bud vases of etched glass, and tapered candles leaned precariously from porcelain holders shaped like doves. The candles showed no signs of having been burned before, and I wondered why Jody hadn't lit them at her own reception six years before. Then again, did I really want to ask? Anything was possible with Jody and Steve. Their cake topper had been R2-D2 and C-3PO from Star Wars.

For the first round of BUNCO, I sat at a table with Lynette, Courtney, and Trish. I was surprised by how much Lynette reminded me of my mom. It wasn't just her shoulder-length, flipped-out hair that was so black and straight, it almost looked blue, or the way she smelled like Chanel No. 5; rather, it was mostly because she claimed to be an e-Bay fanatic and to love anything vintage or antique. As I listened to Lynette talk about her "sales," I had flashbacks to my last few years living at home, when the upstairs hallway was always cluttered with boxes and bubble wrap and Mom's odd e-Bay finds, like the antique dolls that were shipped with the bodies in one box and the heads in another. The rubber of the dolls was so old, it was sticky, and I still have nightmares of them coming to life and chasing me through a garage, only I can't get away because my feet are sticking to packaging tape on the floor. It's because of stuff like this, plus the fact that no furniture in my childhood home was less than a hundred years old, that I steer clear of anything "gently used."

Soon the conversation switched to Trish's wedding plans, because that's the direction all brides-to-be steer conversations. And like romance-starved lunatics, we probed her for details about every last thing: What kind of dress did she want? How many bridesmaids would she have? Buffet or sit-down?

But Trish seemed primarily (for the moment) focused on the idea of music, and only wanted advice on that: Should she use a DJ or a band? What did we think about having someone sing during the ceremony?

Courtney told Trish about her wedding at the United States Naval Academy. It was a story I had heard a thousand times, and I wondered why married women feel compelled to tell brides all about their weddings. It must be the same compulsion that makes us tell pregnant women about our ruptured membranes and mastitis. We have so few opportunities to be experts, I suppose.

"What songs did you guys use for your first dance?" Trish wanted to know, and after Courtney finished her long-winded, off-topic tale about the canapés at her reception, I told Trish that Dustin and I danced to "The Long and Winding Road," by the Beatles.

"That's an interesting song to dance to," Lynette said. "What made you pick it?"

"Sarah and Dustin have known each other since they were babies," Courtney said, obviously pleased to know so much about me that she can finish my own sentences. Although I never had a sister growing up, I imagine if I had, she would have been like Courtney.

"Really?" Lynette and Trish said in unison.

I took the dice and rolled my turn. "Yes, it's true. Our dads flew together in the same squadron, and our moms were in the Spouse Club. So when I was born, Mrs. Smiley came to Mom's baby shower and they became friends. Dustin was one year old at the time, and my dad was on deployment, so technically I met my husband before I ever met my dad."

Lynette put a hand to her chest. "That is the sweetest story I've ever heard! So you guys grew up together?"

"Show them the picture," Courtney said.

I got my wallet from the kitchen and flipped through pictures of Ford and Owen and Tanner until I came to a yellowed snapshot of two toddlers standing on a pier. I passed the picture to Lynette. "That's us," I said. "I was three and he was four. Our dads were leaving for deployment that day."

"Look at how he has his arm around you!" Lynette cried. "That's adorable." She passed the picture to Trish.

"So why 'The Long and Winding Road'?" Trish asked.

"Well, there's a line in the song that goes something like, 'I've seen that road before. . . . It always leads me here . . . leads me to your door.' "

I felt awkward speaking words that clearly sound better sung, but Courtney took care of that and started singing the verse in a breathy voice.

"Anyway," I said when she was finished, "the song reminds us of growing up together, not seeing each other for a few years while we were in high school, and then meeting up again in college. It seems no matter which way we go, we always wind up back together again."

"That is just so sweet," Trish said. "So what did you use for your father-daughter dance?"

Apparently Trish had a one-track mind.

I had to think about the father-daughter song for a minute. "Hmmm," I said, looking up at the ceiling. "My dad's not much of a dancer—he's really quite shy—so I remember we only danced for, like, half a minute and then my brother Will—or was it Van?—took over. But what was the song? I can't believe I don't remember this . . ."

"It was 'The Way You Look Tonight' by Frank Sinatra," Courtney said. "At least, that's what's playing on your wedding video."

"Oh, yeah, that's right," I said. "I've always loved that song. It's perfect for a father-daughter dance. I just wish Dad and I had danced together longer. Maybe someday when he's old and senile he'll forget he doesn't like to dance and I can trick him into dancing with me at his old-folks home."

Courtney smiled at me in a familiar, sympathetic way. Only she could have known there was more—much more—to what I was saying. But Trish and Lynette just laughed.

Trish handed me the photograph, and before I put it in my wallet, I stared at it and thought about my and Dustin's wedding day.

We were married in a small wooden chapel in Fort Monroe, Virginia. It was the middle of July, but the weather was unseasonably mild, without a cloud in the sky. The only glitch in the whole event was the fact that I had broken my right leg walking in platform shoes six weeks beforehand. The first time I walked without crutches was just days before coming down the aisle. Yet anyone who didn't already know never would have guessed; there was so much adrenaline coursing through my legs that day, I walked down the red-carpeted aisle without the faintest limp.

I remember Dustin was especially handsome in his military choker whites and fresh haircut. The smile on his face as Dad escorted me toward him shined like a lighthouse guiding me through the haze of relatives and friends who stared at me and whispered, "Good luck," as I passed by.

Luck? Was I going to need that? Why not just love and happiness?

My hands were shaking, so Dad patted them and said, "Don't be nervous. It's just a bunch of people we know."

Then, at the altar, he gave my hand to Dustin and kissed me on the cheek. In that moment, I was transformed from an "03"—Navy lingo for "third-born child"—to a "30"—"first spouse." I was officially someone else's dependent.

"BUNCO!" Jody yelled from across the room at the head table and rang a bell. It was time to switch tables. Lynette and I had won, so we moved up to table number two, joining Melanie and Sasha, who wore a cropped top to flaunt her new navel ring and flat tummy. The bell rang again and Sasha threw the dice. Everyone was quiet and awkward for a moment. It's always hard to switch tables and start a new conversation. Kind of like speed dating for friends.

Finally Lynette broke the silence. "So do a lot of the wives in the Club have children?"

"Paul and I have a daughter," Melanie said. "We'd like to have more though."

Sasha handed the dice to me for my turn. "I have four children," she said. "Three girls and a boy."

I was afraid Sasha might start her woe-is-me-I-have-four-children talk and never stop, so I spoke up before she could continue.

"I have two boys," I said. "Ford is two and Owen is two months old."

"Wow, a newborn," Lynette said. "I have three children myself. Two boys and a girl."

Again I thought, just like Mom, who had me and my two older brothers. I was sure any minute Lynette would say she was also from Alabama, drank four Diet Cokes a day, and took bowling in college.

"My son is also two years old," Lynette said. "We should get him and your son together sometime."

"That sounds great." I passed the dice to Melanie.

"Tell me honestly," Sasha said, looking at Lynette. "Would you ever have guessed Sarah has two kids?"

I jolted in my seat. I knew Sasha couldn't mean "Can you believe she's had two kids and looks so skinny," because I was clearly postpartum and about twenty pounds overweight. Sometimes Sasha simply had no filter. Thoughts came right from her brain and out through her mouth, and I was afraid of what she might say next.

Lynette looked at me confused. "Well, I don't know. I didn't really think about it, I guess."

"I guess you'd have to know Sarah to know what I mean," Sasha said. "This is the girl who sat on a table at a Ronald McDonald concert when she was eight months pregnant and the table actually broke beneath her!"

Melanie was holding the dice in her hand and staring at Sasha.

"This is the girl," Sasha continued, "who has broken her leg twice and arm once . . . for no good reason! I mean, at least you've got to have a good falling story, but no, Sarah's are always about tripping over a baby gate, or—"

"I really think that's uncalled for," Melanie said.

"What?" Sasha shrieked. "I'm just telling the truth. Sarah's like a walking calamity."

"If you can't say something nice—" Melanie started to say, but I stopped her.

"It's all right, really. Honestly, it is amazing I haven't accidentally burned down the house yet or something."

Melanie looked at me pleadingly, as though she were the one who needed rescuing. I knew she wanted to say more—that she wanted to defend me—but I expected as much from Sasha, and oddly, I really wasn't that hurt.

Sasha was like a tornado: You know you should get out of the way, but you can't stop gawking. She was loud and obnoxious, but, to her credit, you could never say she was a fake. And despite my difficult relationship with her, I admired how she didn't feel compelled to hide anything about herself. In fact, she embraced it all.

Courtney and I stayed late to help Jody with the cleanup. I was washing dishes and Courtney was drying when she said, "So how was your exam with Cute Doctor? I can't believe you went through with it!"

"What was I supposed to do?" I said and handed her another clean plate.

Courtney raised her eyebrows. "Um, like, change doctors!"

"Have you ever tried to change Navy doctors?" I said. "The paperwork alone could take years!"

Jody came in from the living room and put another stack of dirty dishes on the counter. "You know," she said, "I've decided it's kind of sweet the way Sarah thinks about Cute Doctor. I mean, her dad was gone so much when she was little, I bet he's like a father figure for her."

"A 'father' wouldn't do your pelvic exam," Courtney cried. "Good grief!"

"It's not like that," I said. "He just makes me feel good about myself, I guess."

Courtney rolled her eyes and threw a handful of plastic cups into the trash. "Well, for cryin' out loud!" she said. "You aren't supposed to feel *good* about yourself—you're a married woman, for God's sake!"

I turned off the water and dried my hands on a dish towel. "The whole thing reminds me of those Hawaiian dancers," I said. "The ones who wear coconuts to cover up their . . . well, you know."

"Their breasts?" Jody said.

"Yes, those."

Courtney threw up her hands. "Now I've heard it all! How on earth does your ob-gyn remind you of grass skirts and coconuts?"

"Haven't you ever seen the way men look at those women?" I said. "It doesn't matter if the dancers are a hundred years old, if they're married, or if they have twenty children. While they're onstage wearing those coconuts, the men love them. They're hypnotized."

"So this is about needing a pedestal," Courtney said.

I frowned. "I actually have one of those coconut bras. Did you know that? Dustin bought it for me in Hawaii, and he used to ask me to put it on all the time. But now? Now it just sits collecting dust in the top of the closet. He's probably forgotten I even have it."

Jody was tying up a bag of trash. She stopped and looked up at us. "You know, I kind of get what she's saying. I can't remember the last time Steve looked at me the way he used to back when we were younger."

I tried picturing Jody in a grass skirt and coconut top.

"I can't believe you two!" Courtney cried. "Especially you, Jody! Have you lost your mind? Make your own damn pedestals! Go buy a new pair of shoes. Highlight your hair. Do something—anything! Just don't get all giddy for your ob-gyn!"

I stared dreamily at them and shrugged. "I'm Dr. Ashley's coconut girl. I'm a coconut girl."

I walked home in the cold, trying to figure out in my mind how
much to pay Lauren. Did Dustin say five or six dollars an hour? I
wondered. And what to do about the additional forty-five minutes? I wished my BUNCO night had ended on the hour. It
would make figuring out the money so much easier.

Lauren was sitting on the couch watching *The Bachelor* when I
came in the front door. Her face and the room was tinted blue
from the glow of the television.

"Hey," she said, looking surprised. And then, "What time is it?"

"Almost ten. I'm sorry I'm so late."

"Not a problem at all," she said. Then she nodded at the television. "You ever watch this show?"

I looked at the screen and saw a row of women in black
dresses waiting patiently for a rose from the bachelor.

"Uh, yeah, I've seen it a few times," I said; then I riffled
through my purse. "Will thirty dollars be enough, Lauren?"

"Yes, ma'am," she said, standing up from the couch to
straighten her denim miniskirt with a tattered hem.

"Ma'am"? Was I really old enough for that?

"Please, call me Sarah," I said.

Lauren smiled. "OK, Sarah it is, then." She slipped on a pair of
bejeweled flip-flops and started toward the door. I followed behind. At the entryway she turned around and said, "Oh, my gosh,
Mrs. Smi—I mean, Sarah—I looked at your wedding album—I
hope you don't mind. It was sitting on the piano—and wow! Mr.
Smiley is *so* cute!"

At first I thought she meant my father-in-law and I must have
looked surprised.

"I mean, your husband," she said. "He looks just like Tom
Cruise!"

"Oh, my goodness," I said, laughing. "Well, people do tell him that a lot. But if you knew him . . . I mean, looks can be deceiving . . . I mean . . ."

Lauren looked at me, confused.

"Never mind," I said. "Anyway, it's actually quite frustrating being married to someone prettier than me."

"Oh, stop!" she said, waving her hand. She opened the front door and started to walk out. "Please call me anytime, Mrs.—I mean, Sarah."

I closed the door and said aloud to myself, "Mrs.?" Could I be that much older than Lauren? Wasn't I just like her only a few years ago?

I had just closed my eyes and gone to sleep when the telephone rang. The pulse of the ringer startled me and I shot up in bed, looking around confused. Then I glanced at the clock. It was ten thirty.

The phone rang again, and this time Tanner got up from her pillow and stretched.

"It's all right, Tanner girl," I said. "It's just the phone. Go back to bed."

I picked up the receiver on the bedside table. There was static on the other end.

"Sarah? Is that you?"

My heart nearly flipped over. "Dustin? I can barely hear you. Is that you, Dustin?"

"It's me, babe. Did I wake you up?"

There was a delay in the connection and our sentences were overlapping each other. Until then I had forgotten how hard it is to talk from overseas.

"I can't hear you very well, Dustin. Can you speak up?"

It sounded like a disco in the background. I heard people yelling and singing over the rhythmic thump of music.

"I'm sorry. What did you say, Sarah? I can't hear you."

"Are you at a nightclub?"

"We're in Spain right now. I'm out with the guys. It's a little hard to hear."

I heard someone's voice in the background: "Come on, Dustin, another round of—"

I blinked and rubbed my eyes. "Are you drunk, Dustin?"

"What, babe?"

Dustin never calls me "babe" unless he is drunk.

I decided to ignore his slurred speech. "Hey, Dustin, listen for a minute. I need to ask you something."

"Go ahead, I'm listening. But you'll have to speak up," he said.

I was worried about waking the kids, especially Owen, who was finally sleeping in six-hour stretches, but I raised my voice anyway.

"Dustin, do you think I'm a little—how should I say this— flighty?"

"What? Why do you ask?" There were hoots and hollers coming from the background.

"Sasha called me a 'walking calamity' tonight."

"Did you say a 'walking calamity'?"

"Yes, a 'walking calamity.' "

Dustin laughed. "Well, you always have been my little fire-cracker. Especially that last night at home. Wow!"

I rolled my eyes.

"Hey, Sarah," he said, "you wouldn't believe this place. It's amazing. The wine flows like water. The women—oh, my gosh, the women! They flock to us Americans. We're like rock stars. I practically had to beg them to quit asking me to dance."

My jaw dropped open. I had to remind myself to breathe. Was he really telling me this?

"Dustin, you're drunk," I said more firmly than I had meant to.

"Oh, I'm totally drunk, babe. How are the kids?"

I couldn't find any words. My throat was closing in and tears came to my eyes. Here I was diapering babies and cleaning dishes, and my husband was gallivanting around the world having a great time.

The injustice of it all was astounding, and I couldn't bear to hear Dustin's voice any longer.

"Sorry, Dust. I can't really hear you that well," I said. "I think the connection is breaking up. Can you call me back another time?"

"Sure, babe. Is everything OK?"

I pretended not to hear. "What's that, Dustin? I can't hear you. . . . The connection must be bad. . . ."

"Connection's fine on my end," he said.

"Sorry, Dust. You're breaking up. I'm going to go now. Talk to you soon, I guess. Bye." I bit my lip and hung up the phone.

After the charger beeped and Tanner settled back down on her pillow, the house was painfully quiet, and I realized I was alone.

"Tanner?" I whispered. "Tanner girl?"

Tanner poked her head out from under the bed and I reached down to scoop her up, feeling her frail rib beneath my palm. Then I put her next to me as I lay on my back and patted her fluffy fur, trying to picture Dustin in Spain. *Was it really as glamorous as it seemed? And what was that he said about the women?*

A tear rolled out of the corner of my eye and dripped sideways into my ear.

Through the static of the baby monitor, I heard Owen stir in his crib and whimper.

No, don't wake up. Not yet. Just let Mommy get some sleep.

I lay tense and motionless, willing Owen to go back to sleep. But his whimpers soon escalated to full-blown cries, and I slid out of bed to get him.

The kitchen and living room were completely dark, and I had

that feeling of being a child and running to your parents' room after a bad dream. I could have sworn I felt someone on my heels, chasing me as I walked, and then double-stepped, through the room.

I got Owen out of his crib and brought him to the couch. When I snuggled his warm body against me, I felt the muscles in my jaw and neck release. I hadn't been aware they were tense. I stared at Owen's pink cheeks and round, searching eyes and momentarily forgot how mad I was at Dustin.

"Your dad may be visiting exotic ports," I whispered to Owen, "but he's missing this."

When Owen heard my voice and looked up at me with big watery eyes, for the first time I felt sorry for Dustin instead of envying him.

The clock in the kitchen ticked noisily and Owen's sucking slowed. Soon he was drifting back to sleep. His wrinkled, delicate fingers were balled up in fists, but the muscles in his mouth had gone lax and his lips glistened with saliva and milk.

I turned onto my back and settled into the throw pillows. Owen snored faintly, and I could feel his thin breath on my neck.

How long has it been since someone hugged me? I wondered. Sure, Ford gave me hugs, and Jody and Courtney occasionally draped their arms around my shoulder or patted my back to say hello, but when was the last time someone gave me a tight, meaningful hug? The kind that squeezes your ribs and makes you feel compact?

So often we take human contact for granted, I think, until we realize we haven't had much of it for quite some time. I lay there stroking Owen's fine, fluffy hair and thinking about a study I once heard about children who fail to thrive and grow if they don't receive enough contact with another human being. Would the same thing happen to adults? I wondered. Could an adult actually fail to grow and thrive without enough affection?

I was fading in and out of sleep, and each time my eyes fell shut, I had visions of Dr. Ashley's blue eyes and the dimples on his cheeks.

That night I dreamed Dr. Ashley was guiding me into Dustin's favorite restaurant with his hand at the small of my back. Then we were sitting at a table together and he reached over to pat my hand. "There's no other place I'd rather be right now," Dr. Ashley said. He leaned across the table, placing his hand on the side of my cheek, and kissed me slowly, until I had chills down my back and warmth in my stomach.

7

I GUESS YOU COULD SAY I KNOW MY &%$@ NOW

The last Tuesday in January, Jody and Courtney came over to watch the president's state of the union address. Under normal circumstances, when our husbands were home, the three of us would ditch the men and get together to watch *Sex and the City* or *Friends*; it was pretty funny that now we were gathering over wine and chocolate cheesecake to watch politics.

Yet no one was laughing when President Bush announced the United States' plan to attack Iraq even without support from the United Nations. His words seemed to wash over us, and none of us dared say aloud what they might mean for our husbands and our families. None of us mentioned "war." It was as if we had detached ourselves and were living in a realm separate from our normal lives. Time lost all meaning. I couldn't remember what day Dustin had left, or how long he had been gone. But it seemed like forever already.

Everything—the detachment-turned-sudden-deployment, the tension in Iraq—just sort of happened, the idea of it seeping into my consciousness like a creaky floorboard, so that when people began talking in line at the grocery store about "the war with Iraq" and "troops heading to the Middle East," it felt like old news to me. It was like watching friends and family *ooh* and *aah* over a newly announced pregnancy, when the mother-to-be has known all along—since that first twinge in her belly and funny taste in her mouth—that she is expecting.

"My husband will be in a war" was all I could think. And the thought never stunned me. It was almost as if the circumstances were meant to be a part of my and Dustin's lives all along, yet we were only just now remembering.

The most painful sort of déjà vu.

It was around this time that I began to feel sick with loneliness. Like grief, the reality of deployment hits everyone at different times, and my time was now. My trigger had been pulled, and the reality of a long deployment with a yet undetermined ending seemed unbearable. I had hit my "wall," as it is sometimes called, and momentarily felt I couldn't go on.

Days were running into nights and I often couldn't remember if it was Monday or Tuesday or Sunday. But what did it matter anyway? Weekdays are for work and weekends are for family. But I wasn't working. And my family wasn't together. I had slipped through society's loophole and was neither a single girl who could go out and party with her friends, nor a married woman making dinner for her family every night. It was as if my life was on hold, and the long days feeding into restless nights—made even more restless with a newborn baby—began to make me feel heavy and tired.

If only I could curl up in bed and sleep away the next few months, I often thought. But then Ford or Owen would do something really cute, or they would smile at me in a way that was oblivious and innocent, and I knew I had to muster the courage to go on. If only for them.

Ford began asking lots of questions. "Where is Daddy?" he

would say, and "Why did Daddy leave us?" How do you explain "serving the country" to a two-year-old? I wondered. My answers—"Daddy's on that big ship, remember?" and "He's away doing his job"—always seemed to leave Ford more confused than ever.

I felt myself spiraling down to depression. I was so mentally and physically exhausted, my bones ached.

My one saving grace was the toilet.

No, really!

A mental buffer military spouses can depend on is the fact that household chores continue despite all else. The car doesn't stop needing gas. Filters continue to need cleaning. And windows still need washing.

Most military spouses eventually find comfort in these daily tasks. One might even say they become a distraction, whether you realize it at the time or not.

My first "distraction" was the guest bathroom toilet that wouldn't stop running. At first I tried ignoring the steady swooshing sound—which sounded a lot like a miniature waterfall—coming from the bathroom. I even tried willing it to stop. (I had seen something once on *Oprah* or CNN about using brain power to cause things to happen.) But by midafternoon I had had enough and picked up the phone to call the old safety net: my mom. Who, in turn, passed the phone to *her* safety net: Dad.

"Check and see if the chain is hanging from the arm," Dad said.

I put my hand in the cold water of the tank. "What arm? What chain?"

"There should be a thin metal chain hanging from a bar, and a rubber cap on the end of it," he said.

I will point out here that I am adamantly against toilets. Not that I don't use them, of course. But I use them for their purpose and move on. I find no pleasure in hanging around, reading a magazine, and having more contact with the toilet than necessary. In college once, my roommates submitted me to the worst kind of torture by tying my arms and legs and placing me bare bottomed on a public commode.

Porta Potties are my enemy.

So it was no surprise then that I winced when I put my hand farther into the water and sloshed it around. "I can't feel it, Dad," I said.

"Feel it? You should be able to just see it, Sarah! Are you looking in the tank?"

"No," I said. "I'm afraid to. I don't want to see what's in there!"

"Sarah, it's fresh water!" I pictured Dad's eyes bugging out of his ruddy face, the way they do when he gets impatient. "And you've already got your hand in it anyway!"

After a long, painful five minutes of Dad failing to see the humor in my fear of toilet water but walking me through the process of plumbing repair anyway, the toilet was fixed, and I felt proud of myself, like I had won a battle or faced one of my worst fears.

But I don't think Dad laughed when I closed the lid of the tank and said with a grin, "So I guess you could say I know my shit now, huh, Dad?"

"Uh, do you need to talk to your mother?"

The following Sunday, Tanner woke me up early. Despite being a patient, even-tempered dog who could almost be overlooked, she was so quiet, at six a.m. she was barking and scratching her paws on the wood of the back door.

I got out of bed and walked hunched and shivering into the living room. The silvery morning light coming through the windows in horizontal beams made me squint and, unfortunately, highlighted all the dust on top of our television. When the stress of deployment hits, useless household tasks such as cooking and cleaning are unfortunately the first to be forgotten.

Tanner was standing with her nose pressed to the door.

"What is it, Tanner?" I asked.

She barked again and her hind legs nearly came out from under her.

My teeth were chattering. "Do you need to go out? At this time of the morning? Or is there a squirrel somewhere in the bushes?" I peered out the window but couldn't see anything.

Tanner cocked her head and whimpered. Clearly she needed to go, and in a hurry.

"Well, let me get some clothes on," I said and started to walk away.

But Tanner whined and barked louder. I was afraid she would wake up the boys, so I turned on my heel and said, "Shh! Quiet, girl!"

Her eyes were pleading now, and I knew there was no time to put on clothes. I looked down at my nightshirt with cowgirls on the front, which came down just long enough to cover my rear end. But the backyard was fenced, and who will see me? I thought. So I slipped on a pair of pink flip-flops and headed toward the door again.

"All right, Tanner," I said. "Have it your way. But make it quick."

I pressed buttons on the alarm system keypad and waited for it to beep and flash green before I opened the door. A burst of cold air brushed across my legs and the wood blinds banged against the door.

"Go on, girl," I said, and Tanner scurried over the threshold, limping slightly on her right hind leg. This was a new ailment, adding to the growing list of signs that my childhood pet was aging.

Tanner hurried toward the fence and did her business in the same spot as always: right beside the flowers I'd planted last spring and seen die sometime around Halloween. Lifeless bare twigs poked up through the ground where thriving plants were once covered in tiny blue flowers.

Why that same exact spot? I wondered as I watched her. She could be so neurotic sometimes!

I laughed to myself thinking about the time Tanner chased a leaping gecko into our living room from the back porch. I had run around in my bathrobe trying to catch the lizard in a plastic cup, while Ford squealed with delight, "Mommy, it's not gonna hurt you. The wizard just wants to sit on our couch!"

I had always thought Tanner was mocking me as she watched me hop and leap across the room, screaming each time the gecko got away. She sure could get spiteful!

"Come on, Tanner, let's go!" I called out from the doorway now. She seemed to be finishing up. But after glancing in my direction and seeing me standing there with bare legs and that ridiculous nightshirt, she quickly got interested in sniffing around a pile of discarded seeds under our bird feeder.

I was worried about a cold draft making it into the house and waking the boys, and because this was apparently turning into a morning jaunt, I stepped out onto the concrete patio and closed the back door behind me.

Birds were beginning to chirp from nests high in the trees, eyeing the pile of seeds Tanner was nosing, no doubt. I jogged in place to warm my bare legs, but goose bumps were already spreading from my shins, up my knees and to my thighs. Thank goodness for the privacy fence: I didn't even have on a bra.

"Come on, Tanner!" I called. "Let's go back in."

She turned and stared at me.

"Come on, Tanner! Now!"

She sat on her haunches and stared.

"I'm not kidding! Come on!"

I involuntarily stomped my right foot—a common signal to Tanner (and Dustin) that I am getting mad. But Tanner just lay down and placed her muzzle on her front paws. She looked at me with sad eyebrows that dipped in the middle.

"Oh, all right," I said. She could be so demanding. And manipulative!

"Want a treat?" I yelled and she bounded toward the patio.

What a sucker I was! I mean, who had trained whom here? I patted her head and said, "Good girl," and tried to open the door with my other hand. The shiny gold doorknob was stiff and wouldn't turn. "Oh, come on!" I said and kicked the stoop. Tanner looked up at me and blinked. She seemed to be laughing.

"It's not funny, Tanner! The door won't open."

She whined and turned in a circle.

I tried the knob again and pushed on the door with my hip. Nothing.

"No!" I said under my breath. "No, no, no, NO!"

Tanner sat back down on her haunches and looked up at me.

"We're locked out, Tanner."

I stared at the door in silence for a moment, trying to think of all the neighbors who might have a key to our house. Jody did, of course, but I'd have to walk past three houses to get to hers, and I may *sleep* in a cowgirl nightshirt, but I do have my modesty.

I tiptoed through the wet grass, toward the boys' bedroom window. The blinds were closed, but I smooshed my head against the glass trying to get a glimpse between the slats. I couldn't see anything except the yellow glow coming from the Superman night-light Lauren had given Ford.

Owen would wake up soon, and then, like dominoes, his crying would wake up Ford, who would be scared when he couldn't find me in the house. I had no choice but to leave the backyard and the safety of the fence to find someone to help.

When I came around to the front yard, Brent and Danielle's house still looked dark and sleepy. There weren't any lights on as far as I could see.

But maybe that's a good thing, I thought. Then they'll be too tired to notice my pajamas and unshaven legs.

I rapped my hand on the glass door and pulled on the hem of my shirt, trying at least to bring it far enough down to cover my panties. Puffs of white breath escaped between my chattering teeth. I hopped up and down to warm myself.

Several seconds passed and no one answered.

I knocked again, a little louder this time.

Still, no one came to the door.

"Oh, for Heaven's sake!" I said and rang the doorbell.

A few more minutes passed; then lights started coming on, one by one, until I could see Brent's silhouette shuffling toward the door.

I waved sheepishly, then pulled down on my hem again.

Brent opened the door and squinted. "Sarah? What's going on?" he said.

I shivered in the cold and hugged myself.

"Come on in," he said, waving his arm toward the foyer and taking a step back. "Danielle's still sleeping, but—"

"I can't," I said. "The boys are inside. I've locked myself out."

A smile came across Brent's face as he looked me up and down. "For some reason I thought you'd be a flannel jammies kind of girl."

I laughed. "Well, usually, yes. But my heater is stuck on high and I can't figure out how to reprogram that little computer thingy on the wall. So it was hot last night, but freezing this morning. I don't understand it. . . ."

Brent rubbed his chin and smiled.

"Anyway," I said, "please tell me you have a key to my house."

"I'm really sorry," he said, "but I don't think we have one."

"You're kidding, right?"

"Afraid not," he said. "We had one when we took care of Tanner while you were on vacation, but I'm pretty sure we gave it back. You want me to call a locksmith or something?" He opened the door wider. "Please, come on in."

"I can't . . . the kids . . ." I looked back in the direction of my house and saw Tanner going to the bathroom again, this time on Danielle's chrysanthemums.

"Oh, no! Tanner, get out of there!" I yelled, but she didn't hear.

"Don't worry about it," Brent said. He was looking past me, out across the yard at Tanner. "The flowers will be fine. But, Sarah, is Tanner sick?"

Sick? I stared thoughtfully at Tanner in the middle of the flower bed. "Well, I don't know," I said softly. "I hadn't thought about it, really."

Tanner was old, for sure, and she seemed to be aging even faster since I had children. But she couldn't be sick . . . could she? Tanner and I had been through so much together: high school, my first car, going off to college (she went with me), marriage, two deployments, and two children. At times she felt like an extension of myself. She was part of me. The idea of her being sick or dying was as unfathomable to me as a parent's imperfections are to a child.

I looked back up at Brent and realized how pathetic I sounded for not knowing whether or not my own dog was sick. So I shook my head and said, "But, gosh, no, she's not sick. Of course not."

Brent went inside to call a locksmith, and I went to comfort Tanner. When he came back out, he was carrying one of Danielle's bathrobes and two plastic lawn chairs. He had thrown on an Old Navy sweatshirt, but he was still wearing flannel pajama bottoms and slippers that looked like men's loafers. I wrapped myself in the bathrobe and hugged my knees to my chest as I sat in the chair on the driveway. Brent went to the backyard to look in the boys' window.

"Still asleep?" I asked when he came back around the corner.

"I can't see anything," he said. "But I don't hear them crying either. I'll go back and check again in a minute."

He sat down and pulled out a pack of cigarettes. "Want one?" he said, and I shook my head. He offered every time, even though I never accepted.

I watched him strike a match and light the end of a cigarette until it was aglow and crackling. Just the sight of the red fire seemed to warm me. He blew out the flame and placed the used match inside his pack of cigarettes; then he pulled Tanner up into his lap and stroked her back. No one else ever paid so much attention to Tanner. Well, except for me . . . and my dad, who in his quiet way, seems to have a kinship with animals. (I once saw Dad calm down a rattlesnake at the zoo just by staring at it through the glass.) When I was still living at home, Dad always took Tanner out with him when he rolled up under the cars to change the oil or fix the brakes. "How's life treating you, Tanner Wanner?" he would say, as if someday she would finally answer. Sometimes, in a weird sort of way, I think I was jealous of the attention Dad gave Tanner.

Brent puffed on his cigarette and blew smoke at the sky. "Beautiful day, isn't it?" he said.

I looked out at the chilled grass. The neighborhood was so quiet and still, I felt like I had cotton in my ears.

But it was freezing.

And it was early.

Yet, still, Brent was smiling.

"Yes, I guess it is," I said and smiled to myself.

Brent had such an optimistic view of the world, a perpetual smile on his face. Sometimes when I asked, "What are you guys planning to do this weekend?" he would say, "I don't know, but whatever it is, it's going to be fun." Nothing seemed to get him down, and he was capable in every situation. I was sure his marriage was perfect and that Danielle was one of the luckiest girls around.

"Hey, Brent," I said suddenly, "how long do you think a marriage is supposed to stay—how should I say this?—romantic?"

"What are you asking?" he said, squinting in my direction.

"Oh, I don't know. I mean, do you still feel in love? Do you ever wish for something more?"

I could feel Brent studying my profile. He puffed on his cigarette and exhaled. "Sure, we're happy, I guess. Although we don't get to have all the romantic homecomings and separations you and Dustin do," he said, laughing. "That's got to be one heck of an experience!"

I sighed and looked at the concrete. It would be humiliating to tell him about Dustin's less-than-romantic phone call from Spain. Civilians have such a Hollywood view of military life. Maybe it's the movies, or too many World War II photographs, but most people think having a husband "off at war" is somehow romantic. I hated to disappoint Brent and reveal the true nature of—the reality of—my and Dustin's life, so I just said, "Oh, sure—I'm just tired, I guess," and left it at that.

We sat in silence for several more minutes before the police arrived.

"You called the police?" I said, looking over at Brent.

"Just in case. I wanted to make sure if the locksmith didn't show up before I have to go to work—"

I smiled. "Thanks, Brent. Really. And remind me to give you a key for the next emergency."

Clearly I was his damsel in distress.

The police officer swaggered up the driveway in heavy black boots. It seemed like he couldn't lay his arms flat against his sides, but I couldn't tell if that was because of all the gadgets hanging off his uniform, or because of bulky muscles under his shirt. He had a mustache that looked like a Brillo pad, and his thick leather belt creaked as he came toward us.

Brent stood to shake hands. "Good morning, Officer," he said. "Thanks for coming out."

The officer hooked his thumbs through his belt loops. "What seems to be the trouble?" he said.

"My friend Sarah here has locked herself out," Brent said, "and her children are asleep inside. A locksmith is supposed to be on his way."

The radio clipped to the officer's shoulder squawked and he paused to listen. "Already on the scene. Over," he said into the receiver; then he looked up at me again. "Well, ma'am, never mind the locksmith. Let's go ahead and get you inside before all the neighbors wake up and see you sitting out here in your bathrobe."

Brent laughed. "Oh, most of us have seen her laundry flying out the front door anyway."

The officer looked back and forth between the two of us and my face turned hot. He was imposing and strong in his navy blue suit. But uniforms can be so misleading, can't they? People see a doctor's white coat, or a policeman's badge, and they instantly feel safe. They are comforted by an image or, rather, by their expectations of an image.

So what impression do people have when they see Dustin in his flight suit? I wondered. And suddenly it occurred to me that somewhere there was a policeman's wife waking up alone while her husband was across town on my driveway taking care of me. She had sacrificed time with her husband so that he could serve the public. Kind of like I was living alone so my husband could defend the country.

But did that wife mind being alone? Did she resent so many people needing her husband? Did she want him there to take care of her, instead of here taking care of me? Was she better equipped for the sacrifice than me? Would she collapse under the pressure?

And, most important, did she have a Cute Doctor?

The boys were still sleeping when I got back inside, so I went to the computer to check e-mail. I had heard from Courtney, who heard from Sasha, who heard from Kate, that e-mail was working on board the ship now, and a few wives had already received messages from their husbands.

I sat down in a noisy wooden chair borrowed from the kitchen table and pushed aside a stack of bills and mail before booting up the computer. Our system was outdated and needed replacing, but as I sat there watching the flashing monitor come to life, I knew during the next few months, it would become my "spouse." By the time the deployment was all over, I'd feel more connected to my in-box and the expectation of e-mail than I would another human being. The concept of "Dustin"—the man I used to smell and feel next to me in bed—would merely become a collection of e-mails stored in a folder marked "Dusty."

At least, that was the way it had been for Dustin's previous deployment.

Mom liked to tell me that I "have no idea what it was like for spouses before e-mail, when the only way to communicate with your soldier was through the postman!" When Dad first deployed, Mom relied on handwritten letters, often delivered out of sync, to keep her in touch with him.

But at least they didn't have to deal with the *expectation*, I've often thought. Mom couldn't realistically expect instant communication with her husband thousands of miles away, which eliminated the frequent disappointment and pain today's military spouse feels when she opens her in-box a million times a day ("just in case!") and finds nothing.

But that morning I was lucky. Once the screen was in focus

and the computer had retrieved my messages, the words SMI-LEY, DUSTIN H., LT appeared in bold type. I clicked on the link.

Dear Sarah,

Surprise! Our e-mail is finally working!

How are the boys? Is Owen doing anything new? I can't believe I'm going to miss his first smile, and probably when he begins to crawl. I missed all that with Ford also, remember? We'll need to have another baby just so I can see what the first year is actually like!

Hey, I want to apologize for the phone call from Spain. I was really drunk (I guess you knew that), and Steve said I made an ass of myself when I was talking to you. I know you were probably hoping for something more. Maybe I can call again soon and make it up to you.

Work is really busy, as you can imagine. I rescued two pilots yesterday. Their jet had gone off the side of the carrier and I was up in the helo, so my crew performed the rescue. What an incredible feeling to help someone like that!

Other than that, it's the same old grind here. We never get a day off, and we're pretty much working from the time we get up until the time we go to sleep.

I think of you often and wish our last few days/nights together had been better.

Love you,

Dustin

I printed up a copy of Dustin's message and took it to the kitchen, where I poured myself a Diet Coke with ice and reread each sentence line by line. I was still angry about the phone call from Spain, but seeing Dustin's familiar words, and the way he formatted the message perfectly, just like a real letter, made me smile.

I returned to the computer, put my drink down on top of the stack of bills, and wrote my reply:

> Dusty . . . You won't believe what just happened to me! When I took Tanner outside this morning, I accidentally locked myself out . . . and I was wearing my cowgirl nightshirt! Brent had to call the police. It was pretty embarrassing. Thankfully, the boys slept through it all and are still asleep now.
>
> That's great about your rescue. Will they print up something in the newspaper? If so, be sure to send me a copy.
>
> Ford and Owen are doing OK. Ford has a lot of questions about where you are and when you're coming back. Owen, of course, is oblivious. He grinned for the first time a few days ago. Ford was pushing him in the swing, and all of a sudden he flashed this meek, one-sided smile. It was great! Then again, maybe it was just gas.
>
> Remember the way Ford's first smile took up half his face? He had that huge half-moon thing going on and no teeth for like a year. I guess some kids need to grow into their ears or noses; Ford has grown into his smile.
>
> Anyway, Owen had his six-week checkup a few days ago. Everything was fine and he is growing on schedule.
>
> Well, speaking of, I hear Owen waking up now, so I'd better go feed him. Love you. ME

I left to feed Owen, and when I returned to the computer several hours later, not only did I not have a response from Dustin yet, but the ice in my drink had melted and condensation dripped down the glass, soaking the bills beneath it.

"Damn!" I said and stomped my foot. Although I wasn't sure if I was more upset about the wet papers or the words on the computer screen that read "No New Messages."

I took a deep breath and promised myself, "I will not write Dustin again until he writes me first!" *Hmpf!*

Interestingly, I felt very mature and in control when I left the room. Go figure.

8

YOUR DOCTOR CALLS YOU
BY YOUR FIRST NAME?

Finally—because it was only a matter of time—in the first week of February, Mom decided I wasn't doing well. She based this on one phone conversation during which I cried hysterically because I thought there was a raccoon stuck in my attic. So she planned a trip to Florida to rescue me.

The timing was perfect because my dad was leaving for a two-week detachment on board—coincidentally enough—the same aircraft carrier Dustin was on. In his position as a Navy Admiral, Dad made frequent trips to visit the carriers, but this would be the first time he and Dustin were on the same one together, and it placed Mom and me in an unusual situation: We'd be our own mother-daughter Spouse Club.

But I knew Mom's "rescue" might also involve the overwhelming temptation to return home to Virginia Beach, Virginia, which probably was the best, most logical idea, but one I'd never concede to. Going back with Mom would mean giving up, and it would affirm to everyone (including me) that I am not capable of taking care of myself. So I steeled myself for Mom's visit by repeating the mantra "I am an adult, I can do this; I am an adult, I can do this."

But, of course, as soon as I saw Mom's familiar brown hair with streaks of yellow-orange, I regressed to the mind-set of a four-year-old, and cried into the lapel of her red blazer, "Take me home with you. Please, Mommy, take me home with you!"

"Get ahold of yourself, Sarah," she said. "You have the boys to think of."

And with that, she spun into the kitchen and, in minutes, magically whipped up some egg salad for Ford and had Owen gurgling at her "ga-ga-goos."

I stood in the corner and leaned against the refrigerator for support.

Mom has a way of making things happen . . . instantly. And her energy knows no limits. I remember her cleaning bathrooms at two and three o'clock in the morning when I was a little girl and Dad was on deployment. She said it relieved her stress. But as I lay in bed and listened to the clank of the toilet lid and the squeak of the sponge, I often wondered, "What motivation gene am I missing?" Sometimes it takes all I have in me to get up and move wet clothes from the washer to the dryer. And often the clothes never get much farther than that. I simply use the laundry room as my closet and select clothes straight from the dryer. But not Mom; she is the definition of efficient.

"What we need to do is make a list," Mom said as she rummaged through my kitchen drawers for paper and a pen. She was opening and closing doors and mumbling something to the effect of "Don't you ever clean this place? How can you live like this?"

"A list?" I said. "What on earth for?"

"A list to get you motivated, Sarah. If we can just get your life organized, everything will be OK."

I wondered if Mom remembered who she was talking to—her child who dropped out of Girl Scouts after only one day and quit piano lessons if the teacher made me practice. How busy did she think I was that I needed a list?

"Mom, I can make that list for you right now, without the paper. Number one, my husband needs to come home, and number two, I need animal control to set traps in the attic."

Mom shut a cabinet door and turned to look at me. "Sarah, are you depressed?"

I sighed and rolled my eyes. "My husband's gone, Mom. What do you think? Of course I'm depressed. I'm functioning in a constant state of sleep deprivation and mild depression. But I'm growing quite fond of my condition, really. Now, about the raccoon—"

"There are no raccoons in your attic!"

She walked out of the room and went around the corner. A few minutes later, she came back with a yellow pad of paper and a pen. She sat on the edge of a kitchen chair, poised to write, with her back as straight as her hair. Ford stared at her, his mouth full of yellow egg salad. He had never seen anyone make a list.

"Number one," Mom said aloud as she wrote. "First thing tomorrow we're going to get some paint."

"Paint? What for?"

"For your front room," she said flatly. "Number two—"

"Whoa, wait a minute, Mom. What's wrong with my front room?"

"Oh, nothing really," she said. "It just needs some color is all. Now, for number two, we'll be going to Target to get some floor cleaner. Those stains on your linoleum are terrible. How do you live like this?"

I looked down at the floor and didn't see any stains.

"Number three," she said. "We need to get some plastic bins for storage."

I was afraid to ask what needed storing.

There were ten items on Mom's finished list, but not one of

them mentioned mental help, which I knew was what I really needed. Most of Mom's solutions involved cleaning supplies and magazines about living an organized life. Frankly, her list gave me a headache.

That night, I played hooky and read fashion magazines on the couch while Mom took care of the boys. I realized it's probably a good thing I don't live in the same city as my parents, because then I'd exist in a perpetual state of immaturity and helplessness. It seems whenever Mom is around, I can't take care of myself—much less my children. It's so much cozier to go limp and curl up on the couch under a blanket and call out occasionally, "Moooom, could you please get me some cookies . . . and hot cocoa . . . with marshmallows . . . and whipped cream . . . oh, and a straw . . . pretty please?"

After Mom was done putting the boys to bed, she came to sit on the couch with me. I lifted my stretched-out legs to make room for her, then promptly rested them in her lap and had the same warm feeling in my chest of being ten years old and home from school with a cold. Back then I'd sit on the couch while Mom watched Phil Donahue, and when the Loving Care commercial came on, we'd sing together, "I'm gonna wash that gray right out of my hair." I think I pretended to be sick sometimes just to have those days with her.

I caught myself dozing off as Mom patted my legs in her lap. She was watching CNN's *Crossfire*, which was like a virtual sleeping pill for me, but then again, I never sleep well when Dustin is gone, so I was exhausted. In fact, I feel like I don't sleep at all when I'm alone. Sometimes it seems like I simply have one eye shut and one eye open for five hours at a time. I suppose this is due to my overwhelming sense of being on guard: The responsibility of being the only adult in the house makes me anxious and restless.

On that night, however, as I listened to the noise of the television and felt the occasional pat of Mom's freckled hands, I was relaxed for the first time in weeks. My bones sank into the couch. My eyelids were like lead. And there was almost nothing that could disturb me—not even the sound of Mom calling Doris and making arrangements for her to join us in Florida. Having the three of us—me, my mom, and her mom—in the same house was always scary. It was somewhat like a bickering three-person sorority, except I was the only one still menstruating, and therefore had a legitimate excuse.

I raised an eyebrow briefly when I heard Mom say, "Just get on a train, Mother, and you'll be here by the end of the week." But my tiredness was too great and I fell back asleep.

I woke up at eleven o'clock the next morning. Sometime during the night, Mom helped me move to my bed, and while I know I'm too big to be carried, I had no memory of switching locations. That's how tired I was.

The house was eerily quiet—except for Tanner scratching her neck with her hind leg and jingling her tags—and I had the sense that Mom and the boys were gone, that they had started their day without me.

I walked out into the living room and saw that I had obviously slept past the boys' breakfast (pancakes with heavy syrup for Ford; oatmeal for Owen) and one of Mom's cleaning compulsions. The first thing I noticed, after the breakfast dishes neatly stacked in the kitchen sink, was the bookshelf and the way all my paperbacks were now placed side by side on the top shelf, organized according to size and possibly theme (although I was too scared to actually look and see if they were alphabetized). The basket of toys beside the television chest was adjusted ever so slightly to the left to cover the electrical wires that had been visible since the day we moved in. And Tanner's food and water bowls, which were always in the way, had been moved to a far corner of the kitchen.

Why hadn't I thought of these changes myself? I wondered as I stood in the middle of the room and scratched at my bed-head hair. And how does Mom always seem to put my life in order?

I thought about how many times I had tripped over Tanner's food bowl, yet it never occurred to me to move it. Tanner was curled up under the kitchen table and saw me looking at her new eating place. I can't be certain, but I think she had an I-told-you-so look on her face.

"Oh, mind your own business," I told her.

A note from Mom with a new list was waiting for me on the kitchen table.

Good morning, Sarah!

I've taken the boys out to Target to get a few things. I'll do the dishes as soon as I get back. When you get a chance, why don't you start on the following:

1. Continue straightening and organizing the books on the shelf (I've already done the paperbacks but left the hardcover and oversized books for you).

2. Vacuum under the sofa cushions; you wouldn't believe all the crumbs I found there!

3. Go through the stack of papers on the computer desk (did something spill on these?), and when I get back I'll help you optimize that work space.

I'll be coming home with fresh mulch and hope you and I can spread it around the shrubs this afternoon.

Anyway, try to rest and enjoy this time when you have me here to help.

I Love You, MOM

I chewed on the inside of my mouth as I read. Then I folded up the note and left it on the counter. I didn't even bother getting dressed, just threw on a zippered sweater over my flannel pajamas, put on some shoes, and went to Jody's house, because I needed a dose of reality.

It felt like therapy to walk into her cavernous house, smell the rubber of playground balls and athletic equipment and sit on the worn plaid couch. I noticed that Jody's bookshelf was not only unorganized—it was leaning slightly to the right and had nothing but children's books on it.

How did she get away with that? I wondered.

Jody brought me a Diet Coke, then sat on the couch opposite me.

"So how are you, Sarah?" she asked and leaned closer, with her elbows on her knees.

I was about to open my mouth and speak when I had an odd thought: Despite knowing Jody for more than two years, I knew very little about her. She knew me the way a psychologist knows her patient, and yet, I didn't know what made her tick. What were her biggest fears? Did she have any insecurities? Did she really want to carry a gun?

For a moment I felt exposed and unable to talk. I hated the way I was such an open book. Had I always been such a child in front of Jody?

But I can never contain myself for long (it's the baby of the family in me), so I said, "I told you about Dustin's phone call from Spain, right?"

"Yes, many times. What about it?"

"I just feel angry again, that's all."

Jody smiled and leaned back in her seat. "You need to let that go, Sarah. They were drunk off their asses. Do you remember the first deployment, when Steve sent me a roll of film to get developed for him?"

"Vaguely."

"Well, when I picked up the pictures at Wal-Mart, there was a photo of Steve posing with some topless girls on a beach in France."

"Oh, my gosh! I would have killed Dustin!"

"Nah," she said, waving her hand. "It was hilarious. So Steve posed with half-naked girls on a beach, but he *loves* me. Heck, if I saw a man walking naked down the street, I'd probably snap a picture, too."

I laughed because I knew Jody wasn't lying. In fact, hadn't I seen pictures like that in the pile of photographs stuffed in her kitchen junk drawer?

"So my mom's in town," I said, "and I feel like a kid again. I mean, really, am I truly this helpless?"

"Maybe sometimes," Jody said.

"How come Mom can do four loads of laundry before I've even made my own bed!" I sipped my Diet Coke and looked at the floor. Then I groaned and said, "Oh, Jody, I'm a mess, aren't I? Sasha was right. I'm a walking disaster."

"Sasha's a bitch," Jody said without blinking. "Did you know that she has a maid? And her parents live here in town. So you know what that means—"

"She has free babysitters?"

"No," Jody said, laughing. "She has a safety net. She doesn't have to do this all alone. Imagine knowing, in the back of your mind, that your parents were just a drive away when things got bad?"

"My house would be so clean!" I said.

"Yes, but you'd also be carrying less responsibility. Without our parents close by, you and I subconsciously feel like we're doing all this crap alone. And that's a lot."

She picked up a tennis ball and tossed it back and forth between her hands. I watched her for a moment and tried to imagine living in the same city as my parents. Would I be more moti-vated? Would my life suddenly become clearer?

Jody had a point about Sasha and her parents, but she had missed something important: Without my mom nearby, *Jody* was my secu-rity. Late at night, when I suddenly felt all alone and scared, I was comforted by the thought that Jody was just a few houses away.

I was about to point this out when another startling thought occurred to me: Did Jody feel the same way? Was it comforting to her knowing I was down the street?

There was a lump in my throat when I realized the answer was probably no. Jody never called me at four in the morning crying about some noise in the attic. And she hardly ever asked me to babysit her kids. Maybe she thought I couldn't handle it. Maybe she was afraid to leave them with someone who accidentally puts cereal boxes in the refrigerator on a regular basis.

I looked up and saw a greeting card propped up against a travel alarm clock on top of Jody's television, right next to Mr. Squirrel. The card was glittery, with flowers printed on the front. I knew it must be from Steve, but I played dumb anyway.

"Where did you get that card?" I said, nodding my head in the direction of the television.

"Um . . . ah . . . that?" Jody scratched at her head and seemed to be searching for words. But I knew she was searching for a lie. Most military wives are reluctant to boast about mail from their spouses until they are sure others have received just as much.

"It's from Steve, isn't it?" I said.

She smiled apologetically. "Yeah, it is, Sarah. But he only sent it to me because he knew Michael had been sick and I was feeling really stressed out."

I looked back at the card. Dustin would never think to send me a card "just because." The year before he had even forgotten my birthday! Why don't I have a husband who sends me cards with glitter on them?

I remembered a story Dustin's mom often tells, about how when he was four years old he brought her a peanut butter and jelly sandwich in bed because she was sick and her husband was deployed. "Wasn't that so thoughtful of him?" my mother-in-law likes to say, apparently taking pride in the fact that her young son had the wherewithal to take care of his ill mother. But the story just gives me the willies. First, *should* a young child be expected to take care of his mother? Should he be the man of the house just because Daddy is gone? And second, when did Dustin lose this ability to be so attentive to others? Why now, as an adult, did he seem to defiantly avoid any situation in which he is the father?

"Well, anyway," I said, slumping back into the couch, "just so long as Dustin's mother doesn't get a card before I do! After all, she got to talk to him on the phone when he should have been in bed with me."

Jody smiled. "And how is your mother-in-law?"

"Same old, same old," I said, and then, "I bet I wouldn't have all this trouble with Cute Doctor."

"But you're not married to the doctor," Jody said. "You're married to Dustin."

So diplomatic!

"And you're happy about that, right?" she said.

"Right."

When I got back home, there was another note from Mom waiting on the counter.

> Sarah, I've taken the boys to get new shoes. Be back later to make dinner. There's a message for you on the answering machine, and I think there's an e-mail from Dustin, too. Hope you don't mind. I got online to check my e-Bay auctions. Mom

I went to the computer first. Mom had already straightened the stack of bills there, and I almost couldn't find the mouse because she had tucked it away behind the computer monitor.

I opened my in-box and felt a twinge of excitement in my stomach when I saw a message from Dustin, waiting in bold type, like a present ready to open.

Dear Sarah,

Thanks for the message. It's good to get updates about the boys. Sorry to hear you locked yourself out, but I'm glad Brent was there to help. Wish I could have seen you standing there in your cowgirl shirt.

Things are still busy out here, but I'm eating better than I have in my life. A lot of the guys complain about the food, but I'm just glad to have three meals a day and something different every night. I had fish yesterday. Have you ever thought about learning to bake fish? You'd probably like it.

I heard your dad will be coming on board the ship with us tomorrow. I hope I get to see him.

Got to run to a brief for my next flight.

Love, Dustin

I reread the message a few more times, trying to read between the lines. But I should have known better; Dustin is rarely that manipulative.

I hit REPLY and stared at the blank screen, with my hands hovering over the keys. I didn't know where to begin or what to say. I had been so anxious for his reply, and depressed each time I checked my messages and found nothing. But now I was frozen. How do you truly stay close to someone who is so far away? Are e-mail updates really enough? Could I actually tell Dustin all my thoughts and experiences in one message? How does a marriage survive on e-mail alone? I was beginning to feel closer to the people who were physically near me—Jody and Courtney, my neighbors, my children, and, yes, Dr. Ashley—than I was to Dustin.

I reread Dustin's message again. This time it seemed sterile, like something you'd expect from a stranger. Who addresses his wife as "Dear Sarah" anyway? I thought. Why didn't Dustin write "Hi, Honey" or "Hey!" or something more personal like that?

I clicked out of the message screen, deciding not to reply, and closed my in-box. When I went back through the kitchen, I decided not to listen to the phone message blinking on the machine. Instead I lay facedown on the living room floor and kicked my feet against the carpet. I must have fallen asleep there, because the next time I opened my eyes, Ford was crouching down beside me and looking directly into my face.

"Mommy?" he said. "You asweep?"

I blinked and tried to bring his face into focus.

"Got new shoes, Mommy," he said, pointing to a shiny white tennis shoe on his left foot.

I pushed up onto my knees and pulled him into my lap, pressing my nose against his wispy brown hair. He smelled like sleep and graham crackers and orange juice. Then he reached up his pudgy hand and grabbed my hair hanging down in front of his face. I hugged him tighter.

"Will Daddy be home this day, Momma?" he asked.

"Not today. But Mommy's here and I love you very much. You know that, kiddo?"

My mom came in from the garage with Owen asleep in her arms. I stood and met her in the kitchen, where she hurriedly handed me Owen and went back out the garage door, mumbling something like "Hardly have time to make dinner" and "Won't be able to put down the new mulch."

She came back in with an armful of groceries, which she unpacked and put away in what I figure must have been record time. Before I knew it, Mom was chopping vegetables for dinner.

I hadn't even moved from my spot against the wall holding Owen.

When we finally sat down to plates full of spaghetti and warm bread, I was exhausted just from watching Mom's whirlwind of activity.

"Well! What a day!" she said, smearing butter on her bread. "I feel like we got a lot done, don't you?"

"Um, sure." I leaned over to cut Ford's noodles into bite-sized pieces. "But about the paint—"

She looked at me confused. "The paint? . . . Oh, yes, for the front room. What about it?"

"Do you really think I need it? I kind of like the color I have in there."

"Oh, no! Gosh, no! It's way too dark and it clashes with the oil painting Doris gave you." She took a sip of iced tea, then smiled. "But, of course, if you like it that way, it's fine with me."

Ford grabbed a stick of butter and squished it in his palm. Without hesitation, Mom started wiping his hands with a cloth. I thought how I might have left the grease there until he was definitely done.

"So what did Dustin have to say in his e-mail?" Mom asked.

"Not much, really. Same old stuff."

"Those things are always disappointing," she said. "Same with phone calls and letters."

Here it comes, I thought, the speech about being grateful we even have e-mail!

But Mom surprised me when instead she said, "When your dad would call from overseas, I always felt deflated for a few days. Funny how you look forward to hearing from them, but it never lives up to your expectations."

"Just like the prom," I said, and Mom nodded her head in agreement.

There was a brief silence and then Mom said, "Hey, did you ever check that phone message?"

I looked across the kitchen to the blinking red light. "No, I forgot, actually. I'll check it later. It wasn't Dustin, was it?"

"No, but it was a man," she said.

"Oh," I said absently. I was cutting pieces of bread for Ford.

Then, after hesitating a moment, Mom said, "I wasn't listening closely, so I'm not sure, but I think it was your doctor."

I nearly dropped the knife. "My doctor?"

"I think so. You'll have to listen to the message. But I think that's what he said."

I got up from my place at the table and walked toward the blinking light like someone being drawn to a UFO. What I wanted to do was listen to the message alone, but now Mom's eyes were following me and it would be too obvious. She would never accept it if I said, "Well, I'll just listen to it later." And she would be curious if I took the machine into my room and closed the door.

So I pressed the blinking button.

"One new message," the automated voice said. "Message number one."

There was a beep and a pause, and then Dr. Ashley's smooth voice was filling up the kitchen and echoing off the walls.

"Hey, Sarah, this is Dr. Ashley. Just want to see how you're doing since your last visit. If you need anything at all, just give me a call. You have my number. Guess I'll see you soon. Take care."

The machine beeped again and the light stopped blinking. I looked over my shoulder at Mom. She was watching me closely and I felt awkward, unsure what to do or say next.

"Your doctor calls you by your first name?" she said.

I turned to face her. "He's not much older than me, so he probably feels weird calling me 'Mrs.' "

Mom knitted her brows. "But he calls you at home to check on you?"

I tried to act casual but realized I was rubbing the sides of my head, where a migraine was beginning to form. "Oh, Mom! Why are you getting all weird about this?"

"It just seems strange," she said. "Don't you think? I mean, is this a Navy doctor? Is he your doctor? The kids' doctor?"

I groaned. "Yes, he's a Navy doctor. He's the kids' doctor and my doctor—a family doctor."

Mom turned to face Ford again. "I don't want to pry, but it just seems strange."

"Well, it's not, Mom, so drop it."

I went to my room and closed the door. Why did she always have to be so reasonable?

Late that night, once I was sure Mom had gone to bed, I snuck back into the kitchen and replayed the message from Dr. Ashley. I had the volume turned down to its lowest setting, so I had to lean in close to hear. His voice was familiar and much more soothing when it wasn't bouncing off the kitchen walls for everyone to hear.

Was it strange that he called? I wondered. *Should* he call me Mrs. Smiley? Or was it OK to be just "Sarah"?

I played the message three more times—I guess on the theory that maybe he might say something new on the second or third run-through—then I picked up the cordless phone and went straight to my closet.

"You awake?" I asked when Courtney picked up.

"Of course," she said. "What's up?"

"I'm sitting in the closet."

"Oh, dear!" she sighed. "What now?"

"Do you really think my friendship with the Cute Doctor is inappropriate?" I chewed on my thumb and waited while she chose her words.

"Let's just put it this way," she said. "I couldn't bare my chest to a doctor who seemed anything less than asexual to me. Doctors are supposed to be invisible. They aren't supposed to be sexy or cute or involved. They're supposed to be like parents—only not your parents. They're supposed to be there for you, but without even the slightest hint of sexuality. It just isn't right."

"So what am I supposed to do?" I said.

"Um, hello!" she cried, her voice getting all uppity. "You could switch doctors! That's what I've been telling you to do for months!"

I started to say, "It's not that easy—" but Courtney interrupted: "It's not easy because you like him. Because you're his grass-skirt girl or whatever. Because you, my dear, need a pedestal."

The next day, Mom and I loaded the boys in the car and went to the train station to get Doris. The terminal was in the middle of downtown and covered with the familiar smog and soot of most urban buildings. Inside it smelled like greasy metal and travelers who hadn't bathed, and as always, I found myself wishing I had a personal gas mask for such environments.

We took our seats on benches that were fitted with thick, oily plastic and I reminded Ford, "Don't you touch a THING!" (I had my waterless soap just in case.) He was fidgeting and kicking his feet against the bottom of the bench, a blatant rebellion against me. Mom sat with her stiff leather purse held tightly in her lap and rocking Owen's baby carrier on the floor with the toe of her shoe.

Neither of us spoke as we stared out at the bustling station. The only noise between us was the thumping of Ford's shoe against the seat.

"Ford, stop kicking," Mom said.

And he did.

When an announcement came over the loudspeaker that the "train from Birmingham" had arrived, we collected our belongings (there's always so much baggage when you have kids) and headed toward the double doors leading to the tracks. Passengers wheeling suitcases whizzed past us without nodding or acknowledging us, much like they do in airports, with only one distinct difference: Train travelers are usually gritty from the long trip and they walk with a slant, as if their equilibrium is trying to adjust to a motion other than the clickety-clack of the tracks. They have no business being so hoity-toity, and I smiled and said hello to every one of them just to prove my point.

In the distance, through all the hurried travelers in suits, I saw Doris stepping down from a passenger car with the help of a tall, skinny porter dressed in a gray uniform. I smiled when I saw her faded chambray skirt and white top with the sailor collar: She had been wearing the same outfit since I was six years old. She had on a pair of old Nike tennis shoes (hand-me-downs from me) and a purple wool sweater wrapped around her neck like a scarf and covering her brittle silvery hair. She refused to have her hair cut at a beauty parlor like most grandmas, and therefore it always looked a lot like a bird's nest. Today was no different.

Even though she was still too far away, I knew she had on white panty hose with no socks, and that her deceased father's tie clip was fastened like a brooch to her collar. It was her "uniform" of sorts, and I never expected anything less. Only Doris could get away with wearing panty hose, tennis shoes, an old wool sweater, and an antique tie clip all in the same outfit.

She walked toward us, a subtle frown on her soft, wrinkled face and her full skirt swishing behind her, then gave us her typical hello: "Well, I declare! I've never seen such gooney people in all my life. I tell you, I'm never traveling by train again."

I hugged her around the shoulders and could feel her frail bones beneath my arms. "Hello, Doris," I said. "Good to see you."

"How are you, dear?" She pulled back from my embrace and studied my face. "Am I ever happy to be here! Lord willing, I'm never riding by train again. Did I already say that? I've never seen such goofy people in all my life."

She bent at the waist to look at Ford and coo at Owen. Mom and I each picked up one of the Adidas duffel bags at Doris's feet and started to lead her toward the door. I knew Doris would complain about the trip the whole way home, and that she would say a few more times that she would never travel by train again, but neither Mom nor I believed her. Doris is terrified of flying—a trait she has passed down to her daughter and granddaughter—and though she would talk about all the "gooney people" on the train, after the shock of the trip wore off, suddenly she would tell us they were the most magnificent and interesting people she had ever met. "In fact," she'd say, "I think I'll write a book about them."

From the backseat, Ford was mesmerized by Doris's commotion— her loud voice and nonstop chatter—reminding me of the way I felt as child . . . like Doris was a one-woman circus.

Doris had never been to my new house, and I was both excited and anxious to see her reaction. When my grandfather Big Jack died two years before, Doris had to move out of her home of more than thirty years and take up residence at a "retirement apartment." During the transition, she gave me many of her most treasured belongings that wouldn't fit into the new place. Those pieces—an antique sideboard standing against my red wall, an oil painting of a basket of flowers hanging above, and Mom's old red rocking chair from when she was a baby—filled the front room of my house with the comforting smell of baby powder and old wood I remembered from Doris and Big Jack's home. On the piano's ledge, next to the metal lamp, was a framed picture of Big Jack standing on the beach, waving hello with his hat, and a brittle sand dollar Doris had found in the sand for me when I was younger.

We stepped inside the front door and Doris put a hand to her chest when she saw the room. "Lord, have mercy!" she said. "It's gorgeous. Absolutely gorgeous!"

"So you like it," I said. "You like the red? Mom thinks I need to change it."

"Heavens, no!" Doris said, tightening the wool sweater around her neck and throwing a loose end over her shoulder. (She wears a sweater at all times—even indoors and in the heat of summer. She says it makes her "sinuses feel better.")

"See, Mom," I said. "I knew that color was perfect. Even Doris likes it."

"Now wait a minute," Doris said, her face suddenly turning into a scowl. The jowls on the sides of her face shook. "I didn't say nothing about likin' that red wall. Don't you be dragging me into the middle of this. I meant that my piano is gorgeous. Simply gorgeous."

I sighed with defeat.

Late that night, after Mom and the boys had gone to bed, I stayed up to sit with Doris on the couch. Doris never sleeps in a bed. Even before Big Jack died, she slept on the couch while he went upstairs. It wasn't that she didn't want to be with Big Jack—even if he was a Republican—it was more about Doris's anxiety, or her "sinuses," as she liked to say. The couch was her personal crutch, and when she settled into the throw pillows on my sofa, I knew she wouldn't be getting up again for the rest of the trip, except to get a cup of coffee and to use the restroom.

"How are you, dear?" she said and patted my knee. Tanner was lying nestled against her shoes. She had always been fond of Doris, and seemed to be the most comfortable near her.

"I'm fine, Doris. Just fine." I looked down at her hands, the loose skin and spots of brown across them.

"Sarah! Herren! Rutherford!" she said, squeezing my knee hard. "Don't you be thinkin' you can just say 'I'm fine' to me. This is your grandma Doris talking. Don't you forget, I can see right through you like Saran Wrap."

I laughed as I watched her set her lips in a determined frown meant to prove her stubbornness.

It worked. There was no use hiding anything from Doris.

"I just feel overwhelmed sometimes," I said. "I'm not sure I'm cut out for this. I'm not a strong military wife like Mom has always been."

"Sarah Herren," she said. "You mean to tell me that little girl who organized all the neighborhood children to make a homemade sequel to *Gone With the Wind* isn't capable of this? Don't you be telling me you can't make it without a man! Lord, have mercy, you rule this roost anyway! What makes you think you can't survive without that ol' Dustin? I don't call you Madam Queen Bee for nothing."

She paused for effect and looked me directly in the eyes. "You are Sarah—Sarah Herren Rutherford. There isn't anything in this world you can't do. And don't you forget it. And don't you forget that your momma—as high and mighty as she may seem—has had her moments, too. She just doesn't talk about it like you and me. You know, you and me, we're talkin' folk."

I patted her hand. "Yes, Doris, yes, we are . . . talkin' folk."

Doris has this way of seeing through me. Sometimes I'm afraid even to have the slightest thought in front of her because I know she'll be able to read my mind in an instant. I wouldn't dare think about sex in her presence! If anyone has ever truly had telepathy, it would be Doris. She says the ability is something she inherited from her grandmother, but I don't know, sometimes I think Doris is merely a reflection of myself, and vice versa. No one can keep me in line better than she can.

Doris adjusted the sweater around her neck and sat back into the cushions. "Did I ever tell you about the time Big Jack moved me all the way to Boston, away from my daddy, and we didn't even have a car?"

She had told me the story many times before, but I didn't say so and let her reminisce.

"There I was with a newborn baby," she said. "I didn't know a soul in the whole darn city. And where was Big Jack? Off studying law. Can you believe that? After all those years being away with the war, then he comes back and hides away in an old law library. I felt certain that old man was having an affair on me. One night I found a phone number in the pocket of his jacket. I said, 'Jack, whose number do you have in your jacket?' and he just smiled at me. I said, 'You old bird, tell me whose number this is or I'm going to stay up the entire night singing "I'm Henry the Eighth"!' And wouldn't you know your grandpa didn't answer! No, he let me sit there singing all night like a fool. The next morning, he was walking out the door, on the way to that old law library, and he said, 'Doris, the number in my pocket is ours.'"

Doris laughed and put her palms against her moist cheeks. "Lord, have mercy!" she said. "That old man, I tell you. What a fool I was. I didn't even know my own phone number. Talk about being stupid! Boy, was I ever unprepared."

She sighed and bent down to pat Tanner at her ankles. "Oh, but I miss that old bird," she said. "I miss him every day. There's not a day in my life I would change . . . not for all the money in the world."

Tanner moaned happily and turned onto her side so Doris could pat her belly.

"Speaking of money," Doris said, "I hope you don't let your husband give you an allowance."

"What? What do you mean?"

"I mean, don't just sit there like a fool and let your husband do everything while you wait on him hand and foot, cooking and cleaning and . . . and . . . and being stupid. It's not 'his money' or 'your money.' It's your money together. And don't you forget it." She frowned. "Do you own a calculator, Sarah?"

"Well, of course."

"Do you know how to use it?"

"Doris! Don't be silly."

She stopped patting Tanner and folded her arms across her chest. "I'm just sayin' you wouldn't believe all the women who have no idea about their family's finances. Some women go their whole lives letting the man do everything, and where does it leave 'em? It leaves 'em at my retirement apartment helpless and pathetic without their old bird. You don't want to end up some ninny who can't take care of herself, do you?"

She paused and looked up at me real hard, squinting her eyes, and making me feel transparent again. Had I thought something out of line?

"What?" I said defensively.

"Oh, I've been watching you, honey," she said. "The way you stare off into space at the kitchen table. The way you mope around when someone mentions Dustin. Oh, yes, I've been watching you."

Her gray eyes, which always have a white light in them due to cataracts, looked me up and down. She drew in her bottom lip and set out her chin, almost pouting.

"And that answering machine message," she said.

"What? What are you talking about?"

She was nodding her head slowly now. "When you and your momma were out getting the boys' dinner tonight, I played the message on your machine from that doctor person." Her eyes narrowed. "And I know *exactly* what's on that mind of yours, Sarah. I can read you like a book. But you listen to me. You've got a beautiful family, a fine husband, and this gorgeous house. Don't you dare go doing something stupid and mess all that up."

Her thoughts pierced me. I stumbled for words. But there weren't any. She would see through any attempt I made to disguise myself. So instead I leaned over and placed my head on her shoulder. She patted the side of my head with her bony hand and said, "There, there," just like she used to when I was little.

I listened to her soft breathing and faint heartbeat, and suddenly the fear of losing her someday struck me. I had nearly fallen apart when Big Jack died while I was pregnant with Ford. Big Jack had been like a second dad to me. He called me "Miss Scarlett" and "Miss Punkin" and his "favorite granddaughter" (I was his only granddaughter), and he sent me silly cards "just because." I felt like the most beautiful and special person in the world with Big Jack.

It would be doubly traumatic to lose Doris.

"I love you, Doris," I said, looking up at her.

"I love you, too, darlin'." She patted my head again. Then she pulled me upright and looked me in the eyes. She was scowling again. "Now you remember what I told you," she said. "Don't you go messing anything up. You take good care of those babies and Dustin. And never forget that God is love. Do you hear me?"

I nodded my head, swallowing back a lump in my throat.

"And, Sarah?" she said.

"Yes?"

"Grow out your eyebrows, child! For Heaven's sakes!"

I laughed. "OK, Doris. OK."

9

GOD IS GREAT, GOD IS GOOD; LET US THANK HIM . . .

I never called Dr. Ashley back (although I did replay the message often, looking for clues—a tone in his voice, a word I had missed). I'm not sure why, except that calling him felt wrong.

Like a strange dream that leaves you feeling icky about a particular person the next day, each time my fantasy and reality of Dr. Ashley met in the middle, I chickened out and was unable to follow through. For all the daydreaming I had done about Dr. Ashley, you'd think I would have been thrilled to call him back. But no, I just settled for listening to his message over and over and over again, until his voice started to sound like a chipmunk's.

It was pathetic! I had never seen him outside the hospital, and I wasn't even sure I'd recognize him without his blue scrubs and white coat, yet there was an undeniable connection between us, one of those confounding "sparks" you feel but can't explain.

Or was it just me who felt this? Was the connection really between *us*? Or was it all in *my* head?

Doris and Mom left the next week. Dad was returning from

his detachment and Mom wanted to be there when he got home. She would drop off Doris at the train station on her way out of town. As they pulled out of the driveway, Doris waved and I could see that Mom was crying. I held back tears myself, watching from the front door with Ford on my hip. I was both excited to have my house back again, and scared . . . to have my house back. Each time my mom leaves, it's like flying out of the nest all over again.

I couldn't wait to talk to Dad and hear about his trip to the ship. But when I called him a few days later, he was downright bland with the details: "He looked like the same old Dustin to me," Dad said.

I don't know why I expected more. If I wanted the real scoop, I'd have to send my mom or Doris out to the ship. Why did I think Dad—a man—would give me the answers I really wanted: Did Dustin look happy? Was he thinner? Heavier? Did you see him talking to any women? Did he talk about me?

But no, Dad just told me the basics and then said, "Uh, I don't know—do you want to talk to your mother?"

That weekend, which was Valentine's Day weekend—the most dreaded of holidays for lonely wives—the Spouse Club was having a baby shower for Leslie, who had had her baby shortly after the men left. With all the commotion, no one had had a chance to do anything for her, so we combined the February Spouse Club meeting with a baby shower and a Valentine's Day pity party. Melanie volunteered her home.

Courtney and I met at Jody's house so the three of us could ride together. Melanie had instructed everyone to bring her favorite dish with a Valentine's theme. This stretched even Courtney's creative abilities: There just aren't many "Valentine's Day" foods. Well, there's chocolate, obviously, but there are only so many ways to dress up chocolate so that you can outdo the other wives.

I was impressed when Courtney showed up with a bottle of wine covered with a homemade label: LOVE POTION #9. And Jody was arranging weenies on a tray when we walked in. One by one, she gouged a toothpick into the links, and then affixed a sign to the tray: SCORNED LOVER.

"Very nice, Jody," I said. "And somehow, not surprising at all."

"Yeah? And what did you bring, Mrs. Smiley?"

I laid a glass bowl filled with fluffy pink marshmallows and goo on the table. "I brought pink salad."

"What *is* that?" they both said together, wrinkling up their noses.

I pulled back the tight Saran Wrap to give them a dose of the cold, fruity smell. "It's my dad's favorite," I said. "His mom used to make it, so when I was growing up, he made it for Thanksgiving and Christmas."

They both stared at me.

"What?" I said.

Jody shook her head. "Nothing. It's just that, well, how does pink salad relate to Valentine's Day?"

I put a hand on my hip and stomped my foot. "Oh, come on! Pink. Valentine's Day. Get it?"

"No, we need to come up with a better name," Courtney said. "Something more clever." She put a finger to her pursed lips and looked up at the ceiling.

Jody laughed. "How about 'bleeding heart salad'?"

"No, I've got it!" Courtney said. "We'll call it pink passion-ate fruit. Jody, grab a pen!"

So the two of them were busily redoing my handmade label when Jody's telephone rang.

"Could you grab that, Sar?" Jody asked without looking up.

I lifted the receiver and started to say hello when I heard heavy breathing on the other end.

"Jody?" a strained voice said.

"No, it's Sarah. Can I help you?"

"Sarah, it's Melanie."

I put a finger in my ear to block out Jody and Courtney's howling laughter in the background. "I'm sorry. Is that you, Melanie? I can hardly hear you."

There was a moaning sound, and the phone dropped. I snapped my fingers at Jody and Courtney to get their attention. Their laughing wound down to a sigh when they saw my face.

"What is it?" Jody whispered. "Who is it?" She and Courtney crowded around me.

"Melanie? Melanie?" I said. "Pick up, Melanie. Are you still there?"

"I . . . can't . . . get to the . . . phone . . ." she said between breaths.

I started to feel faint and passed the phone to Jody. Cold chills ran down to my toes and up through my neck. Courtney put an arm around my shoulder to steady me. "Don't worry. Jody will take care of it," she whispered. "Whatever it is."

"Melanie!" Jody yelled into the receiver. "Pick up the phone and tell me what you need."

Melanie must have responded because Jody was listening and squinting her eyes real hard. After several seconds, she started barking orders at Courtney and me: "Melanie's having a miscarriage," she said. "Sarah, go to her house and take her to the emergency room. Courtney, get on the phone and start calling the guest list. The baby shower will be over here now."

I stood blinking and numb. "Me? Me go get her? But . . . but why me?" I followed close behind Jody, nearly clipping her heels, as she hustled back and forth between the kitchen and den. "Jody, I can't possibly handle this. Please, you take her. I'll stay here and do the party."

Jody spun around and looked at me with an expression I had never seen on her face before. Her eyes and mouth were set so tight, I thought the blood vessel in her temple might rupture. "There's no time for this, Sarah," she said. "Go get Melanie and take her to the emergency room!"

My eyes filled with tears, and just as if I was in a bad dream, I felt unable to move. "But I didn't even know she was pregnant. Did you?"

"Now, dammit!" Jody yelled and threw my car keys at me.

When I got to Melanie's house, she was lying on her bathroom floor with a pool of blood seeping from between her legs and making a puddle around her drenched nylon slip.

"Hi, Sarah," she said in a weak voice and tried to lift herself up. I rushed to grab her arm. "I'm glad you came."

I tried not to look directly at her or at her exposed undergarments. "I think I should call an ambulance," I said.

Melanie put up a hand. "No. I don't need an ambulance. Just drive me to the emergency room. OK? Everything will be fine."

"Melanie, I don't think I can handle this. I don't think—"

"Sarah," she said. "I asked Jody to send you. I need you."

Me? But why?

I was unsure how to act as I got Melanie into the car and drove. Did she want air, or no air? Music, or no music? Christian music, or regular music? It seemed that everything I said or did was clumsy and awkward. But Melanie didn't notice. She mostly sat with her eyes closed and her head lolling back and forth on the seat each time I turned. She was sitting on a pile of towels and I tried not to look at them for fear of getting sick. But the heat radiating from her body was beginning to make me feel feverish anyway. I was even starting to have cramps.

At the hospital, the double doors pulled apart, forcing a gush of heated air—mixed with the smells of vomit and peroxide—across our faces. Melanie didn't seem to notice. She was hunched forward, one arm protectively around her waist, the other arm embraced in mine for support.

"We just go straight to the nurse triage," she said and pointed me in the direction of a small cubicle to the left of the waiting room.

A nurse with Mickey Mouse scrubs saw us coming and rushed to take Melanie's arm. Once her weight was released from mine, I began to feel dizzy and sank onto a hard plastic chair. I was dressed in red high heels and a skirt—for the baby shower—and felt, shall we say, a little out of place. From across the room, I watched the nurse take notes and fit Melanie's arm with a blood pressure cuff. Melanie doubled over in pain a few times, and beads of sweat formed on her temples. She was sitting on a pile of towels, the same ones she had sat on in the car, and they were already soaked with red blood. The nurse didn't seem concerned about that, so I started to relax, but when Melanie's face suddenly turned pale and pasty, the nurse put down the clipboard and laid Melanie on a gurney.

Everything happened fast from there, with words like "hemorrhage" and "shock" shouted across the room. I followed the nurse and her squeaky tennis shoes as she wheeled Melanie through a narrow corridor with harsh fluorescent lights. I had to hurry to keep up, and my high heels echoed down the hall, making me feel intrusive and clumsy. I tried walking on my tiptoes but then I fell behind and had to run to catch up again. I was holding my pearl necklace against my chest with one hand to keep it from bouncing up in my face.

At a pair of swinging doors, the nurse turned to me and said, "You'll have to wait in the waiting room now. I'm sorry, but only family can go beyond this point."

Melanie grabbed for my hand and squeezed it. "I'll be OK," she said. "Call the Red Cross and get a message to Paul."

The nurse pushed the gurney through the doors, which flapped closed behind them. I stood with my arm still outstretched and reaching for Melanie's.

I walked back to the waiting room in a daze and found a phone to call Jody. I had no idea how to contact the Red Cross, and if she didn't know, Courtney certainly would. The baby shower was in progress and I could hear voices and laughter in the background. Obviously Jody hadn't told them about Melanie. She probably didn't want to make Leslie feel awkward about the party, and that made sense, but I knew I might not have been as tactful. For instance, how did Jody explain the last-minute change of plans? These things just don't occur to me. Maybe that's why they sent me to the hospital instead.

After passing off the responsibility of calling the Red Cross to Jody, and promising to keep her informed of Melanie's status, I hung up the phone and went to find a seat in the waiting room. There was a pile of wrinkled magazines on a faux-wood end table, and I flipped through them mindlessly. My choices were either to read or eat Peanut M&Ms (not a good idea), but there was nothing on the table except *AARP* magazine and *Retired Officer*. So I did what any hypochondriac on a diet would do: I found a brochure about GERD (Gastroesophageal Reflux Disease), got a pack of M&Ms from the vending machine, and settled into a chair. The intercom above me blared occasionally about some doctor who was needed on a particular floor, but I only became concerned when I heard things like "code blue." That was when I noticed my breath quickening considerably. I was waiting for them to call "code red" for fire because I've rarely been to the Navy hospital when there wasn't a fire emergency or false alarm. I was even the cause of the "code red" once. I had asked a health administrator to help me with my insurance form, and his computer actually caught on fire. That was the last time I ever tried to understand the military's insurance system.

But there were no code reds this night. In fact, the waiting room was unusually empty and quiet. Every once in a while a nurse squeaked by in stiff leather shoes, but there were no other patients. Each time the doors swung open and closed, I looked up eagerly, hoping for the nurse in Mickey Mouse scrubs to come with news. But for long stretches of time, there was no one except an occasional custodian, who whistled while he mopped.

Sometime around nine o'clock, I had fallen asleep and was woken up by someone shaking my shoulder.

"Mrs. Smiley? Mrs. Smiley?" a voice said.

I opened my eyes and saw a nurse, but no Mickey Mouse scrubs.

"Mrs. Smiley," the voice said again. "Your sister would like to have you come back now."

"My sister?" I said, confused. Then, "Oh, yes, of course—my sister."

I followed the nurse back to the emergency room. Most of the patient beds were settled behind partitions with curtains, but Melanie was in a private ob-gyn room, with the shades pulled down over the windows. She was curled up on her side under several layers of white hospital blankets when I came in, and she lifted her head and smiled as I came to her bedside.

"Your sister?" I whispered once the nurse had left.

Melanie winked and reached for my hand. "They wouldn't let anyone except family back here."

"How wonderfully naughty of you," I said, laughing, but immediately covered my mouth and apologized. It felt a little unseemly.

Melanie squeezed my hand. "Thank you, Sarah. Thank you for bringing me here. Where are your boys?"

"Don't worry about that, Melanie," I said. "They're home with Lauren, and Jody will go get them after the party. They can sleep at Jody's house if they need to."

Melanie's eyes were bloodshot and dark purple half-moons hung below them. For the first time, she looked her age.

"But what about Hannah?" I said. "Do you need me to go get her?"

"No, stay here with me," she said. "The babysitter will take care of it." She paused a moment to sip some water. Her lips were dry and cracked. I helped her get the cup back on the table beside the gurney and she said, "No one knew I was pregnant. Except Paul, of course."

I was relieved she brought this up first, so I simply nodded and listened. Her eyes were wet with tears. "This is my second miscarriage. I don't know if you knew that or not."

I shook my head and felt guilty for getting so much personal information. I had no words to say, so I shifted on my feet awkwardly. I couldn't imagine someone more deserving of a baby. Melanie embodied everything that was motherly. She even knew how to make oatmeal cookies and had visible purple-blue veins on her hands.

"How do you go on?" I blurted out, feeling a little childish. "How are you not totally breaking down right now?"

"Because obviously this is the plan for me," she said. "It's not in the plan for me to have more children, and I'm learning to be OK with that."

"But . . . how . . . I mean . . ." I was stuttering and flustered.

Melanie put a finger to her lips to hush me. "I have faith, Sarah," she said.

There was a knock at the door.

"Yes?" Melanie said softly, and the heavy wood door began to creak open.

"Is it OK for me to come in?" a familiar voice asked.

"Yes. Please," Melanie said. Then she turned to me. "This must be the doctor."

I saw the shoes first—running shoes that looked like they had taken more than a few laps around the hospital. Then I saw blue pants and the white tie that held them at the waist. And finally I saw his face staring at me with a surprise I can only guess was visible on mine as well.

"Sarah?" Dr. Ashley said.

"You two know each other?" Melanie asked, looking back and forth between us.

I was aware that my face had turned hot and probably red. "Um, yeah . . . kind of. I mean, yes, this is my doctor . . . er . . . Owen's doctor . . . and my doctor."

Dr. Ashley stepped forward to the other side of Melanie's bed. "I'm Dr. Ashley," he said, extending his hand to her. "It's nice to meet you, Melanie."

Thin sprouts of hair were sticking out of the V-neck of his scrubs, and I wondered why I hadn't noticed that before. Or did he usually have on an undershirt? Because surely I would have noticed something as sexy as that.

Shame on me, I thought suddenly, averting my eyes toward Melanie and straightening my posture.

"Well!" I said—probably a little too eager and loud—"I guess I'll just step outside now. I need to make some phone calls."

Melanie smiled and squeezed my hand. "I'll be OK," she said.

Dr. Ashley's eyes traveled up from my hand clasped in Melanie's, to my shoulders and neck, and then finally our eyes locked. "Don't worry," he said. "Melanie's in good hands."

"I know," I said and slipped out the door.

My heart was pounding so hard, I could feel it in my ears when I closed the door behind me and leaned against it with my back. I stared down at the strappy high heels and skirt meant for the baby shower. How did it look now, outside the context of a girly party with petits fours? Did Dr. Ashley think I knew he'd be here? Did he think I had dressed up for him? I shook the thoughts from my mind and my long, beaded earrings bounced against the sides of my neck. God, I was ridiculously overdressed for the military emergency room.

I wasn't sure when it would be appropriate to go back into Melanie's room—the worst possible scenario I could imagine was walking in during her exam with the doctor . . . *my* doctor—so I went to the waiting room and watched *Growing Pains* reruns on a television with bad reception. Eventually I made a bed for myself by combining some chairs, and I managed to fall asleep.

Sometime around midnight, I awakened to shoes squeaking on the floor beside me and someone stifling a laugh. I opened one eye at a time and saw Dr. Ashley standing above me.

"Comfortable?" he said and took a seat to the left of my feet with the bright red heels.

I pulled myself up to sit and smoothed my hair. "How's Melanie? Is she going to be OK?"

There was a pile of crumpled M&M wrappers to my right, which, of course, I could never let Dr. Ashley see, so I sneakily tucked them under my leg.

"Melanie needs to stay here overnight," he said. "She's lost a lot of blood and we want to monitor her for a while. I understand this is her second miscarriage?"

"Yes," I said. And then the babbling started. "I mean, I think that's what she said. I didn't know it before. But I know she's been trying for a while."

The word "trying" implied "sex," and I blushed.

Dr. Ashley looked me up and down and I felt the need to stare at my lap. "And how are you, Sarah?" he said. "I called to check up on you but got the machine. Have you gone to see the counselor yet?"

His breath smelled like stale coffee and I tried clinging to that to make him less attractive.

"I can't really think about that right now," I said. "My head is still reeling from tonight. One crisis at a time, you know?"

He put his arm around my shoulders. "I understand. Just remember, you have my number if you need it."

"Yes, it's right beside my phone," I said.

"That's a great place for it," he said; then he stood and reached for my hand to help me up. "I think Melanie wants to see you again," he said. "Nurse Shannon will escort you back in just a moment."

He gave me a thumbs-up sign and turned to leave, and I couldn't help but stare at his cute rear end in the scrubs as he walked away. There was a noticeable pep in his step; then he glanced back over his shoulder and said, "Oh, and, Sarah, you've got some wrappers stuck to the back of your leg there."

Melanie was even paler—and somehow thinner—the second time I went in, and the room smelled like sweat and vomit and blood.

"Thanks for getting the message to Paul," she said. "He called about an hour ago."

"Are they in port?" I asked, already gearing up to be mad at Dustin for not telling me himself, but also berating myself for being so selfish in front of Melanie.

"No, I don't think so," she said. "The CO let him use the phone in his room. It was very quick. . . . We only talked a minute or two."

I sat in a chair beside the bed. I wanted to take off the pinching high heels and massage my feet, but I'd rather have belched in front of Dr. Ashley than let my bare feet touch the filthy hospital floor. So I settled for propping them up on the metal bar of Melanie's bed.

"Your doctor is very handsome," Melanie said, looking at me with such innocence, I felt like a total harlot.

"Oh, well, I guess so," I said. "I hadn't really noticed."

I had to look away as I lied to her.

"He's very attentive, too," Melanie said. "Did you know that he's single? I wonder why someone like that hasn't been snatched up already."

I stared at the ground, and willed her to stop talking about Dr. Ashley, but she continued. "The world is funny, isn't it? So often things don't make sense."

"Like when bad things happen to good people," I said, trying to change the subject.

"Yes," she said, "and how a man like that can't find a wife for himself." She sighed and looked up at the ceiling.

"Is there anything I can do for you right now?" I asked. "Is there anything else you need?"

Melanie didn't hesitate before saying, "You could say a prayer for me."

"Me?" I said. "But, I don't know . . . I mean, I don't really have any . . . I mean . . ."

Melanie smiled and thin crow's-feet creased the edges of her tired red eyes. "Just pray for me, Sarah," she said.

Her eyes were already closed in preparation, so I bowed my head and pulled at my hands. "Ummm . . . let's see. A prayer. Well, OK, here goes." I cleared my throat and began the only prayer I could remember from my childhood: "God is great, God is good. . . ." What was I thinking? "Let us thank Him for our food. . . ." I finished weakly. I peeked out one eye and saw Melanie grinning. I bowed my head again. "Um, I mean . . . OK, let's see . . . ah . . . Thank you, God. Thank you for Melanie and the blessing she has been to me. Please watch over her while she is, ah, sick, and make her well again soon. Amen."

I looked up sheepishly and saw that Melanie was crying.

"Thank you, Sarah," she said. "That was beautiful."

10

THE GIRL IN A COWGIRL SHIRT AND FLIP-FLOPS

E ventually the rest of the Spouse Club heard about Melanie's miscarriage, and an emergency meeting was held at Margo's house to decide who could make dinners and help with child care. Jody and I volunteered to keep Hannah, and she went back and forth between our two houses for several days.

Hannah was an exceptionally easy child to care for, and just as dignified as her mother, so I felt like a slob any time I accidentally burped in front of her. She even walked softly. There were a few times I was afraid I might forget her when we were leaving the house because she was so quiet. It was a condition made even worse during those few days, because although Hannah didn't understand exactly what was happening with her mom, she knew it was something scary. She knew, at least, that neither Jody nor I could make oatmeal cookies or meat loaf to suit her. (When I fed her hot dogs and macaroni and cheese one evening, she said, "Where's the vegetable?" and I tried to remember the last time Ford had eaten anything that wasn't made of bread or noodles.) But given the careful way Hannah looked at me with pouting lips and wide clear blue eyes, I knew she was feeling—possibly fearing—more than she could express, and I dug deep into my maternal instincts to help her.

Taking care of a girl didn't come naturally to me. This should be easy, I thought. I'm a girl. I know girls. I once was a child, too. But the first time Hannah asked, "Where's the Barbies?" I felt horribly unprepared. "This plastic Superman will have to do," I told her, and she wasn't impressed, but eventually settled on playing house, with Ford, of course, acting as the unwilling "baby."

Somehow, having Hannah around made me feel closer to my own mom . . . and closer to my childhood self. Maybe it was Hannah's thin, blunt bangs, which she unconsciously swept away from her eyes from time to time. Or maybe it was the way the bumps of her knobby knees seemed to knock together every time she walked. Or how she called me "Miss Sawah." But whatever the reason, Hannah stirred up in me emotions I hadn't considered in a long time. How would I have felt when I was her age if my mom was sick? How would I have felt if I had to go live with the neighbors?

The truth is, I think I would have nearly died. Losing my mom has always been one of my greatest fears, a survival instinct that surely stems from having a father who was gone more than half my life. Without Mom to fall back on, what would I do?

When I was seven, just two years older than Hannah, I had a neighbor named Shirley whose mother suffered from lupus. I didn't understand the illness at the time, of course; I just knew Shirley came to stay with us unexpectedly when her mom was "feeling sick."

Shirley was my older, more mature friend. She wore a bra—and showed it to me before I knew what one was for—and she was the one who broke the bad news to me about Santa Claus not being real. So Shirley had an exceptional amount of influence over me (as well she should: She wore mascara).

During one of the times she stayed at our house while her mom was sick, Shirley and I were asleep in my antique four-poster bed when there was a knock at the front door. I remember Mom shuffling downstairs in her robe and slippers and asking, "Who's there?" before cracking open the door. Then I heard her saying, "Not now. Not like this." And suddenly a man—Shirley's father—was standing beside my bed. "Your mother has died," he said, and Shirley broke down crying.

What followed was six years of night terrors during which I'd wake up sweating and calling out for my mom. It was something I never got over as a child, and it only increased my anxiety about being left alone.

And now here I was with a shy, scared girl in my care, and the best I could do was serve her hot dogs and macaroni and cheese. Secretly I worried I had failed Hannah. Failed myself.

Then one night, long after her bedtime, Hannah came to sit with me on the couch. She curled up quietly, drawing her knees to her chin, and put her head in my lap. I covered her with a blanket. When she started to weep, I couldn't think of anything else to do but sing: "I'm gonna wash that gray right out of my hair." I sang it over and over again, and Hannah hugged me tight. For nearly an hour I patted her back and sang commercial jingles until she was asleep.

On the last night Hannah stayed with me, it was time for a bath. I know, I know. She probably should have had a bath long before this, but unlike my toddler boy with grass stains on his knees, Hannah seemed unnaturally clean and without need of a washing. But she was returning home to Melanie the next day, so a good bath was in order.

The whole thing seemed like an easy enough process, and Hannah took her bath as quietly and helpfully as she did everything else. But because it's been ages since I had long, straight hair of my own, I didn't know enough to comb through Hannah's wet hair before putting her to bed. And for whatever reason, Hannah failed to mention this very important step to me.

The next morning, she was standing beside my bed when I woke up, and the rat's nest atop her head was at least twelve inches tall. Tangled masses of blond hair were gracing her scalp like a fuzzy ball of yarn.

"Oh, no!" I shrieked, throwing back the covers and rushing to her side. "Your mom usually combs your hair, doesn't she?"

Hannah nodded.

That's it, I thought. I've definitely failed.

But Hannah was staring at me with pleading eyes, her hands neatly clasped behind her back, and I couldn't give up.

"Well," I said, straightening my posture, "we need to take care of this before your mother sees you. That's for sure."

Hannah reached up and felt the pouf of hair with her hand. Tears came to her blue eyes and the bridge of her nose started to crinkle.

I grabbed her forearms and said eagerly, "No, don't cry! It will be all right. It's just hair."

Tears were rolling down her cheeks now as she sniffled.

"I know! Should we pray about this, Hannah? Would that help?"

"Yes," she said in a hushed voice.

I looked around the room anxiously, as if I were searching for someone to help.

A prayer for hair? Why on earth did I suggest that?

I took a deep breath and said, "Honestly, Hannah, I don't know any good prayers for hair emergencies, so why don't you say it? I'm sure you're much better at it than me anyway."

She looked at me doubtfully, but I smiled and nodded, so she bowed her head and said, "Dear God, please make Mrs. Smiley more responsible in the future. Please make sure I don't need to cut off my hair to get out these tangles. And, God, please make Mommy better so I can go home."

Another bath and a cupful of heavy conditioner got rid of the tangles and restored Hannah's shiny blond hair. I took her home to her mom that afternoon, and if Melanie noticed anything amiss about her daughter's hair, she never let on.

A week later, the Spouse Club met at Courtney's house for a "surprise announcement." Everyone had their guesses at what the "surprise" might be, but the most delightful to consider was Trish's theory that maybe the men had come home during the night and would be waiting for us there. Rumors like this are common during a deployment and never (to my knowledge) come true, yet we wives get sucked into believing anyway, like a child who's old enough to know about the tooth fairy but hides fallen teeth under his pillow anyway.

So naturally we were more than a little let down when the only thing waiting for us at Courtney's house was a plateful of crackers and cheeses with names no one except the hostess could pronounce.

Courtney was positively aglow with the possibilities of Kate's surprise. She could be so optimistic sometimes! I arrived early to help set up, but after watching Courtney flutter about her yellow-and-blue kitchen wearing a gingham apron that reminded me of June Cleaver, I found myself feeling a bit useless. She was buzzing here and there, mumbling gibberish about the "cocktail napkins" and "wine charms," while I sat perched on a barstool at her counter.

"You're nesting," I said. "You're getting all domestic because you really believe the news has something to do with the men coming home. Am I right?"

Courtney wiped her hands on a sunflower dish towel and looked at me. "That's ridiculous," she said. "I'm not nesting. And what does that mean anyway?"

"It means you're scaring me with your cheese knives and cocktail napkins. What's gotten into you?"

She turned toward the stove and stirred something in a pot. "I'm just excited about the possibilities," she said, taking a deep breath and gazing up at the ceiling. "Haven't you ever felt in love with a possibility?" She turned around to look directly at me. "I haven't felt this alive since the guys left. And I don't care what Kate's surprise is. I'm just grateful for the idea of it."

Courtney had a point. Ever since Kate's cryptic e-mail arrived in our in-boxes four days earlier, the mood had shifted from one of drudgery to one of excitement. Just thinking about the "surprise" was like a nugget of hope in the middle of a long string of nothing. Instead of sitting around talking about our angst, Jody, Courtney, and I had been giddy over the possibilities of what awaited us.

Yet somehow, now that the night was here, I didn't feel up to it.

I left Courtney to her humming and baking, and went to sit in her wood-paneled living room. It was a muted, dark room with lots of navy blue and gold. Sometimes when it rained and drops hit the skylights in the roof, the living room felt like the under-cabin of a ship, and maybe that's why Courtney chose nautical decor and had lighthouses on the mantel of the fireplace. This was a key difference between Courtney and me: Whereas I try to rid my living space of any reminders of Dustin's job aboard a ship or airplane, Courtney seemed to revel in it.

I sat down on the denim-covered couch and curled my feet beneath me. I knew I should be feeling excited—I'd spent the last few days anticipating the meeting and the surprise—but as I sank into the throw pillows with ship appliqués, I felt a sense of dread. Maybe Courtney was right; maybe none of us really wanted the hoping and guessing to end. Maybe it was the anticipation we enjoyed. It had made the week fly by, and I didn't want that to end. What would get me through the next week?

The rest of the spouses arrived soon after. Usually there are a few stragglers who take their time getting to the meeting—and make everyone else angry in the process—but not on this night. By five after seven, everyone was seated around Courtney's coffee table and whispering anxiously. Some wives were definitely dressed sexier than usual, and I felt a twinge of triumph when I saw Sasha struggling to sit comfortably on the floor in her miniskirt and boots. Despite her usual insistence that she knows military life better than anyone, she had obviously fallen prey to the rumors about the surprise.

Kate sensed everyone's excitement, so she opened the meeting without delay. Her platinum hair was pulled back in a loose knot, and she sat cross-legged on the red brick of the hearth, poised as ever, with a black high heel dangling from her left foot. "Wow, what a great turnout we have," she said. "I guess everyone is eager to hear the exciting news. I'm sorry if I have raised some people's hopes about the men coming home, but maybe what I have to say will be just as rewarding."

I watched Sasha's face go from an electric smile, to a frown, to a blank stare presumably meant to mask how stupid she felt for believing.

Courtney stood in the kitchen doorway, still dressed in the apron and with a slender hand at her throat. I knew she could barely wait to hear the news, but I also knew she'd experience a letdown once the excitement was over. I knew because I was already feeling deflated and I didn't even know what the news was yet.

Kate smiled playfully and continued. "I've received word that the ship will make one last port call in France before heading to the Persian Gulf, and the CO and XO have deemed this stop safe enough for the spouses to fly over and meet them—"

Before she could say anything more, women jumped to their feet and started hugging one another. They were clapping and shouting, and I swear Courtney was already talking about what she was going to wear. "France, can you believe it?" she said to no one in particular. "Think of all the shopping . . . and the cheeses . . . and the wine!"

I stayed on the couch and sank farther into the cushions. I knew this day would eventually come. One of the highlights of military life is the opportunity to fly overseas and meet your spouse in a foreign port, usually with groups of other wives, making it yet another bonding experience. My own mom had once participated in this age-old tradition when I was a baby. She flew to the Philippines to meet up with Dad and left me and my brothers with Doris and Big Jack. I have no memory of her leaving or returning, but I do know she never went on another overseas flight again. Apparently Mom's fear of flying (handed down from Doris) kicked in, and for the rest of Dad's military career and various deployments, she said, "No, thanks," when the other wives planned trips to go abroad.

I couldn't have imagined Kate telling us anything worse, other than that one of the guys had had an accident. Besides the whole flying issue, I wasn't sure I wanted to go to France. I wasn't sure I wanted to see Dustin. Which surprised me because I had just spent the last several days hoping he'd be at Courtney's house that night.

When Jody spotted me on the couch, she pushed her way through the excited women and came to sit down next to me.

"Aren't you excited?" she said.

I looked at her, confused. "Excited? You know me better than that. There's no way I can go. Unless you know of any boats to get me there."

"We'll get you some medicine," she said. "And some beer. You'll never even know you've been on a plane once you get there. Come on! You can't miss out on this."

I shook my head. "I can't, Jody. There's just no way. It would take a lot more than medicine and alcohol to get me on a plane."

"What then?" she said. "What would it take? Just tell me and we'll do it."

I looked at her and smiled. "It would take your hitting me over the head with a two-by-four and knocking me unconscious."

"Great!" she said. "I can do that."

That night, Dustin called. I knew it was him because the caller ID read "US Government," but I didn't answer. I couldn't answer. I knew, without a doubt, he would try to convince me to fly, and I didn't know what to say. Then, sure enough, when he left a message, I knew I had done the right thing:

> "Hey, Sarah, I was hoping to talk to you. Guess you've heard the news by now. I hope you'll consider flying out here to meet me in France. Just consider it. That's all I'm asking. We'll get you whatever you need—medicine, tranquilizers. Just please come. Love you. Bye."

I had no trouble going to sleep at a reasonable hour (one a.m.) that night. Perhaps I was emotionally drained, or maybe the anxious grinding of my teeth ever since I'd left Courtney's house had made me tired, but once I got in bed, my eyes shut, and I was asleep.

An hour later, I woke to a startling noise. A blaring siren whirled in the hallway, bouncing off the wood floors and echoing so that one piercing sound fell into the next. I sat straight up in bed and put a hand to my chest. The noise was deafening, and I imagined it circling around my brain, swirling around my ears. The bedroom was completely dark, and I couldn't see anything, except one flashing red light on the wall near the door.

The burglar alarm.

My heart was beating in my throat and banging against my chest. I had gone from being peacefully asleep to feeling like I had drunk twenty cups of coffee.

I reached for the phone beside the bed and dialed 911, but got it backward and ended up with 1-9-9. "Dammit!" I yelled and threw the phone down. The siren was getting louder and the whirling seemed to be getting closer and closer. My hands were cold and wet.

I fumbled with the phone and tried the number again: 9-1-1. This time it rang.

"911, what's your emergency?" a dispatcher said in a drone voice.

"Someone's in my house," I yelled. "Please, help me!"

"What's your address?" The dispatcher sounded calm, almost bored, as if this were routine.

"I don't know right now. Call my neighbor," I said.

"I'm sorry, I can't hear you. You need to turn off your alarm."

I screamed louder. "CALL MY NEIGHBOR!"

"Who's your neighbor, ma'am?"

"Brent!"

"Brent who?"

"I don't know—just call him!"

The dispatcher tried to be patient, but irritation came through her staccato words: "Ma'am, I can't call Brent unless you give me his last name or phone number. Now I need you to stay calm and answer some questions for me. Are you alone?"

My hands shook the phone. "No," I said. "I have two children in another room."

"I need you to put down the phone and go get your children," she said.

My breath caught in my chest. "I don't think I can move."

"Listen to me," she snapped. "Put down the phone and go get your children. I won't hang up and I'll be here when you get back."

My legs were like weights. It was like a bad dream when you want to run but can't. I felt frozen. "I can't move," I said and started to cry. "I don't want to see what's happened to them."

Just then a dark shadow came across the floor outside my bedroom door. I screamed into the phone, "Help me! Help me! Oh, God, please! My children!"

Then I looked up just as Brent came out of the shadows and stepped through the door. He was bare chested and wearing a pair of SpongeBob SquarePants boxer shorts. He had a baseball bat in his hand.

"The police are on their way," he said. "You're going to be OK."

I threw down the phone and ran to him.

When the red-and-blue lights of police cars lit up the cul-de-sac like a disco party, neighbors stepped out onto their front stoops in bathrobes and squinted their eyes to see across the street. There's nothing like a mysterious emergency in the middle of the night to bring out the community spirit in everyone.

Brent bundled me and Ford and Owen in blankets and brought out chairs for everyone to sit on while the police searched the house. I was still shaking, but I had stopped crying . . . until I remembered Tanner. "Oh, my gosh, Brent!" I yelled. "Tanner! Tanner's still inside."

Brent dashed back inside to get her, like a fireman running into a burning building.

I pictured Tanner shaking and whimpering under my bed. I pictured her crying because I hadn't thought to bring her out with the kids. I pictured her hating me for the rest of her life. She'll never get over this, I thought. She'll be scarred and frightened forever.

But when Brent came back out a few moments later, he was holding a very irritated and sleepy Tanner with fluffy bed head sticking out in all directions.

She was less than scared—she was indignant.

"Where was she?" I cried, reaching out to hold her.

"Asleep under your bed," Brent said. "Have you had her hearing checked lately?"

A police officer came out of the house and I recognized his stiff walk and mustache. He was the same one from before, and here I was again in my driveway . . . in my pajamas. Thank goodness I was wearing flannel this time.

"Looks like you have a warped back door," the officer said as he scribbled notes on a pad of paper. The radio on his belt clicked on and off with nothing but static and mumbling voices. "It probably popped out when the temperature changed tonight," he said. "And that was just enough to trip the alarm. But everything looks good and we've reset the system."

I sighed with relief and clutched Tanner closer to my chest. "I can't thank you enough, Officer," I said.

He smiled as he flipped the pad of paper closed. "Don't worry about it. We're glad to help. But hey, you might want to get a better watchdog for yourself." He laughed and tousled the fur on Tanner's head. Then he looked at my face and his eyes brightened. "Wait a minute," he said. "Aren't you the girl—the girl in the cowboy shirt and flip-flops?"

"Cow GIRL," I said. "It was a cowgirl shirt. But yes, that was me."

He looked me up and down, then smiled sympathetically. "A single mom?" he asked.

"No, actually, my husband is serving overseas," I said.

The officer smiled. "Oh, well . . . Hey, next time you talk to him, send him our best, and our thanks."

He swaggered back down the driveway to his police car, waving at all the onlookers as if he were a rock star.

Why is it that women go crazy for a man in uniform? I wondered. How can a uniform totally mask every other flaw so that we believe the man inside is near superhuman and infallible?

The officer was probably going back to his wife, back to his children. There he would take off his thick leather belt and shiny badge and transform back into "husband" and "dad" until the next shift. I turned to look at my house. Every light was on and there was a definite glow from the front window lighting up the darkness outside, yet the house still seemed empty and cold to me. I would go back inside and put the kids to bed and try to go to sleep, but it would still be months and months before Dustin's uniform rested on the floor of our bedroom again.

I couldn't help but envy the policeman's wife.

Once I was back inside and had put the kids to bed, I called Courtney, but not from the closet this time.

"You won't believe what just happened," I said. "My freaking burglar alarm went off in the middle of the night!"

"No way!" she said. "Is everyone all right?"

"Yes, we're fine. The police came to check everything. I'm still kind of shaking. I don't think I can go back to sleep."

"I'd think not," she said. "I'd probably pee my pants if the alarm went off."

I was a little taken aback by this. First of all, it was stunning to hear Courtney say "pee." But also, I had always thought Courtney was fearless—or at least unconcerned—in most situations. She's the kind of person who never jumps to conclusions about strange illnesses when she is sick. So it didn't occur to me that she might sometimes be scared—by something other than my bad manners.

"Were you crying hysterically?" she asked.

"Oh, yeah! Of course. But I handled it. I'm actually kind of proud of myself."

"Way to go, girl!" she said. "See, now you can get on a plane and fly to France with us!"

"Nope, no way."

"Sarah!" she cried. "It just won't be the same without you. You have to come. Dustin will be so disappointed."

"I know, I know," I said, "but I just can't—"

I stared at our black-and-white wedding picture on the bedside table and took a deep breath, finally realizing how tired I had become.

"Look, Courtney, I'm starting to feel exhausted now," I said. "I should probably get some sleep before the boys wake up again."

"OK, so long as everything is all right," she said. "If you want me to watch the boys while you sleep tomorrow, just give me a call."

I hung up the phone and saw the Viagra notepaper with Dr. Ashley's phone number on it next to the charger. The house seemed quieter than it ever had before. I could hear the kitchen clock ticking outside my room. *Tick, tick, tick.* Usually ticking clocks are soothing and help me to sleep, but now the noise was bothersome, and with each *tick* of the second hand, I was reminded of my loneliness.

Where is Dustin? I wondered. What country? Which ocean? I had no way of knowing. But did it really matter anyway? He was a world away in all respects.

It was strange to think about our parallel lives, the way I was going about my business in the same city and town he knew, while he was thousands of miles across the ocean, experiencing a world I had never been a part of. What is he doing right this minute? I often wondered. But I couldn't begin to guess. I had no point of reference for his days and nights and what his schedule might be like. I didn't even know what the rack he was sleeping on looked like.

Dustin was living somewhere I had never been. Were there any reminders to make him think of me? I thought of Dustin every time I passed his favorite Italian restaurant on Twentieth Street or saw his pickup truck sitting in the garage. But what did he have to remember me?

I looked at the Viagra notepaper again. I wanted to hear Dr. Ashley's voice. I wanted to tell him about what had happened. I wanted to hear him say again that I can take care of myself. But why? Why did I need that? Why him?

Had I become—*gasp!*—dependent on Dr. Ashley?

I picked up the paper and bit my lip.

"Oh, what could it hurt? I'll just get an answering service anyway."

I dialed the number, and my palms began to sweat when I heard the ringing.

Maybe I shouldn't be doing this, I thought. What was the purpose anyway?

And then someone picked up the other end.

"Hello?" Dr. Ashley said.

"Um . . . uh . . . I . . ." I was speechless. Had he given me his private office number?

"Hello?" Dr. Ashley said again. "Is someone there?"

"I'm . . . ah . . . looking for Dr. Ashley."

"Sarah?" he said. "Is this Sarah Smiley?"

I winced. "Yes, it's me. I didn't think you'd be there. I thought I'd get an answering service."

"I'm on call tonight," he said. "What's up? It's pretty late—er, early—for you to be up."

Suddenly I was crying. Maybe it was hearing his voice. Maybe it was the inevitable release of all my adrenaline. But when I tried to speak, my voice cracked and I started sobbing.

"Sarah?" he said. "Sarah? What's wrong?"

"I'm . . . I'm not . . ." I wiped away tears with the back of my hand.

"Sarah?"

"Um, Dr. Ashley," I said between sniffles. "I . . . ah . . . think I need to come in and see you. I think I need— Oh, I don't know what I need. I just need to come see you."

He was quiet, and then: "How about first thing in the morning? As soon as the office opens?"

"OK." My voice was shaking.

"Damn, wait a minute," he said. "I won't be in tomorrow. Can you come at eight o'clock on Tuesday?"

"Yes."

"And you're sure you'll be OK until then?" he asked.

"Yes, and thank you," I said, wiping my nose with the back of my hand. "Thank you for always being so kind to me, and for . . . for . . . um . . . taking care of me."

We both were silent. I felt awkward and wished I hadn't called.

"Well, I guess I'll see you then," I said.

"Yes, see you then. And, Sarah?"

"Yes?"

He paused. "I'm glad you called."

11

TAKE A NUMBER AND SIT DOWN

The next day I was plagued by two thoughts: What does "I'm glad you called" mean? And why am I more concerned about that than the fact that I haven't talked to my husband in weeks?

Jody and Courtney came over for pizza so we could analyze the situation.

"It can mean so many different things," Jody said. She was sitting on my living room floor, mindlessly rolling a Matchbox car back and forth in front of her. "It could mean 'I'm glad you called because I don't want you to suffer alone' or 'I'm glad you called because hearing your voice reminded me I need to put in a refill for your prescription' or—"

Courtney flopped back into the sofa and put her hands up in disgust. "I'm glad you called because I was just thinking—inappropriately, I might add—about you? I mean, really! It's all in poor taste, if you ask me."

I picked at a piece of Pop-Tart stuck on the carpet and thought it over for a minute. "But really, guys, what do you think he meant by it?" I said. "Am I reading more into this than I should? What will I say when I see him again?"

Courtney leaned forward on the couch. "Don't tell me you're actually thinking about going to that appointment."

"Why wouldn't I?" I said. "He's my doctor."

"Oh pa-lease!" Courtney snorted. "Are you kidding me? Sarah, his behavior has become untenable! After all, he *knows* your husband is on deployment, for Heaven's sake!"

"Well, we are only hearing Sarah's side of the story," Jody said. "So we can't condemn the man on hearsay alone." She paused and twisted up her lips. "Although it does sound like the doctor has crossed some sort of gray line."

"Do you really think so?" I said. "I mean, do you really think I'm not imagining this?"

My voice must have sounded more excited than concerned because they both looked at me and frowned disapprovingly. And then Courtney said, "Seriously, Sarah, why do you care what another man meant by 'I'm glad you called'? Why does it matter so much? Are you, like, in love with this man or something?"

"What? Well, that's absurd!" I said. "I don't even know him! And besides, I'm married!"

"Well, you're certainly not talking like a married woman," Courtney said.

I looked at Jody for support, but she smiled apologetically and said, "I have to agree. This is beginning to seem like more than a flirtation. It just doesn't seem right with Dustin being gone and everything."

"What are you saying?" I asked. "Are you guys mad at me for this?"

"Not mad," Jody said. "We're just trying to understand."

But Courtney shook her head disapprovingly and said, "You're unbelievable—you know that? Our husbands are serving their country, fighting a *war*, and all you can think about is this torrid infatuation with your gynecologist."

I felt myself growing angry. It was an uncomfortable feeling because I was usually more hurt than mad around Jody and Courtney. I didn't know how to react to these new emotions. Who was I to argue with the always-right Courtney or the insightful Jody?

So I surprised myself when suddenly I said, "Oh, so just because my husband is serving our country I'm supposed to excuse him for any bad behavior? Does the wife of a man with prostate cancer suddenly allow him to disrespect her because he's sick? Do you tell someone with a terminally ill child they can never again complain about something as petty as a broken toe or a grocery store who sells them expired milk?"

"Of course not," Jody said, looking at me in amazement.

"So why does everyone expect me to suddenly deem everything else in my life null and void just because my husband is in a war? Do I not still have feelings? Can't I be angry? Don't I still bleed from a paper cut?"

Courtney chuckled. "Well, it would be a bit trivial to cry about a paper cut with all that's going on in the world right now." She looked at Jody with a here-Sarah-goes-again smirk.

But Jody tilted her head thoughtfully and said, "Would it be, Courtney? What if your house burned down tomorrow? That wouldn't be trivial, no matter what else is going on. There are people starving and dying of disease every single day. Someone always has it worse. Yet our own pain still hurts."

"Hell, Courtney, I guess you think serving the country is a man's ticket to eternal pardon!" I said. "How lucky for Derek! He can never do any wrong now."

Courtney blushed and put a hand to her chest. "Well, Sarah!" she said. "I see your point—really I do—I just cannot condone your feelings for another man. And I think the two are exclusive of one another. It's one thing to be real and acknowledge that sometimes we feel sorry for ourselves, but it's quite another to lust after another man."

I was beginning to feel tired and frustrated. My voice grew softer. "Well, all I mean is that Dustin serving overseas in a war doesn't erase the problems in our marriage."

Courtney and Jody exchanged glances, and then Jody said, "I understand what you're saying, Sarah. We're just worried about you. That's all."

And then Courtney said, "Tell me, Sarah, when was the last time you thought about Dustin?"

Feeling defensive again, I rolled my eyes at them. "Oh, well! I happen to think about him all the time," I said. "Why, just yesterday I thought about how he doesn't send me e-mail nearly as much as your husbands. And a few days before that, I thought about his mom sending him a dozen cookies right after she heard I had already sent him some, and—"

"No, Sarah," Jody interrupted. "When was the last time you thought about Dustin . . . when you weren't angry at him?"

I was speechless.

I arrived at the hospital at seven forty-five on Tuesday morning. The lobby was nearly empty except for a child in the corner huddled next to his mother and coughing into wadded-up tissue. Each time he wheezed, I held my breath and was glad the boys were staying at Courtney's (even if she did say it made her feel like she was "aiding and abetting the enemy"). But I smiled at the child's mother and pretended not to notice the red splotches on his face when she caught me looking over my magazine at them. I wondered how tacky it might be to wear a surgical mask to the hospital next time . . . just in case.

I tried believing I wasn't nervous, and I excused my trembling knees by telling myself I was cold. So why did I find myself chewing on the side of my mouth when Dustin suddenly crossed my mind?

I looked up from my magazine and saw Dr. Ashley coming around the corner in his light blue scrubs and gold-rimmed glasses. He smiled and waved. I wanted to wave back, but it was as if my hand had forgotten how, and I ended up smiling awkwardly instead, with my lips closed. He was coming closer. Then, as if in slow motion, he walked to my chair and put a hand on my shoulder. I could almost feel each of his fingers individually as they brushed across my shirt.

"I'll be with you in just a minute," he said in a hushed voice. "I've got something to take care of real quick, but it won't be long."

"Thanks" and "OK" were the only words I could get out. "This is so wrong," I thought, and I considered running for the door and not coming back. But then I watched Dr. Ashley walk away, and he was so darn cute with his boyish build and baggy scrubs. I smiled to myself and quickly looked around to make sure no one else had seen.

My hands shook the pages of the magazine. Was I only imagining Dr. Ashley raised his eyebrows when he touched my shoulder? Maybe he's just a friendly doctor. It probably means nothing, I thought. After all, this is the man who has seen all my stretch marks and the dimple underneath my breast. How could he possibly think I'm attractive?

Was Jody right about the doctor having crossed a line?

Several minutes later, Dr. Ashley returned and personally escorted me to one of the exam rooms. I sat down in a plastic chair against the wall and wrapped my arms around my purse in my lap. I wasn't sure where to look—at him; at the wall; at the diagram of an infected ear—so I kind of looked up at the ceiling and pretended to be in deep thought while he gathered up his clipboard and sat down on the spinning stool.

"So," he said, and smiled in my direction.

"So," I said back, looking at him and then quickly away.

He chuckled and wheeled the spinning stool closer. "I'm worried about you," he said finally, putting a hand on my knee. "I was scared when you called that night. What was going on?"

I shook my head. "Oh, nothing, really. It was stupid. My burglar alarm went off and I was feeling really scared. I'm sorry I called so late."

"You should have told me," he said. "About the burglar alarm, I mean. I might have been able to help. Was there someone in your house?"

He was staring into my eyes with a look of concern. Had Dustin ever looked at me with such compassion? Then I realized I hadn't even told Dustin about the burglar alarm yet. In fact, I hadn't told Dustin much of anything that had been going on. It was like I had separated myself from him. But did he even notice?

"No," I said, shaking my head. "It was just the back door. It warped in the night when the temperature dropped or something."

"Do you need it fixed?" he asked.

Oh God, what was he implying?

Suddenly there was a nauseous twisting in my stomach. I thought I might throw up.

"Already taken care of," I said, but it was a lie. Brent was supposed to come over later that week to fix the door. But I was afraid to tell Dr. Ashley the truth, and I wasn't sure why. Was I afraid he might offer to help? Or that he wouldn't?

Then Dr. Ashley reached up, gently pulled my purse from my grasp, and set it on the floor, brushing my hand in the process. Until then, I wasn't aware how tense I had been. I released the muscles in my shoulders and arms, looking for a new place to stow my hands now that the protection of the purse was gone, and I could feel the relaxation spread across my back. Funny how you never realize you're tense until you're not anymore.

"How's your friend Melanie doing?" he asked.

I was relieved by the distraction. "She's doing much better," I said. "In fact, she's back to doing step aerobics and jogging and putting all the rest of us to shame. You should see that woman in a bathing suit! You wouldn't guess it by the way she dresses, but I certainly don't want to be the one standing next to her at a pool."

I was rambling, so I blushed.

Dr. Ashley laughed. He was looking at me with such intensity, I had to look away.

"Sarah," he said finally, "I can't help you unless I know what's going on in there." He touched the side of my head. "Do you think you're having some postpartum depression? Do you find yourself crying often?"

"It would seem that way, wouldn't it?" I said, laughing. "I think I've cried the last few times I've seen you, at least. You seem to have that effect on me lately."

I smiled, but Dr. Ashley didn't smile back.

"That's my concern," he said. "You used to be able to talk to me. We'd laugh and joke around. But something feels different now. Something feels different from you."

Oh, no! I was so obvious! Was it the red shoes in the ER?

I stood abruptly, knocking his hands off my knee, and paced across the floor. I was so confused. Did I have feelings for this man? Was it just textbook transference? Was something wrong with my marriage? Had I finally gone crazy? Was it all in my mind?

I started to cry and buried my face in my hands. "Why are you so nice to me?" I cried. "Why? Why?"

"Sarah, tell me what's going on," Dr. Ashley said and got up from the stool.

Of course, I couldn't tell him exactly what was going on, because that would mean admitting that I had dreams about him instead of my husband; that I wished he was the one who had come into my house in the middle of the night when the alarm went off; that I looked forward to my visits with him; and that I wasn't sure what all of it meant for my marriage, or why he represented everything my husband was not. So I went for the safe confession.

"I'm just not cut out for this," I said. "I'm not cut out to be a military wife. I hate it. I hate that my husband has missed half our marriage and most of our children's lives. I hate that my own dad was gone most of my life. I hate that Dustin calls me from foreign ports, when he's laughing and having a great time, and I'm here dealing with the boys and feeling so alone that I'm terrified!"

I was talking more emphatically than I had meant to. Did I really want to tell this man all my innermost thoughts? I felt as exposed as . . . well, as a girl in a backless hospital gown.

But Dr. Ashley was watching me with that same lips-turned-down thoughtful stare I had grown to expect from him. "These are all very natural reactions," he said. "And don't forget that you have a newborn baby, so your emotions are a little out of balance right now."

"No," I cried, pacing back and forth. "It's not my hormones. Don't say it's my hormones."

"What is it, then?"

"It's that I'm raising two kids by myself, and I'm living alone, and I feel so disconnected from my husband right now. We're more than oceans apart. We're light-years apart."

I sat back down in the plastic chair with my shoulders slumped forward. Again, I felt a release in the muscles of my back. Dr. Ashley handed me a tissue and I dabbed at my eyes.

"You know what happened to me one day?" I said through sniffles. "I locked myself out of the house. And you know who had to help me? My neighbor Brent and a policeman, that's who. Two married men with wives and families of their own. Someone else's husband had to come help me because mine's not here. And I know you'll say Dustin's serving his country and that he's making sacrifices and protecting our freedom. I know all that. But frankly, none of that made me feel any better when I was standing on the back patio in my nightshirt and flip-flops!"

I saw Dr. Ashley bite his lip. Probably trying to keep from laughing, I thought. Why was I always the clown?

I grew more angry and determined. "And at BUNCO one night, my friend called me a 'walking calamity.' And you know what? She's right. I'm someone who needs help . . . a lot of help. I'm no good by myself. It's a wonder I haven't gotten lost on my way to the grocery store or something. I don't even mow my own lawn. My neighbor does it for me."

Dr. Ashley put his hand on my knee again. "I think you're stronger than you realize, Sarah. In fact, I think you are one of the strongest patients I've got!" He laughed. "You can be a pistol sometimes—do you know that? I've never had such a hard time getting someone to take their medicines. And not many of my patients research their prescriptions as well as you do."

"Oh, see, you have me mistaken again," I said. "I do all those things because I'm afraid—afraid of everything. I won't even get on a plane to visit my husband in France."

"We have drugs for that," he said. "I can get you a prescription."

I groaned and stood up again. "I'm not even sure I want to go, even if I wasn't afraid of flying." I was pacing again. Then I shook my head. "You know, I've gone my entire life being under someone else's care. I went from my parents, to a sorority, to Dustin. I've never taken care of myself. Do you realize that? It's pitiful."

"Of course you have. And you're an excellent mother, too."

"Well, besides my children, who don't know any better, who would actually depend on me?"

"You did a great job taking care of Melanie that night in the ER," he said.

I rolled my eyes. Hadn't I tried everything to get out of taking care of Melanie?

He was scratching his chin and staring at me. I looked at the floor. "Anyway, Sarah, it doesn't matter why you do the things you do," he said. "What matters is that you do know how to take care of yourself. So what if your neighbor mows your lawn? At least you're getting it done. Everyone has their limits. You may not recognize this, Sarah, but it's a strength that you know what yours are."

I collapsed into the chair again and thought it over. I felt a rush of relief like the giddy feeling after an important test is over.

Then I looked up and smiled at Dr. Ashley. "How do you always know exactly what to say to a woman?"

He laughed. "I don't always know. Otherwise I might actually be married!"

"Getting married has nothing to do with saying the right thing," I said. "Otherwise Dustin would still be single."

Dr. Ashley looked at me and cocked his head to the side. "Are you going to be all right?" he asked.

I rubbed at my eyes and took a deep breath. "Yes, I'll be fine. I may look like a mess, but that's just the state of my life, really."

Dr. Ashley looked at his watch and frowned. "I have another appointment waiting, so I need to go, but I want to see you again soon."

"I'd like that," I said.

He gathered up my chart and tapped it on the counter to straighten the pages. "Take care of yourself and call me if you need me," he said, and then, "Go to France and see your husband. It might be just what you need."

I went to pick up the boys at Courtney's house and she invited me in to split a turkey sub—real, homemade subs, with fresh turkey, unlike the frozen chicken tenders and hamburger patties I had been eating at home.

"Dr. Ashley actually suggested I go see Dustin overseas," I said with my mouth full. "Why would he say that?"

"Because you're married," Courtney said. "And because all the other wives are going. Because obviously he's not caught up in this same fantasy with you."

Her observation crushed me. Was she saying Dr. Ashley didn't like me after all? Why didn't she also just go ahead and tell me that reindeer can't fly or that frozen yogurt is low-fat but not low calorie?

"You really believe that?" I said. "You don't think he likes me?"

Courtney put down her sandwich and stared at me with a look of disappointment and frustration.

"Are we going to go through this again?" she said.

"Go through what?"

"This whole thing—that's what. I mean, what do you want me to say, Sarah? What is it you want?"

"I don't want anything. I just—"

Courtney shook her head. "Do you want me to say the man is in love with you? Do you want me to say you should leave your husband? Is that what you want me to say?"

"What? Of course not, Courtney! You know I love Dustin."

She rolled her eyes.

"Why are you so angry at me?" I asked.

"Sarah, do you think you're the only wife who's suffering? Do you think you're the only one who's lonely? Do you think the rest of us don't hate that our husbands are gone six months out of the year? Do you even think about anyone else at all? Because, honestly, Sarah, I think you're using this whole doctor thing as an escape. You're using it to hide from what's really going on."

Tears welled up in my eyes. "Courtney? What do you mean? I . . . I . . . I'm sorry. . . ." I didn't know what else to say.

Suddenly she stood up and pushed her chair away from the

table. "You know what I think, Sarah? I think you need to grow up! Quit relying on other people. Quit waiting for a rescue. I mean, really!"

She stomped out of the room. I waited for her to come back and tried to think of an apology, but when I heard the bedroom door slam closed, I knew I should leave. I gathered up Ford and Owen and quietly closed the front door behind me.

I was shaking on the way home. From fear or anger, I don't know, but my head was spinning, and I was beginning to feel overwhelmingly tired.

Where is Mom when I need her? I thought. Oh, how I longed for her to visit again and help me get things in order.

When I opened the front door of the house, there were three piles of dirty laundry on the floor in the foyer. There were stacks of dishes towering in the sink, waiting to be cleaned, and a mountain of mail—mostly bills—was scattered across the sideboard underneath Doris's oil painting.

Tanner sulked around the corner and I knew immediately by the way her tail was pushed between her legs and her head was hanging low that she had done something. Something bad.

"Tanner," I said with my hands on my hips. "What have you done, girl?"

She whimpered and cowered behind the legs of a chair.

"Tanner? What's going on? What did you do?"

I crept around the corner, walking slowly and watching the ground with each step. Then just as I came into the living room, I saw a pile of brown vomit on the carpet. Tanner rarely had accidents, and I couldn't remember the last time she had gotten sick in the house. I closed my eyes and sighed.

Ford ran off to his room, talking a mile a minute about Superman and Batman and the Flash. I put Owen in his crib for a nap; then I went back into the living room.

Tears rolled off my cheeks as I scrubbed at the stained carpet.

There was so much that needed to be done. The bills. The laundry. The dishes. It was all piling up and making me feel tired. I wanted to go to sleep.

Then I heard Tanner making coughing sounds in the other room and I paused to listen. She was getting sick again. My heart beat faster. Somehow, in the back of my mind, I knew. . . .

I walked toward the sound coming from my bedroom and saw Tanner lying on her pillow under my bed. But she was facing the other way, and I couldn't see her eyes. The air smelled like vomit.

"Tanner girl?" I said softly, but she didn't move.

"Momma, come see Superman," Ford yelled from the living room.

"Just a minute, honey," I said over my shoulder and walked farther into the bedroom.

The room was cool and dark—I had forgotten to open my blinds that morning—and Dustin's alarm clock cast a greenish light across the bed.

"Tanner?" I said, crawling under the bed toward her.

She didn't move. She was lying with her head in a pool of spit-up. I instinctively reached out to check her breathing. It was shallow and fast. Her delicate ribs were pumping up and down, but her body was absolutely still.

"Tanner!" I yelled as tears ran down my cheeks. I slid her pillow out from under the bed with her still on top and bundled her in my arms. Her body was limp and she sighed when I pressed her against me. I sat back against the dresser and buried my nose in her fluffy fur.

"Tanner, no," I cried. "Hold on, Tanner. Don't leave me now. Not now, girl."

She was whimpering, but the sound was weak and almost inaudible. I stroked her back and cried, "Please, Tanner, not now. Don't leave me now."

"Momma!" Ford yelled, running into the bedroom. "Momma?"

I held up a hand and said as gently as I could manage, "Not now, Ford. Go to another room. Mommy will be out soon."

He considered me for a minute and his eyes got wide. "Momma? Tanner?"

"Ford, go to the other room," I said. "Right now!"

He ran back into the living room yelling, "Superman! *Don dee da* . . . Superman!"

"Please, Tanner, please," I begged, and she started quivering. Her breathing was getting even faster, but her body was as limp as a wet piece of paper. Her bones felt like toothpicks.

I stood up, still cradling her in my arms, and went to the phone to call Jody.

"Jody, Tanner's dying," I sobbed. "She's dying right here in my arms. My Tanner is dying, and I can't . . . I can't . . . I . . . I—"

"I'm coming over," she said and hung up.

Jody stayed with the boys and I sped to the nearest veterinarian. Tanner lay on her side in the passenger seat. I stroked her back with one hand and drove with the other. I could barely see the yellow lines on the road for all the tears coating my eyes, and I was hiccupping from the sobs.

"Tanner girl . . . Tanner girl . . ." I said it over and over again. "We're going to make you well. I promise."

But when I pulled into the gravel parking lot and came around to the passenger door to get her out, I noticed that something in her eyes had changed.

She didn't have strength to lift her head; it was flat against the seat. But she moved her watery black eyes toward me, and with one tired, graceful arch of her eyebrow, I knew what she was saying: It's my time to go now, Sarah.

She died inside the vet's office, as I stroked her back and cried into her fur. I was too choked up to speak, but Tanner didn't need words anymore. She didn't need me to talk for her.

Tanner would never see Dustin again. She would never see my

boys grow up. She would never again look at me with those bossy, temperamental eyes. She had brought me to this point in my life, but now she was gone, and that moment in the vet's office may have been the loneliest I've felt in my life.

The vet came back into the room. Clearly it was time for me to say good-bye and leave. But how could I go back home without my Tanner? How could I leave her there? After all these years together, how could I just walk away?

The vet put a hand on my shoulder. "You must have lost a childhood pet when you were a kid, too. So you know that time heals and soon you'll have all the happy memories of Tanner."

I looked at him with wet, stinging eyes. "Tanner *was* my childhood pet," I said and turned to leave.

Back inside the car, I leaned my forehead against the steering wheel and closed my eyes.

"Why me?" I cried. "I can't take it anymore!"

I wanted to sit there forever. I dreaded going home to the piles of mail, dishes, and laundry, and the thought of waking up in the morning and taking care of the boys and the house all by myself again made me cry harder. There seemed to be no end.

My head began to ache. I leaned it back on the seat and sighed. I can't go home. Not right now. But I couldn't sit in the parking lot forever either, so I took a deep breath, straightened my back and wiped my eyes with my fingers, which still smelled like Tanner's fur. I was holding her green-and-white collar clutched in my left hand. I kissed it and said, "Good-bye," one last time; then I laid the collar on the passenger seat beside me and started driving. I didn't know where I was going. And I didn't care either. I just wanted to keep moving.

Eventually I wound up at the Navy base. I toyed with the idea of going up to see Dr. Ashley, but in one unusually clearheaded moment, I decided to go to the Fleet and Family Support Center instead. It was almost closing time, and the waiting room was empty, so I went directly to the desk of the only employee I saw there. She was a skeletal civilian with permed orange hair pulled back tight in a banana clip. She was busily writing something on a notepad, or possibly simply ignoring me.

"Can I help you?" she said in a smoker's voice and without looking up.

My hands were shaking; it was hard to admit my failures and that I needed help. But I cleared my throat and said, "Yes, I need some help with my finances. My husband—"

"Take a number and sit down," she said, still not looking up.

I glanced around the room. There were definitely no other people waiting in line, and she was the only employee so far as I could see.

"But I'm the only person here, and I just thought—"

The woman finally looked up with a blank expression that punctuated her lack of amusement.

I stuttered and cleared my throat again. "I mean, I just saw that no one else was waiting, and—"

"Read the sign," she said, pointing with her pen to a piece of notebook paper taped to the front of her desk. Written shakily in pencil the sign read:

Familys will be seen on a first come, first serve bases. Please take a number and wait your turn.

"Oh, I see that now," I said. "But I'm the only one here, and I just thought, you know—"

She looked at me hard and raised an eyebrow. The wrinkles radiating from her mouth were like deep valleys, and there was the faintest amount of fuzzy hair above her lip. I felt a little afraid of her.

"Well, OK then," I said. "I guess I'll just take a number and sit down."

I went to a red number dispenser and pulled the tab. Number seventeen. Did numbers one to sixteen go through this same ordeal? I wondered.

There was a makeshift waiting room consisting of a grouping of plastic chairs along the beige cement wall, so I found a seat and sat with my purse in my lap. I wasn't going to get comfortable.

A few moments later, the woman put down her pen and took a breath to speak. I got ready to stand.

"Now taking number sixteen," she said.

You've got to be kidding me! I glanced around at the empty chairs.

"Number sixteen," she called again. Then she waited a minute before going back to her writing.

I was starting to get angry. This is the problem with military facilities, I thought. They follow the rules, whether they make any sense or not. Apparently the woman had been taught that everyone needs a number and everyone has to wait. Why didn't someone empower her to make exceptions when her good judgment called for it?

I shifted in my seat, purposely making noise so she wouldn't forget I was there. But, really, how could she forget?

The woman put down the pen again, looked out across the room, and said to no one in particular, "Number seventeen. Now taking number seventeen."

I jumped to my feet.

"Uh, that's me," I said with what I hoped was a convincing smile and approached the desk again.

She stared at me with the one raised eyebrow.

"Um, let's see." I started riffling through my purse, pulling out the checkbook and a wad of crumpled-up receipts and a few bills. "I'm having some trouble understanding my checkbook, and my husband is deployed. I was wondering if someone could help me make sense of all this."

"I'm sorry, but we're closing in ten minutes," she said.

My kill-her-with-kindness smile snapped into a frown. "You're kidding me, right?" I said. "You made me sit over there waiting, and now you tell me there's no time?"

"I'm sorry," she said again. "But rules are rules. It doesn't matter what rank your husband is. Everyone waits their turn."

That *really* set me off. I was accustomed to this sort of thing when I was still Dad's dependent, because when you're the daughter of a Captain or an Admiral, people assume you want special treatment. In reality, though, Dad always taught us the opposite: to let others go first and respect the privileges we had. I never once expected preferential treatment from this orange-haired witch. Not to mention, as a junior officer, my husband was hardly at the top of the military food chain.

"Excuse me? Did you just say—" I involuntarily stomped my foot.

"I said that you needed to wait your turn, and you did, and now it's closing time."

I was beginning to feel hot with anger. "This is absolutely unacceptable," I said. "It was hard enough coming here to ask for help, and now you're talking to me like this!"

Just then, a heavyset woman with salt-and-pepper hair came out of an office door in the back. I recognized her noisy pant hose and leather shoes at once: She was the counselor who had talked to us at Kate's house.

"What seems to be the trouble out here?" she asked, coming closer.

"This lady made me wait," I began, and my voice cracked. "She . . . she . . . she made me wait . . . for no reason . . . and now she's telling me that . . . that . . . that I can't get any help . . . and my dog just died . . . and I feel so tired . . . and—"

I struggled to take a breath. The counselor came over and put her arm around me. She hugged me to her shoulder and patted my back. "Now, now," she said. "Of course we'll help you. Let's go into my office."

For nearly an hour, the counselor walked me through the process of balancing a checkbook and keeping track of bills. I was absurdly grateful. Why hadn't anyone taught me this before? I wondered. And then, oh, yeah, Dustin tried to teach me several times, but I never wanted to listen. And now I wondered why.

I left the office feeling more empowered than I had in years. I was a woman with a checkbook—a balanced checkbook—and I could take on the world.

I practically high-kicked back to the car, I felt so good. I thought, I can walk past a roach and not be scared! I can feel a bump on my temple and not worry about tumors! I was liberated! I thought I could even get on a plane and fly!

But then I shook my head and came back to my senses. I didn't feel THAT good.

I sent Dustin an e-mail about Tanner that night and was surprised when he called me an hour later.

"I'm sorry to hear about Tanner," he said. "I know that was hard for you."

I thought about our fight the morning before he had left, when he had cursed at Tanner, and the memory made me bristle.

"Well, you know, she was a just a 'damn dog,' right?" I said bitterly.

"Hey, now, that's not fair, Sarah," he said. "I didn't mean it when I said those things. We were both under a lot of stress."

I didn't have the energy to answer, so I said nothing. Where once I might have mustered up the strength and emotion to argue, instead I just felt tired and numb.

But I wasn't sure exactly why I was so mad at Dustin. Obviously, Tanner's death wasn't his fault, and, after all, he did call to comfort me. Yet still I felt abandoned by him, as if he should have been there to hold me at the vet's office.

Dustin cleared his throat. "So have you definitely decided not to come to France?"

"Yep."

I knew he wanted me to expound, but I was too tired. Hadn't I explained the way I felt a hundred times before? Why didn't he listen then? What about the day I wanted to talk at the legal office when we were waiting to make his will?

Dustin took a deep breath and said, "Well, that's awfully disappointing, Sarah. Can't you at least do it for me?"

Do it for him?

I was sitting on the couch flipping through a fashion magazine, only I wasn't reading or paying attention to any of the articles and pictures.

I didn't answer him, so he said, "Sarah? Are you still there?"

"Yes."

"Why don't you tell me what's going on?" he said. "I can tell something's up. It's in your voice."

"Oh, you mean besides my dog dying? Hmmm, let's see. . . ."

He sighed again. "Come on, Sarah. I'm trying to be serious."

I threw the magazine on our weathered white coffee table. "All right," I said. "You want to know what's going on?"

"Yes, I do."

"I'll tell you what's up. I balanced the checkbook for the first time today. And a few weeks ago I set my own raccoon traps in the attic. I even fixed the toilet . . . with my bare hands! I've spent sleepless nights with Owen crying until I thought I couldn't hold my head up anymore. I found my dog dying beneath our bed—"

"I know," Dustin interrupted. "It's definitely not easy, but you knew that when we got married—"

"No, Dustin, let me finish," I said, and the hardness of my voice surprised me. "Yes, doing all these things is stressful, but here's the funny thing. When I sat down to sort through the bills and mail today, I felt more in control than I ever have in my life. You know, I realized, 'I'm not a *dependent*! I'm not dependent on Dustin!' "

"I'm glad you had that experience, then," he said. "But why does that affect your decision about coming to see me?"

Duh! Why are men so thickheaded? Can't they follow a conversation?

I huffed and said, "Because if I were to come see you, Dustin—forgetting all the minor details of flying in an airplane . . . over an ocean!—I would fall right back into that same trap of being your dependent. It's the way we are! I'm changing. My fear is that you—or we—can't change."

Dustin was quiet, as if all this had hit him out of the blue, as if I wasn't making any sense.

Suddenly I could hear the ship's 1-MC echoing through the hallways behind him: "This is a drill: Man overboard, man overboard. Report to your duty stations for mustering purposes only. This is a drill."

"What was that?" I asked.

"The ship's intercom," he said. "We're doing a man-overboard drill. I need to get to the ready room to check in."

His voice was soft, almost a whisper, but I couldn't tell if it sounded more dejected or exasperated.

"OK," I said. "Well, then, I guess we should just say good-bye then."

"Guess so."

"All right then."

The 1-MC blared in the background again: "This is a drill. This is a drill. . . ."

"I've got to go now, Sarah," Dustin said; then he paused, as if he were waiting for me to respond. I didn't.

"I love you," he said and hung up.

12

DID I SAY IT WAS
A STRAY CAT?

The other wives flew to France a few days later.

"I should stay here and take care of things for every-one," I told them, but anyone who knew me well enough knew it was an excuse.

Besides, what did I need to "take care of" anyway? They had all arranged for neighbors to water their plants and check their mail, and Jody's in-laws came to watch her kids. No one really needed me to stay behind, and yet I still couldn't get on a plane and go.

So while Courtney and Jody and everyone else rendezvoused with their husbands in Cannes, I stayed home and agreed to take care of Courtney's black cat . . . to make my "taking care of things" farce seem more legitimate.

And I hate cats. To me, cats are unpredictable. The way they stalk and pounce makes me nervous, and worst of all, I think cats sense my discomfort around them. They seem to study me, circling around and waiting to attack. I just know every cat I've ever met has had it in for me. They must know I'm the dreaded "dog person."

But I thought caring for Courtney's cat would be easy. Courtney said I only needed to go to her house once a day and put out food and clean water. Unlike a dog, the cat didn't need companionship and she wouldn't fetch a ball. She didn't need to be exercised, and Courtney claimed the cat wouldn't even care if I paid her no attention at all.

Perfect, I thought. I'll just put food in the bowl and get out. What could be easier?

But the first day I went to check on Devil Cat—not her real name, but stay with me here—she was more than a little disgruntled about being left alone. I opened the front door and Courtney's burglar alarm sounded a warning signal. I ran to the laundry room to silence it. I didn't see Devil Cat, but I knew she was probably lurking somewhere, watching me and waiting.

"Here, kitty, kitty," I called out, because I had once heard Courtney do that.

I was holding Ford on my hip and had left Owen sleeping in his carrier in the foyer by the front door.

"Kitty, kitty," Ford said and giggled.

"Here, kitty, kitty," we said together.

I was laughing and rubbing my nose up against Ford's when I heard a soft meow.

"Oh, she must be nearby," I said. When I turned around, I saw a scrawny black cat sitting in the kitchen doorway wagging her tail. I thought only dogs wagged their tails.

"Look, she's glad to see us," I said to Ford. "Here, kitty. Come here, kitty."

Devil Cat lifted a front paw and licked it, but she never took her eyes off us.

I looked at Ford and shrugged. The cat seemed pleasant enough. She was wagging her tail, after all.

"Oh, well," I said. "Let's go get the kitty some food."

I turned my back and rummaged through Courtney's pantry.

"Let's see. Courtney said it would be a shiny purple bag . . . and there's supposed to be a spoon . . . and—"

Just then, Devil Cat made a screeching sound like an angry monkey, and before I could turn around to look at her, I felt a pain in my calf like razor blades sinking into my flesh.

"Holy cow," I yelled and jumped up in the air.

Her jaw was clamped to my leg and she yanked at it like a dog does his chew toy. The sensation of her knifelike teeth sinking into my skin still gives me chills, and to this day, I can't stab a piece of chicken with a fork without thinking about Devil Cat.

I screamed again and shook my leg, but her teeth were too far into the muscle. She was attached, and with each shake of my leg, she flailed around like someone on one of those giant swings at an amusement park.

"Oh, my God," I yelled. "Get off me! Get off me!"

Then I kicked my leg forward, more forcefully this time, and the cat released her grip. She went sliding across the linoleum and banged into the cabinets with a thud.

I still had Ford on my hip, and his eyes were like saucers. I clutched him to my chest and jumped onto Courtney's kitchen table.

"Oh, no, Owen!" I yelled. But Devil Cat never seemed to notice him sleeping peacefully in his carrier by the front door. She was decidedly more determined to attack me than anyone else.

After a few moments of shaking her head and meowing, the cat recovered from the slam against the cabinet and started circling the table like a shark.

"Get away, you stupid cat," I yelled and Ford, who up until this point was frozen with fear, burst into tears.

"No, don't cry, baby," I said. "Cats don't jump on furniture, so we're safe up here."

I could have sworn I heard Devil Cat laughing at me at this

point, and with one forceful, silent leap, she jumped up onto a chair beside the table. She was licking her lips again.

"Mommy! Mommy!" Ford cried. "Scary cat! Scary cat!"

There was a fuzzy mouse toy near my foot, and I kicked it hard across the room, toward the back door. Devil Cat leaped from the chair and chased after the mouse. I jumped down from the table and ran to the front door, still holding Ford on my hip. I reached down, grabbed Owen's carrier, and slammed the heavy wood door behind us.

Once I was safe inside the car and had the boys secured in their seats, I looked down at my calf. Bright red blood was trickling from four pinholes in my skin, and everything below my knee was beginning to swell. Normally, for a medical crisis, I would have run to Jody's or Melanie's house, but they were both overseas, darn it!

So I grabbed the cell phone and called my parents. When I told Mom what had happened, she screamed and handed the phone to Dad. Despite being competent and independent, Mom, whenever Dad is nearby, doesn't do well in emergencies. When my older brother, Van, choked on a piece of steak, Mom ran out the front door screaming. Thankfully, Dad was home and did the Heimlich maneuver, but Mom insists if he hadn't, she would have pulled through. "I only fell apart because I knew I could," she always says.

Once Dad was on the phone, I recounted the whole ordeal, barely stopping to take a breath. It's a wonder Dad understood anything I said.

"Was it a stray cat?" he said in a calm, steady voice.

"No, it was my friend Courtney's," I said. "She's meeting the ship in France, and I'm taking care of the cat for her."

"Oh," Dad said, "why didn't you go to France?"

I twisted up my face and huffed. "Dad, you know I don't fly! And besides, let's get back to my emergency here."

"OK, OK," he said. "Cat bites can be really dirty. They harbor lots of bacteria. You should probably go to the hospital and have it looked at. They might want to give you a tetanus shot."

"A shot?" I yelped. "Do you really think it's that bad?"

"Probably not," he said. "It's nothing to get all worked up about. Just go to the hospital and have it looked at. That's all you need to do, Sarah."

He was beginning to sound irritated and impatient. I felt myself spiraling into that all too familiar hypochondria, when no amount of comforting words helps, and though I try to extract information from my unlucky listeners, I never believe their response.

"You think it's bad, don't you?" I said. "Tell me the truth, Dad: You think that cat gave me some disease!"

"It's really nothing to get worked up about," he said. "The cat has its rabies shots up-to-date, right?"

I closed my eyes and put my head against the steering wheel. Visions of Old Yeller spun around in my mind. They'll have to put me in a barn and shoot me, I thought.

"Just go to the hospital," Dad said again. "Everything will be fine."

The base emergency room was packed, but because my leg was swelling and both my children were screaming, the nurse decided to check me in right away.

I knew the hospital would be required to contact animal control about the bite, and if I blamed Courtney's cat, they might confiscate her. So when the nurse asked me to describe the incident, I lied.

"I was walking down the street and this big black stray cat jumped out and bit me in the leg."

"A stray cat?" the nurse said. "Really? It just jumped out and bit you?"

"Yep. It flew out of the bushes and attacked me, just like that."
She scribbled something on a sheet of paper. "We'll have to
contact city officials about this," she said and led me back to the
exam room.

I waited a long time on a bed behind a curtain, trying to keep
Owen quiet and Ford from crawling on the dirty floor. Eventually
I convinced him the bed was a "boat" and he played "pirates" for
a good twenty minutes—twenty minutes I had to contemplate
whether Dr. Ashley might be there, and what I might say if he appeared as my attending physician. But when the curtain finally
slid open, the man standing there in a white coat was definitely
not Dr. Ashley. He was tall—about six three—with gray hair and
a hunched back. His legs were extraordinarily long, and his lips
were set in a firm straight line.

"What seems to be the trouble?" he asked, looking down at the
clipboard.

"Well, there was this stray cat, and I was walking down the
street, and he jumped out from behind a bush and bit my leg. My
dad said I should have it checked out." I twisted my leg around to
show the damage.

The doctor came closer and rubbed the skin near the four
pinholes gently with his finger. "Hmmm," he said. "Looks like a
good bite you got there. Is it tender?"

I winced as he suddenly pressed hard on my calf.

"Yes, it hurts a lot," I said. "Is there any chance my regular
doctor—Dr. Ashley—is here tonight?"

The doctor looked up with a blank expression. "I don't know
of any Dr. Ashley," he said. "Must be a resident. But no, there's no
one here with that name today."

I felt a wave of disappointment, and it occurred to me that I
was now *completely* alone. Dustin was gone. All my girlfriends were
overseas. My parents were in another state. And even my doctor
wasn't on call.

There was no one to help.

The doctor scribbled something on a chart, then peered at the bite again. "So a stray cat did this to you?"

"Yep, it just jumped out of the bushes and attacked me, that vicious cat!"

The doctor frowned. "Well, then, we need to get you started on the rabies series right away. I'll call for the nurse."

"Whoa, wait a minute," I said. "A rabies series? What do you mean?"

"We have no way of knowing a stray cat's vaccination history," he said, "so we need to do the shots just in case."

My heart was beginning to beat faster. I remembered some urban legend about the rabies shot being given with a twelve-inch needle in your stomach.

"Well, actually," I stuttered, "actually, it was really my friend's cat. I'm watching it while she's overseas meeting her husband in France."

"Your friend's cat," he said doubtfully.

"Yes, really, it was. I only said it was a stray before because I was afraid you'd report it and the cat would be taken away."

The doctor frowned at me again and scratched his head. "So a friend's cat did this?"

"Yep."

"And she's out of the country?"

"Yes, sir."

He studied the chart, then pointed at me with his pen. "You have twenty-four hours to get that cat's shot record. And if you can't, we'll start the rabies series. Your tetanus shot is already up-to-date."

He turned to leave, calling over his shoulder, "A nurse will be in to clean up the wound."

That night I racked my brain, trying to remember any snippet of information Courtney might have given me about her travel plans. I tried calling her cell phone, but the call wouldn't go through.

I felt frantic. The doctor's words—"rabies" and "tetanus"—were swirling in my mind and making me dizzy. At midnight, my jaw began to feel tight, and after a quick search on the Internet, I confirmed that "lockjaw" is another word for "tetanus."

I called my parents, and once again, Mom screamed and handed the phone to Dad.

"Sarah, you don't have lockjaw," he said. "The doctor told you your vaccination is up-to-date."

"But my jaw feels really tight, Dad." I was rubbing my ear and shifting my bottom jaw left and right. "Seriously, Dad! It's aching, it's so tight."

He sighed. "You're probably clenching your teeth. You need to relax. The doctor wouldn't let you leave the hospital if he thought anything was wrong with you."

"But, Dad, he actually said the word "rabies"! Why would he say that?"

"He's a doctor, Sarah! That's why."

"Let me talk to Mom again," I said. Clearly I needed to speak to someone a little less collected.

He passed the phone to Mom. Mom's voice was surprisingly patient and soothing this time. But she couldn't fool me. It was all a choreographed facade to make me calm down.

"Sarah, honey, try not to worry," she said. "Remember what I always tell you: 'When you hear hoofbeats, think horses, not zebras.' Just keep telling yourself that."

I rolled my eyes, annoyed at her little game of pretending to be cool. "What does that mean anyway, Mom?"

"Remember your last month of pregnancy with Ford?" she said.

"Yes."

"And remember how you ate three one-pound bags of Tootsie Rolls in those last few weeks?"

"Unfortunately, yes."

"And remember how later you had that pain in your jaw and you went to ENT after ENT asking to have your tonsils removed? You were convinced you had tonsillar cancer. Remember that?"

"Yes, Mom. But it really did hurt! Anyone else would have been scared, too."

Mom chuckled. "Sarah, you were thinking of 'zebras'—or cancer—when clearly it was 'horses'—a pulled muscle in your jaw from all those Tootsie Rolls!"

She had a point, and put that way, it did make my tonsil scare seem rather silly.

"Anyway," Mom said, "I'm sure the cat has had all its shots. You're going to be fine."

At two o'clock in the morning, I did a search online of French hotels. A few in the Cannes area rang a bell and I wrote down the numbers. It was already daytime in France, so I went down the list and called each one. The language barrier was difficult, but one of the concierges recognized Courtney's last name and said, *"Oui, oui."*

"So you know who I'm talking about?" I said.

"Oui, madame. Oui."

"I have a very important message I need you to get to my friend."

"Oui?"

"Her cat . . . er, her feline . . . um, I don't know the word in French. . . ."

"Le chat?"

"Chat?" I said. "I guess so. . . . Um, let's see. . . . It's a big . . ."

"Grand?"

"Yes! Grand! A grand cat—only, just between you and me, this cat isn't that grand—"

"Oui?"

"It bit me. I mean . . . um . . . its teeth . . . eat? How do I say—"

"Manges?"

"Yes, that! . . . I think. Anyway, I need to get the cat's shot record."

The concierge gasped. *"Flingue? Flingue! C'est terrible!"*

"What? What was that?" I said. "I can't understand. Something terrible?"

"A *personne* is shot?" he said.

"Oh, gosh, no," I said. "Not at all. Although it did feel a lot like a shot. But I just need the cat's shot . . . I mean . . . let's see . . . vaccination? . . . vaccination record."

"Oui," he said, audibly relieved. *"Vaccination."*

"Yes," I said. "I mean, *Oui.*"

But I had forgotten what my point was. Why was I even calling this person? Then I said real loud and slow, "Can you . . . leave a message . . . for . . . my friend Courtney to . . . call me?"

"Oui, madame," he said, and *"Au revoir"* and hung up.

The next morning, Courtney called me in a panic. "Has someone been shot? Is the cat OK?"

I laughed. "Yes, everything's OK. I had a little trouble talking to the concierge. See, this is why I don't travel!"

"So what's going on?" she said.

I didn't want to worry her about what had happened, and I definitely didn't want to sound like a sore loser who was taking away their fun. Then again, I wasn't willing to get a rabies shot to spare them either.

"Well, Courtney, your cat kind of bit me. No, actually, she attacked me. I had to go to the emergency room."

"Oh, dear!" she said. "I can't believe this! That's terrible!" Then she paused and said more softly, "But I guess I should have warned you. She gets a little vicious after being left alone."

"Yes, Courtney, that would have been helpful. Then I might have worn pants. But anyway, I just need to get into your house and find the shot records or else the hospital will be forced to give me rabies shots."

Courtney was silent. Then she said, "Oh, dear," again.

"What?"

"There's a little problem," she said. "We've . . . um . . . I don't know how to say this to you, but, um, we've never had the cat vaccinated."

I froze. "You're kidding me, right?"

"No, I'm not, Sarah."

"Isn't there something in that *Miss Manners* book of yours about getting your pets vaccinated before asking a friend to go feed them?" I was beginning to feel angry.

"But she's an indoor cat," Courtney said. "So the chances of her having rabies are very slim."

I broke into a cold sweat.

"Sarah? Sarah, are you there?" Courtney said.

I threw down the phone, gathered up the boys, and drove back to the emergency room.

"No shot record, huh?" a new shorter and plumper doctor said when he came behind the curtain.

"Apparently not," I said. "And you have to understand, I'm, like, the world's biggest hypochondriac! This just doesn't sit well with me."

"Having rabies wouldn't sit well with anyone," he said and laughed. When he showed his teeth, they were as wide and square as piano keys.

"No, don't say that," I cried. "Do you really think I have it?"

He smiled and shook his head. "The chances are very slim. Was the cat foaming at the mouth? Is this kind of behavior unusual for it?"

"I don't think she was foaming," I said, "but still, what if?" My heart was beating so fast, I felt dizzy.

"I tell you what," he said. "Don't go over to your friends' house again for ten days. Will they be back before then?"

"No."

"OK," he said. "We're going to keep the cat 'semiquarantined.' You'll need to find someone to go in and feed it—I don't recommend your going in there again. If the cat shows any sign of illness during that time, we'll collect it and start your rabies series."

Just hearing those words again made me sick. "Why ten days?" I said. "How can we be certain?"

"Rabid animals don't live longer than about ten days," he said. "Your friend's cat will be deader than a doornail in a few days if it has rabies."

So, for ten days, I took Brent with me to Courtney's house and made him climb on a ladder to look inside the windows before sending him in to tend to the cat's food and water. I found it incredibly difficult to relax or go to sleep unless Brent made those daily checks. If Devil Cat showed up dead, I didn't want to waste any time getting my shots, and I knew I was going to need moral support.

Brent sort of enjoyed the task. It made him feel like the Crocodile Hunter or something like that. He did a lot of teasing—coming down from the ladder and pretending the cat was dead—but mostly he thought I and everyone else were overreacting.

At the end of ten days, Devil Cat was as healthy and "normal" as ever. I never had to get the shots, but I did receive instructions to "follow up with my regular doctor," and that meant going to see Dr. Ashley. Which might have been the only good thing to come out of my run-in with Devil Cat. Just the thought of Dr. Ashley touching my leg made me tingle.

13

SOMETHING HAS HAPPENED

When the other wives returned from France, showing off their photographs and stories, I felt like the only kid at school who wasn't invited to someone's birthday party. Except, I *was* invited to this party, and I chose not to go. I only had myself to blame. And there's nothing worse than that.

Courtney brought me some porcelain blue dish towels she bought in Cannes as a thank-you gift—or was it an "I'm sorry" gift?—for watching her cat, and Jody had pictures of Dustin to show me. He looked thinner, and somehow older, not like I remembered. It was becoming more and more difficult to remember our lives together, to remember what a "normal marriage" is like. Some nights I woke in a panic, wondering if I remembered the smell of Dustin's hair, the sound of his voice, or the mole next to his lip. On the nights I couldn't, that's when I cried. Would we even know each other at the end of this?

Jody watched the boys while I went to the hospital for my follow-up appointment with Dr. Ashley. I had asked Courtney to do the favor—after all, her cat did attack me!—but she refused, saying she would no longer take part in my "disreputable behavior," or something like that.

Initially, Dr. Ashley's nurse said he didn't even have any appointments available, but later, Dr. Ashley called and said he'd fit me in on his lunch break. I liked thinking I got some kind of special treatment from Dr. Ashley.

Dressing for the appointment was difficult. I knew he would need to see my leg and, more specifically, my calf, but the temperature outside had suddenly turned cool after a stretch of unseasonably warm weather. If I wore pants I knew I'd have to take them off and get into a gown for the exam, and that might make me too nervous. So I opted for a skirt and black sweater, and ended up feeling—once again—a bit overdressed for the hospital.

Was I beginning to look obvious?

When I got to the family practice wing, a corpsman dressed in camouflage behind the reception desk didn't believe I had an appointment.

"I'm here to see Dr. Ashley," I said, and the corpsman looked up from his paperwork and scowled. "Dr. Ashley is on his lunch break," he said.

I smiled apologetically (or did I just look guilty?). "Yes, I know, but he's fitting me in because he didn't have any other appointments."

The corpsman stared at me through squinted eyes, sizing me up, then went around the corner to verify my story. Military hospitals usually don't have fancy intercom systems; they rely on Post-it notes and the feet of corpsman to deliver messages. It's a slow process.

I sat in a chair beneath the FALLOUT SHELTER sign (because I'm most at home there), and stared up at a television hanging from the ceiling across the room. I could see it was set to the news, but I was too far away to hear anything. A group of nurses and doctors with stethoscopes draped around their necks was standing beneath the boxy television with faux-wood trim. They had their arms crossed and their heads tipped back to see. It seemed a little strange to take a break from work and stare at the news in silence, but when the corpsman came back and escorted me to the exam room, I didn't give it another thought.

After I had waited only a few moments in the cold, bright room, Dr. Ashley came in with a smile and that familiar rush of electric air. He flopped down on a chair and sighed, "What a day, I tell you!" Then he straightened himself and opened my chart. I chewed my nail and watched as he read notes from my emergency room visit. "Hmm," he said as he read, rubbing a hand along his short, Navy-regulation sideburns. Then the corners of his mouth crept upward. "So what's this about a cat biting you?" he asked.

"Yeah, I didn't end up going to France to meet the ship—"

"Really? Why not?" He sounded genuinely surprised. Maybe even curious.

"I just couldn't get on the plane. But anyway, I can't think about that right now." I waved my hand to dispel the topic, which was too uncomfortable to get into with him. Then I said, "So I ended up taking care of my friend's cat, and it bit me the first time I went to feed her. Got me right in the calf." I twisted my leg so he could see. The pinholes were by now covered with tiny scabs, but the skin surrounding them was purple and black.

Dr. Ashley wheeled himself forward with the chair and rubbed his finger along the bruises. He was peering out from above his gold-rimmed glasses. "Hmm," he said. "That cat got you good, huh?"

I could smell his musky cologne wafting up from the V-neck of his light blue scrubs. I felt guilty, and excited . . . and a little bit nauseous. So I pulled back my leg and smoothed my skirt. "Yes, she got me in the muscle, and you know me, now I'm worried about the whole rabies-infection thing."

Dr. Ashley opened my chart again. "Well, the notes here say

that the ER gave you some antibiotics and instructed you to monitor the cat. Did you do that?"

"I did get the medicine, and you'll be proud to know I actually took it."

Dr. Ashley grinned. "And the cat? She's still alive, right?"

"Oh, yes," I said. "She's as alive and crazy as ever. Damn cat."

"Then it looks like everything's going to be OK," he said and patted my knee. "You're good as new."

"So you're positive I don't have rabies? I mean, I don't want to stay up at night worrying about this."

Dr. Ashley stood up and held my records loosely at his side; his face was relaxed and patient. "You don't have rabies," he said. "Trust me. I wouldn't let you walk out of here if I thought you did. You wouldn't be nearly as pretty with foam coming out of your mouth."

Ha. Ha. Ha.

Pretty?

He walked to the sink and washed his hands. Then he turned around, drying them with a paper towel, and said, "By the way, I was thinking about you the other day."

"Oh?" I tried to hide my shock, but I know my eyes doubled in size.

"Yeah, I met this woman and she reminded me so much of you."

He sat back down in the chair and put my chart aside.

Was I dreaming? Did he really just say that? I wanted to pinch myself. Or maybe slap myself.

"Reminded you of me?" I said, but in my mind I was thinking, What girl? There's someone else? I'm pretty?

Dr. Ashley rubbed his chin. "You know, she was just a lot of fun, and real easy to talk to. Just like you."

I stared at him, trying in earnest—like masking a yawn—to keep my mouth from gaping open.

I'm "fun" and "easy to talk to"?

I could hardly believe my good fortune!

"But anyway," he said with a sigh, "at this rate I'll probably never get married. It's tough out there, you know? I see people like you and I think, 'Man, her husband is so lucky. He's got this wonderful wife and kids . . . everything.' It doesn't happen like that for everyone."

I was blinking and, of course, trying to memorize every word so I could repeat it point for point to Jody. I would definitely need her help to analyze his message. Did he know I had a crush on him? Was this mention of another woman a way of letting me down gently? Or was it code for how much he really liked me?

Had I gone totally insane?

I'm not sure I responded verbally to Dr. Ashley because I was too shocked and overwhelmed, but I think I was nodding.

"I hope Dustin realizes how lucky he is," Dr. Ashley said, and I had to try really hard to resist the growing ball of excitement inside me that felt like it might make my stomach burst.

Then Dr. Ashley seemed to pull himself together. He shook his head, stood up, and said, "Well, anyway, when do I see you again, kiddo?"

"At Owen's next checkup, I think."

"Great," he said. "I'll see you then. And hey, Sarah, don't worry about the cat bite. Remember, if you need anything—anything at all—just call me. You've got my number."

I drove straight to Jody's house and walked in without knocking.

"Jody, you're not going to believe this," I said, coming into the living room. She was sitting on the couch in total darkness. Every blind on the windows was closed.

I stopped short when I saw her there. "Where are the kids?"

She pointed toward Michael's room. She wasn't smiling.

I wouldn't exactly describe Jody's normal character as "bubbly" or "perky," so her mood didn't strike me as overly unusual. Whatever had put her in a funk, it didn't concern me, I thought.

"So anyway," I said, flopping onto the couch, "Dr. Ashley said he met this girl and she—"

"Sarah, something's happened," Jody said. She was staring straight at me and not blinking.

"Oh, dear, did Ford spill something? Whatever it is I can clean it up or replace—"

Jody put up a hand and shook her head. "It's not that. Have you been watching the news?"

"Well, no, I've been at the hospital, of course. Why? What's going on?"

"The war, Sarah. It's started. And the ship is headed that way."

I scratched at my head. "What? But, I mean—I thought . . . well, I guess we all knew this was coming. . . ."

I couldn't figure out why Jody seemed so serious. We knew the war was coming, and we knew our husbands would be involved. Yes, it was a bit shocking to hear it in a formal way, to know that it was real, but Jody's face looked like all the blood had drained out of it.

And then she said, "There's more, Sarah."

"More?"

"Steve called while you were at your appointment. He's being sent home early—"

"Coming home early? What do you mean?"

"He's not finishing out the deployment," she said. "There's been a big shake-up at the squadron. Steve said it's total chaos out there right now and a lot of changes are happening since the news of the war."

"But I don't understand. Why are they sending him home?"

"I don't know, Sarah. I mean, we knew we'd be leaving after the deployment was over. . . . I never guessed it would be so soon . . . but then who could have guessed any of this would happen . . . ?"

Jody paused to take a deep breath, and then she said, "They're sending Steve home in a few weeks. His orders have been officially changed."

I thought it over a minute. So what was Jody so upset about? Her husband was coming home!

I sat up and clapped my hands. "Well, that's excellent news, Jody! You must be so excited! And now Courtney and I will have a resident handyman around!"

Jody frowned. "And we're moving to California . . . by the end of next month."

"Oh, come on," I said, smiling. "Real funny, Jody. Is this reverse psychology or something?"

"No, I wish it was," she said flatly. "I have to go to the base tomorrow and set up the move."

I blinked and huffed before stuttering, "But why, Jody? Why is this happening? What changed?"

"I don't know all the reasons," she said, looking down at the ground.

"By the end of next month?" I repeated it again and again and Jody kept nodding.

"Steve couldn't give me all the details over the phone. It's just so—so unexpected."

I put my hands on either side of my head to steady myself. I knew I was going to cry, but I couldn't in front of Jody, because this wasn't supposed to be about me . . . was it?

The phone rang and I waited awkwardly for Jody to answer it. It rang and rang. Then finally, on the fifth or sixth ring—just when I was thinking an answering machine would be nice—Jody got up and went to the kitchen.

"Hello?" I heard her say in a quiet voice. I looked over my shoulder at her. She turned her back and leaned over a countertop. Then she put her forehead in her hand and started to cry. I had never seen Jody cry before.

I pressed my back into the cushions of the couch and tried to be invisible. I felt awkward and clumsy, and I didn't know how to sit or where to place my hands. The round wood clock above the television ticked noisily, and the sound of crashing LEGOs and the kids' laughter floated down the hall from Michael's room. Owen was asleep in a portable crib in Jody's bedroom, where she always put him for a nap at her house—the same place she had put Ford to sleep when he was a baby.

I looked around the living room—at the picture of the moose on the wall, at Mr. Squirrel, at the plastic bin of toys shoved in a corner—and began to wonder how many times I had sat on Jody's couch. I sometimes felt like her living room was a best girlfriend's dorm room across the hall in college. I usually invited myself in without knocking, and I felt as comfortable sitting on her couch in my pj's and ponytail as I did on my own.

"I know, Mom," Jody whispered into the phone. "I will . . . yes, I know. . . ."

I still had my back to her and was unsure about what I should do. Did she want me to comfort her? Did she want me to pretend I couldn't hear her crying?

Damn the military! I was sick of living this way, of growing close to people and falling in love with a city and a way of life, only to move and start over again a couple of years later.

But then again, would I have ever met Jody if it weren't for the military?

"OK, I'll let you know," she said. "I'll call you then. . . . OK . . . I will. . . . Gotta go." She hung up the phone.

I almost didn't hear her walk back into the living room, she was so quiet. When she sat down on the couch beside me, she looked just as awkward and uncomfortable.

What would Jody want? I asked myself. What does Jody need?

Finally I put my arm around her shoulder and said, not totally sure of myself, "How about a girl's night?"

She looked at me and smiled. Her cheeks were wet and splotched with red. "Absolutely!"

Courtney brought the wine, we ordered takeout (plain cheese pizza for Jody and me, Kung Pao chicken for Courtney), and for the rest of the night, the three of us got drunk and reminisced.

"Sarah, remember the time you hung upside down on my couch," Jody said, "and did that Mr. Chin thing with marker on your face?"

"I think I have a video of that somewhere," Courtney said.

I put a hand on my hip. "Oh, yeah, well, I have this vivid memory of a certain someone going to the Albertsons up the street and—"

"Shut up," Jody laughed and threw a chocolate kiss at me.

"What about the time Dustin tried to teach us canasta?" Courtney said. " 'This is a great card game,' he said and—"

"And pulled out the five-hundred-page instruction book," Jody finished.

"It's really a great game," I said, and when I caught myself defending Dustin, I had a familiar twinge in my stomach. I laughed. "Oh, he is terrible explaining the rules to games, isn't he?"

Courtney sighed and looked dreamily at nothing in particular. "Those guys! I wonder what they're up to right now?"

The conversation went on and on like that until the kids had long since fallen asleep and the wine had worn off. I carried both of the boys home at one o'clock in the morning.

The sky was perfectly clear as I walked between our houses, and the stars twinkled above me like tiny pinholes in black paper. I remembered something Dustin once told me about the stars: "Even when I'm far away or across the world, we're still under the same sky. Isn't that amazing?"

But wait a minute, I thought. It was daylight wherever he was.

He wasn't seeing the same stars or the same banana-shaped moon. How could he have gotten that mixed up? He's usually so good at science.

When was the last time we were in the same time zone? What time was it where he was, anyway? What was he doing?

The house was completely dark when I came in. I didn't know I'd be out late, and I hadn't left on any lights. I carried the boys to their beds, and went into the kitchen to make myself some warm milk. Mom always gave me warm milk when I couldn't sleep.

I noticed the red light on the answering machine was blinking, so I pressed PLAY and went about heating a mug of milk in the microwave.

The first message was from my mother-in-law:

> "Hi, Sarah. We just got the best surprise ever! Dustin called and it was so great to hear his voice. He said things are really busy, but he's doing well and hanging in there. Just thought I'd call and let you know. Take care."

I sat down at the round kitchen table with my milk and groaned. If Dustin's mom got a phone call tonight, I thought, this next message had better be from Dustin.

"Message number two," the machine's automated voice said.

"Hey, Sarah, it's Dr. Ashley. . . ."

My heart skipped and I put down the mug with a thud. Dots of hot milk splashed out and landed on the back of my hand.

> You left today without making Owen's next appointment. My schedule is filling up, so I want to make sure I see him on time. Just give me a call at the number I gave you before and we'll pick a date and time. Hopefully I'll see you soon."

I walked toward the machine hanging on the wall and stared at it as if it might burst into flames. Then I played the message again, paying attention this time to the time and date stamp.

"Call received at ten eighteen p.m.," the machine's voice said.

He called at ten o'clock at night? I pulled at my fingers, slipping my rings on and off mindlessly. Then I went to my room and lay on the bed in the dark to think it over. Do doctors usually call their patients at ten o'clock at night?

Then, before I could second-guess myself, and perhaps because I still had more wine in me than I thought, I picked up the phone and dialed his number. My hands were shaking and cold. Maybe I shouldn't be doing this, I thought, but then the ringing stopped.

"Hello?" Dr. Ashley said in a hushed voice.

"On call again tonight?" I asked nervously, but trying hard to sound breezy and offhanded.

He laughed. "And how about you? Any burglar alarms going off over there this evening?"

"No, I just got back from a friend's house."

We were both uncomfortably silent for a moment. And, for me, the only thing worse than small talk is the sound of nothing over the telephone.

"Dr. Ashley," I said suddenly, and he interrupted: "Please, call me David."

Gulp!

"Um . . . ah . . . OK, well, David, I'm um . . ."

I had no plans for what to say. I hadn't even thought about it. Like a nervous jumper going off a diving board, I had just held my breath and dialed without thinking. And now I was talking to him, and I had no idea what to do. So I did what I always do when I'm nervous and uncomfortable: I rambled and said more than I should have.

"Um, let's see—how should I say this?"

"Say what, Sarah?"

"Well, I'm . . . ah . . . let's see . . . I think I'm having some feelings—"

"Feelings?"

"Some feelings about you."

He was quiet again, so I rambled some more. "I mean, I don't understand it all. I'm very confused right now, but I feel like I have feelings for you. And I don't know if it's just postpartum stuff or something more, but I . . . well, actually, no, I know myself better than that, and I know what I'm feeling is real. There, I've said it. I have feelings for you. And I don't know if it's romantic or friendly or what, but it's there and I think . . . Oh, I don't know what I think. I mean, there is chemistry between us, right? Am I crazy?"

Dr. Ashley exhaled noisily. "This can happen sometimes," he said. "What you're feeling is normal, and it's OK. I'm glad you told me."

Normal?

"So what am I supposed to do?" I said. "What do I do with all this stuff I'm feeling? What am I—"

"Stop," he said. "You don't need to explain. I know what you mean." His voice was tender, almost a whisper.

"Should I change doctors? Should I not see you anymore?" I was beginning to feel frantic. Dr. Ashley seemed calm, almost as if he expected this. His even-keeled reaction confused me. Shouldn't he scold me? Shouldn't he tell me how inappropriate my feelings are? Shouldn't he wash his hands of me immediately and send me to someone else?

Or was he enjoying this? Did he feel the same thing?

"I can't tell you whether or not to change doctors," he said. "That's entirely up to you."

He paused as if he was waiting for my answer, but I said nothing. I didn't know what to say. My heart was beating against my back and my ears felt hot.

I shouldn't have called.

But then Dr. Ashley said, "I tell you what. I'm going to schedule Owen's next checkup for eight weeks from today. Take some time to think it over. Figure out what you're feeling, and when you come to Owen's appointment, we'll take it from there. Does that sound good?"

"Sure, I guess. I mean, I don't know. I'm so confused right now, and I'm sorry. I'm just so sorry this has happened."

"Don't be sorry," he said. "I'm glad you told me. And I understand, so don't be embarrassed."

Embarrassed?

"I'll see you soon, Sarah," he said and hung up.

I listened to the dial tone for several seconds, unable to move.

Holy cow! Did I really just do that?

I wanted to call Courtney, but she had had enough of abetting the enemy, as she called it. And Jody was overwhelmed with her own problems. So I went to the living room and tried to calm down by watching television. A correspondent on CNN was interviewing the wife of an Army soldier stationed in Iraq. I listened and watched but felt numb, as if everything was a dream.

Was all this really happening?

I felt guilty for not giving the war more thought. It was almost as if I were watching a movie or reading a book but not really experiencing anything. Each time I looked at the television and tried to focus on the news, my mind went fuzzy and I couldn't concentrate.

And then the telephone rang. I leaped from my seat and ran to the kitchen.

Was it him? Oh, please be him!

I picked up the receiver, and heard static, and then Dustin said, "Did I wake you up?"

"No, I'm awake," I said, almost in a whisper. I wasn't sure how to respond yet. The last time we talked I was angry and combative, but now Dustin's tone was loving. Had he forgiven me? Or had he simply forgotten?

"It's good to hear your voice," he said. "Feels like it's been a while."

"It's good to hear yours, too. I'm sorry about the last time."

"I know," he said. "I'm sorry, too. I realize this has been hard on you, and I've done a lot of thinking about it. You're gaining some independence, Sarah, and I'm glad for that. Really, I am. I just wish you didn't have to push me away to do it."

"I'm not pushing you away, Dustin."

"No, you are," he said. "You're shutting me out. And I don't understand why you need to toss me aside so you can grow up."

Grow up? Did he just say "grow up"?

"What? That is such—" My voice was starting to rise, and I could feel myself getting angry again. Why can't we ever understand each other?

"Oh, let's not start that again," he said. "Let's not fight. It's not what I called for."

"No, Dustin," I snapped. "You've been pushing me away since the day we got married! You shut me out of everything!"

"What are you talking about, Sarah? I go out of my way to make you happy. And you don't even realize that."

Now his voice was angry, too. And how long had we been on the phone? Ten seconds, maybe.

All of a sudden I thought about a time when Dustin and I were working out together at the base gym. He was on the elliptical machine and I was running on the treadmill, and there was a handful of other people exercising between us. I tried several times to catch his eye in the mirrored wall because I wanted to smile at him or mouth, "How are you doing?" But he just stared straight ahead and never looked at me. Not once. And then he finished working out and left the small cardio room without waving or smiling in my direction. I remember thinking, No one else in this room would even guess Dustin and I know each other! And then, a man in a blue tank top approached the skinny woman in front of me on a stationary bike. He leaned down and kissed the top of her head and said, "See you when you're done, honey." I jumped off the treadmill, stormed out of the gym, and sat sulking in the car until Dustin was finished lifting weights. I didn't speak the whole way home, and Dustin could never figure out why.

Thinking of that time now filled me with anger, and before I could get ahold of myself, I blurted out, "I have feelings for someone else."

"Excuse me? Did you just say—"

"I said I have feelings for someone else." My tone was matter-of-fact, and I could feel my confidence growing as I spoke. For once I had the upper hand.

"OK, who do you have feelings for?" Dustin asked.

"I have feelings for Dr. Ashley and I told him so tonight."

"You did what?"

"I called Dr. Ashley and told him that I have feelings for him."

Dustin was quiet for several seconds and I thought he had hung up. But then he cleared his throat and said, "And what was his response?"

"He said he wants to see me in eight weeks."

"What? You're going out with him?"

"No! For Owen's appointment, and to talk about whether or not he should still be my doctor in light of, well, in light of recent developments."

"And if he stops being your doctor," Dustin said, "then what?"

He was hanging on my every word—practically begging me to open up to him—and I wasn't sure what to do with that.

"Then I don't know what," I said.

"You don't know?"

"No, Dustin, I don't. I'm not the same person you left at the terminal that day. It's like I've had an epiphany or something, like I've suddenly become alive."

"You've become alive?"

"Yes, when I see Dr. Ashley, he makes me feel beautiful and funny and . . . alive. I care about what I wear and how I do my hair for the first time in months."

"Oh, so this is about vanity," he said.

I paused and wished Dustin could have seen my angry face. Then I said, "Dr. Ashley makes me feel special. And he looks at me in a way I wish you could. I don't know how to explain it. . . ."

I was starting to cry and my words were breaking apart.

Dustin took a deep breath and exhaled. "So I guess my letter meant nothing to you then," he said. "I'm sorry I called."

"What letter? I didn't get any letter."

There was silence on the other end.

"What letter, Dustin? Did you send me something? Dustin? Are you there?"

But he had already hung up, and all that was left was a dial tone.

That letter from Dustin arrived two days later. The envelope was wrinkled and torn, as if it had been around the world and back again before coming to my mailbox. And judging by the postmark—February 20, 2003—I knew it probably had.

> *Dear Sarah,*
>
> *It's been interesting having your dad on board the ship with us. I hadn't told anyone that he's an Admiral, and I think they were a little surprised. But your dad was really cool about it and kept things low-key, as he always does. I have to say, though, I've never seen our ready room get cleaned as fast as when the squadron heard he was coming down to visit with me after lunch! It reminds me of that time you told me about before we were married, when some junior*

officer hit on you, and you said, "My dad is your Admiral," and the guy ran the other way.

It's funny the perception people (maybe even you?) have of your dad sometimes. They think he will be this rigid, hard-nosed Admiral, and it doesn't help that he's so quiet and reserved anyway. But he's such a different person on the inside. Don't you agree?

When the guys were nervous about his visit, I kept thinking about the way your dad played with Tanner in the front yard, chasing her around like a kid. And I thought of the way he always calls you "Sarah Beth." No one else in your family calls you that, do they?

This deployment has been so crazy. From leaving ahead of schedule, to all the talk of war, it's definitely been a ride. Plus, I realize you and I left each other on bad terms. I hold myself mostly to blame for that. I need to chill out sometimes and be more attentive. I've thought about it a lot lately. I get so wrapped up in the details, about what needs to be done, and I take for granted that you are doing fine and following along with me.

I know I've been a jerk at times, Sarah, and you probably deserve much better than me. But I want to make it up to you when I get home.

I haven't always told you I love you, and I say and do stupid things now and then, but I can't imagine my life with anyone else, Sarah, and I hope you know that.

It's crazy to think about how we met so long ago as kids, isn't it? Sometimes I feel like we've known each other forever, and then I stop and think, "Oh, yeah, that's right. We have!" But maybe that's part of the problem; we've grown complacent.

Anyway, Sarah, I love you. You will always be that funny girl who's not afraid to dance in front of a roomful of people, the girl who can walk on her hands and sing all the words to the kids' cartoon shows.

I'll never see the world the way you do, but I hope you realize my life is better because of you and because of the perspective you give me. Someday, when we're old, you'll be the one who has no regrets, because you're always living in the moment while I'm worrying about the future. That's something I envy, and please don't let the things I have or haven't done change that about you.

I love you,
Dusty

14

YOU'LL DO
THE RIGHT THING

As March turned into April, winter gave way to spring, and the brown dormant grass began to turn green. Oh, sure, the blooming crepe myrtles and yellow flowers were beautiful and the weather was still pleasant . . . *blah, blah, blah* . . . but ultimately, this was a dreaded time for me, because it meant having to take care of the lawn again.

Why mowing the grass was such a problem, I don't know, because I never actually did it. Not once. That's what I had Brent for. Early in the morning once a week, before the break of dawn, I would wake up to the soft purring of his mower clipping past my bedroom window. It was a comforting sound because it meant that all was well, that my house—my world—wasn't actually falling apart around me. If nothing else, I was going to have the best-manicured grass on the block.

Owen was sitting up now and learning to clap his hands. His round face had filled out, and buds of white teeth were popping through his gums. Sprouts of flimsy blond hair stuck up from the crown of his head, making it irresistible to call him "Rooster." Yet he was so thin and small for his age, I sometimes said he was my little kitten—the only cat I would ever like.

Both boys were growing fast, changing like the seasons, and already Dustin had missed so much. Change is difficult for military spouses because it represents time gone by, time that can't be replaced—memories that can't be relived. Life goes on, and children grow up, yet still you're living only to "wait": waiting for the ship to come home, waiting for a phone call, waiting for the next season.

And yes, waiting for the grass to go dormant again so you don't have to mow it.

Dustin hadn't called in weeks, and the ship's e-mail was on and off, so I didn't have any messages from him either. I felt more distant from him than I ever had. And yet, my mind was decidedly more focused on the next appointment with Dr. Ashley and what would transpire there.

I kept Dustin's letter stuffed in a drawer in my dresser because it was too painful to reread. If only I had waited to get it before opening my big mouth! Now I couldn't take back those words. I couldn't even apologize. The connection between Dustin and me had literally been severed. But in a way it seemed easier and safer to be disconnected completely.

Besides, even if I had had the chance, would I have said anything differently on the phone that night? Would I not have told him about Dr. Ashley? I couldn't be sure. But the more I thought about it, the more I wondered, why the heck did I tell Dustin about Dr. Ashley anyway? It's not like I was having an affair. I had nothing to confess or feel guilty about. Did I?

It was a question Jody would certainly know the answer to, if she wasn't so busy moving. Darn it.

One warm, breezy afternoon, she and I sat on the curb outside her house while bearded men in jeans and white T-shirts loaded all her furniture into a rumbling moving van waiting in the driveway. As each item emerged it seemed to trigger an unrelated memory: "Remember when the kids colored Easter eggs and spilled the dye on the kitchen floor?" "Remember Michael's birthday when he ate so much ice cream he started shivering?" "Remember when the guys came back from that bachelor party and Dustin had glitter all over his face?"

The sun beat down on our backs, but there was a soft breeze across our winter white skin. It would still be a few more weeks before the oppressive Florida summer weather began.

"You're getting out just in time," I said, shading my eyes from the sun. "You'll totally miss the humidity."

Jody had a perspiring water bottle between her feet on the pavement. "Oh, I wouldn't say we're getting out just in time," she said; then she took a sip of water and looked up at the sky.

Another load of boxes came out the front door and down the sidewalk. Jody looked over her shoulder at the sweaty men coming toward us, but I couldn't stand to see another piece of her house loaded into the truck, so I stared forward.

"I don't know what I'll do without you here," I said.

"You're going to be fine, Sarah. So long as you keep your head on straight."

Steve poked his head out the open front door. "Jody, do you want to pack up the wedding pictures? Or are we taking them in the car?"

The last week had been strange, with Steve home. The dynamics of our group tipped out of balance in the presence of male testosterone, and in many ways, Steve was a hindrance to my relationship with Jody. He wasn't even fond of *Sex and the City*, if you can believe that! But Courtney and I wasted no time pressing him for every detail ("Has Dustin lost weight? He looks thin in those pictures." "Is Derek doing much flying? Did he talk about me?"). I'm sure Steve was as ready as ever to move, if just to get away from all us women.

"I'll be there in a minute," Jody yelled over her shoulder at Steve, and then to me, "I'd better go help him. I'll be right back."

She got up from the curb and wiped the back of her pants as she sauntered to the door. She was in no rush—apparently the novelty of Steve being home had already worn off. After she disappeared inside, I realized she had become "one of them"— a woman with a husband.

When all the boxes had been loaded and the moving van finally left its obtrusive spot on the driveway, Jody and Steve and the boys piled into their minivan, which was already packed to the roof with suitcases and supplies for the trip across country.

"Where they goin', Momma?" Ford asked. "Are they coming back?"

I didn't know how to answer him, but in my own mind I wondered if I would ever see Jody again. What are the chances we'll be stationed together next time? I wondered. And even if we are, would it ever be the same? We were closing a chapter in our lives, moving on to the next era, a feeling similar to a college graduation, when you say good-bye to the people who were your closest friends for the past four years, knowing you might never see them again.

I felt change on the horizon.

Boy, was I tired of change.

Jody closed the back door of the minivan and walked over to me. She seemed awkward, and I knew she was unsure whether or not to hug me. So I hugged her first.

"Now my house probably *will* burn down without you here," I whispered over her shoulder.

She pulled away from my embrace and waved her hand. "Nah, you'll be fine." Then she glanced behind her to make sure Steve and the boys weren't listening. "And hey, keep me updated," she said. "About the doctor, I mean. And about Dustin, too. Are you going to that next appointment?"

I shaded my eyes and shifted on my feet. "I can't really think about that right now. One crisis at a time, ya know."

"Well, anyway," she said, "I know you'll do the right thing—whatever that is."

We hugged again, and she was more relaxed and natural this time. "Bye, Sarah," she said, but I just waved. I couldn't say good-bye. My eyes filled with tears and Jody touched my shoulder. "You're going to be fine," she said. "And I'm always just a phone call away."

Then she climbed into the van and settled in her seat before rolling down the window. "Don't go feeding any more cats," she called out. "And remember, dead batteries don't 'whine.' "

I smiled and waved. "Bye, Jody."

"Take care of yourself," she said, and Steve eased the purple van out of the driveway.

I stood in the middle of the street and watched them drive away, until they turned the corner and I couldn't see the van anymore. When I turned back around to walk home, the road between our two houses had never seemed longer. A lone bird chirped happily in a tree above me.

"Oh, shut up," I said under my breath.

"What'd you say, Momma?" Ford asked and I stiffened my posture.

"Grown-up stuff," I said. "That's all."

Several times during those first few days after Jody was gone, I picked up the phone and dialed her number before remembering and hanging up again. And when I took the boys for a walk and passed her house, I couldn't look at it for fear of seeing the dark windows, which looked uninviting and impersonal without Jody's lighthouse curtains.

I stayed in my pajamas for almost a week straight, which really wasn't a problem, except when the UPS man came to the door with a package and I was still not dressed at two o'clock in the afternoon.

"You all right, ma'am?" the burly man in a brown uniform asked.

At first I was surprised and wondered what he meant. Did I look sick? Then I peered down at my bunny slippers and blushed.

"Oh, my husband's on deployment," I said. "That's all."

I felt like I needed a disclaimer tattooed to my forehead: "Don't bother asking why—my husband is deployed!"

On another depressed afternoon, I was sitting watching *Oprah* with my feet propped up on the coffee table when I heard the purr of a lawn mower coming closer in the distance. Must be Brent, I thought and strained my neck to see out the blinds of the back door.

But to my horror, when the purring got close enough that it vibrated picture frames on the living room wall, I saw that it was Danielle, not Brent, who was mowing my lawn.

It was one thing to let my male neighbor take care of me while my husband was away, but even I couldn't accept letting a female neighbor do my chores while I sat on the couch sipping iced tea.

So what did I do? I ran and closed the blinds before Danielle saw me. Then I immediately cursed myself for being such a loser.

I hid away in the darkened room until the sound of the mower had stopped and I knew Danielle was done. But when I dared to creep back out and open the blinds, there Danielle stood at the door with grass-stained shoes and a pair of clippers in her right hand.

"Oh, I was just about to knock," she said when I reluctantly opened the door. I wrapped my arms around my waist, trying to hide my pajamas.

Danielle looked me up and down and said, "Are you sick, Sarah?"

"A little under the weather," I said, feigning a cough.

She pulled a white envelope out of her back pocket and handed it to me. "The postman accidentally put this in our mailbox the other day," she said.

I looked at the return address, which was a series of letters and numbers (FPO AE dash something or other) with no actual words.

"Is it from Dustin?" Danielle asked.

"Yes, I think so."

"Oh, that is just so sweet," Danielle said in a high-pitched voiced. "How romantic!"

How romantic? I stared at the envelope. "Mrs. Dustin Smiley" and the address were neatly typed and centered. Dustin always addressed letters to me that way, which, along with his habit of carrying a neatly folded handkerchief, often made him seem a bit uptight. Frankly, I thought "Mrs. Dustin Smiley" was a bit formal and cold, but to have it typed—on a stiff envelope, no less—was over the top!

I folded the envelope and shoved it in the pocket of my pajama pants.

"So do you need any help out there?" I said, peering over Danielle's shoulder and hoping she'd say no.

"Nope. I've got it covered," she said. "You just go and rest. Do you have some soup or anything for that cough?"

"Huh?" I said before remembering. Then I covered my mouth and coughed again. "Oh, no, I'll be fine. But thanks anyway."

Danielle went back to her gardening and I went back to the couch. Then about a half hour later, there was another knock.

"I thought you might need this," Danielle said when I opened the door, and she handed me a dark bottle of cough syrup.

The rest of the day was filled with joys like Ford drawing on the living room furniture with a highlighter, so I nearly forgot about the letter in my pocket until late that night, after the kids had already gone to bed. I opened the envelope slowly, almost afraid to look inside; then I settled into the pillows on our bed to read. But when I pulled the folded piece of paper out, I was surprised to see DEPARTMENT OF THE NAVY embossed at the top. This wasn't a letter from Dustin; it was from Margo's husband.

Dear Mrs. Dustin Smiley,

On behalf of the United States Navy I wish to inform you that your husband, Dustin, has been recognized for his superior performance during three at-sea rescues during this deployment.

We are proud to have your husband aboard, and would like to personally commend you on the positive influence you have made in Dustin's life and the support you have given him.

Sincerely,

The Commanding Officer

I bit my lip as I reread the words: the positive influence you have made in Dustin's life and the support you have given him.

Dustin had never given anything less than 100 percent at work. He was the go-to guy, Mr. Dependable. So I wasn't surprised that he was being honored in such a way. But I was shocked at the twinge of fear I felt.

All he knew how to do was rescue people, I thought, and I don't need to be saved.

So where does that leave us?

The following week, the Spouse Club had a garage sale on Lynette's driveway as a fund-raising event. Folding tables covered with plastic tablecloths and cotton bedsheets that snapped in the breeze littered her walkway and yard. They were loaded down with knickknacks and old books, and, frankly, lots of other junk.

We were making an impressive profit as word got out in the community that "soldiers' wives" were raising money on Thornton Street. Most of our customers left with items I wasn't sure they wanted, but they smiled with subtle sympathy and said, "God bless and protect your husbands."

Courtney fluttered through the throngs of people like Vanna White on too much caffeine: "Have you seen the beautiful set of goblets for sale on the table by the curb? And don't forget about the treadmill we have in the garage. It's a wonderful price!"

I hung toward the back and agreed to collect the shoppers' money so I could stay quietly wrapped up in my own thoughts— thoughts about Dr. Ashley and Dustin.

The weather was still mild, although getting hotter. I sat back in the chair at the folding table "checkout stand" and fanned myself while watching the other women help customers.

Spouse events weren't the same since Jody left. I missed her cynical comments and blatant disregard for the rules. Without her there, I even toyed with the idea of dropping out altogether. After all, I felt a little dishonest talking with the other women about our husbands and how much we missed them when my mind often drifted to . . . other things.

Margo was absent for most of the sale, and that caused some contention among the wives. How could the CO's wife just abandon us during the big fund-raiser? we all wondered. Well, the rest of them thought that, I guess, because I honestly didn't care. I felt flat, almost frozen. I was simply going through the motions.

But Margo arrived around noontime with an undeniable energy about her face and posture. She was nearly skipping up and down the driveway, checking in on the profits and patting everyone on the back.

"Something's up," I said to Courtney when she came by my table. But she just rolled her eyes and said, "You are so paranoid." Then we gossiped about Sasha, who was wearing a cropped top to show off her pierced navel again.

Finally, at one o'clock, when late-morning garage-sale shoppers had stopped trickling in, we started breaking down tables. Everyone was rushing to get home to their kids and pay babysitters. Danielle and Brent were watching mine.

Then Margo clapped her hands and said, "Gather round, ladies, gather round."

"Told you so," I said to Courtney. "Here it comes." I didn't know what "it" was, but I knew it was something big. Maybe Margo is pregnant, I thought. She had that glow about her, like she was keeping a secret.

We all gathered in a circle around her on the driveway, wiping our brows with rags and slapping at insects on our legs and arms. The Florida heat was on its way.

"Ladies," Margo said, "I have some very exciting news for everyone." She waved her hands as if she couldn't possibly contain herself. But we all just stared back at her, so she collected herself again and smoothed her denim skort with her hands.

"OK, well, first of all, the base has set up for us to do video teleconferences with the ship. Does everyone know what that means?"

I looked around the group. Some wives were nodding; others were shaking their heads and saying, "What's that?" to the wives beside them.

"In a few days," Margo said, "you will have the chance to go on base and talk to your spouse via satellite in a teleconference. It's like a phone call, only better, because you'll actually get to see him in real time."

Margo jumped up and clapped. "Isn't that absolutely wonderful?"

The group was slow to respond, like people who don't know how to act after a bad joke. "Oh, that *is* wonderful," a few of the women said. But I knew they were thinking, "Although not exciting enough to clap for." I could have sworn I heard Sasha say, "Oh, my gosh, what on earth will I wear?"

But Margo raised her voice and put up her hands. "Now wait a minute," she said. "There's more."

A few *shhs* scattered through the group, and Margo waited for everyone's attention. Then she said, "You're probably wondering why our husbands are able to do this since we are in the middle of a war. Which brings me to the best news of all—are you ready for this? Our men are coming home! Another U.S. carrier is on its way to the Gulf and will be relieving our husbands. They will be home in June."

The group exploded into shrieks and screams and hugs. Courtney and Kate cried and pressed white tissues to their noses. "Are you serious?" a few women asked. "This isn't a joke?"

"I wouldn't joke about something like this," Margo said. "They're coming home!" She jumped up and down again and all the women shrieked . . . again.

I just stood there at the back of the driveway. When Melanie noticed me, she came and put her arm around my shoulders. "Aren't you excited?" she squealed.

I slowly shook my head.

"Sarah, this is great news! Maybe you're just in shock."

"No," I said, still shaking my head and staring at the concrete. "I'm not in shock. I'm just not ready."

"Not ready? How could you not be ready?"

Her voice was getting loud and I didn't want to cause a scene, so I shh'ed her. She leaned in closer and said much softer, "I mean, sure, most of us would have liked to lose more weight and maybe get the house painted before they came home, but this is such a blessing, Sarah! We've been blessed!"

She was smiling at me and squeezing my shoulder. Her breath smelled like mint and her hands were so moisturized, they felt like wet clay on my bare arms.

I pulled away and squinted my eyes to look at her. "Damn you and all your 'blessings,' Melanie!"

A hush fell across the driveway as the other women stopped seemingly midjump and midshriek to look at me.

Melanie put a hand to her chest. "Sarah?"

"No, Melanie. This isn't a blessing. Maybe for you, but not for me."

"Oh, brother!" Sasha said. "Another day in the life of Sarah."

I ran across the yard to my car parked on the other curb. Courtney ran after me. "Sarah," she yelled. "Sarah, come back." But I jumped in the Explorer and drove away.

Brent was mowing my lawn when I got home. Ford and Blake played ball on the driveway, and Owen was sitting up in his playpen in the shade. He clapped his hands and cooed when he saw me get out of the car.

"Hey there!" Brent yelled and stopped the mower. "What's up?"

I couldn't hide the tearstains on my cheeks or the splotchy red marks that had popped up around my eyes.

"Hey, why the sad face, Smiley?" he said coming closer.

As soon as I opened my mouth, I started crying again. "The guys . . . are coming . . . home . . . next month . . . and—"

"Wow, that's great!" he said and stepped forward to hug me. Then he must have remembered his bare chest covered with sweat and grass clippings, because he stopped short, smiled instead, and said, "Wow!" again.

"I know, I know." I put my head in my hands. "And . . . and . . . and I should be excited . . . but . . . but . . . I'm not ready."

"Not ready? Girl, you've been ready since the day he left!"

I shook my head.

Then he must have realized I was serious, because his voice got quiet and he said, "Hey, I'm sure it's a big adjustment to have him come back, but maybe you'll feel better about everything once you get some rest and maybe have a nice cold beer."

"I don't think so." I looked out across the yard, at Ford and Blake kicking the ball back and forth. My sobbing slowed to sniffles and hiccups, but my muscles felt tense and I could feel a nervous energy in my arms and legs. I felt like I could run and never stop. I had to keep moving.

I turned back to Brent. "Hey, do you mind if I finish mowing the grass myself?"

He jerked his head back. "You? You mow the lawn?"

I nodded and smiled.

He put up his hands. "Hey, who am I to stand in the way of a woman and her lawn mower?"

That night I couldn't stop thinking about Dr. Ashley, and when I fell asleep, I dreamed I was at his house and it was covered with pictures of airplanes and aircraft carriers. There were waves beating on the windows outside and I screamed for him to save me. But he kept laughing, because, well, I was naked except for my tennis shoes. Then I was transported—in a magic, dreamlike way—to Kate's house, where the Spouse Club was in the middle of a meeting. Everyone except me had gotten mail from their husbands. I started to cry, and when I looked down, I was still naked . . . except for my tennis shoes.

I woke in a panic and sat up in bed. My hair was damp with sweat. I looked at the phone on the dresser beside me. The piano in the front room settled with the house and made an eerie creaking sound. I paused to listen. Then the house was quiet again, except for the ticking clock in the kitchen.

I pulled the covers up under my chin and lay back on the pillows, letting the loneliness and quiet wash over me until I was asleep.

15

THANK YOU FOR
CALLING ME MRS. SMILEY

Jody called on the day I was supposed to do the video teleconference with Dustin. She and her family were already settled into their home, but I couldn't picture her anywhere else except down the street. When I talked to her now, I still pictured her on the purple-and-green couch, sitting under the moose.

"So are you excited about the teleconference?" she asked.

I looked up at the kitchen clock. It was almost three o'clock in the afternoon; my teleconference was scheduled for three forty-five.

"I'm not going," I said and twisted a strand of hair at my temple.

"Not going? Sarah, why not? This is your last chance to talk to Dustin before he comes home. And you guys have so much you need to talk about."

"But I'm not ready," I said. "I can't think of what to say to him. It would be too awkward."

"Have you guys even talked since you got his letter?"

"No, we haven't." I sighed and tapped my fingers on the table.

"I don't know, Jody. I just feel different. I mean, I even mowed the lawn. Can you believe that?"

"Sure, I can believe it. And Dustin will, too."

"And I went running a few nights ago. I couldn't even remember the last time I went running, and then yesterday I—"

"You're changing. It's true," she said. "Every marriage does, eventually." Then she paused. "Is this about Dr. Ashley? Have you been talking to him lately?"

"No!" I said defiantly, failing to add that I was counting down the days to our appointment next week.

Jody's tone suddenly changed and became more serious. "I just want you to know something," she said. "When Steve came home, he told me that Dustin was a wreck the day you told him about Dr. Ashley. All the guys were really worried about him. They said he wasn't himself."

"Oh, that's ridiculous," I said. "Haven't you ever fought with your husband? That's all it was—an argument!" But inside I was thinking, Did I really have that effect on him? Is he capable of such emotion?

"You crushed him," Jody said. "And I think it's time you knew that. Sure, Dustin hasn't always been the most sensitive, but he loves you, and you hurt him. You hurt him bad."

"Why didn't you tell me all this before you left then?"

"Because I was hoping you'd figure it for yourself."

My other line beeped and I groaned. "That's my call-waiting, and I guess I should probably take it . . . just in case it's Dustin—" (Or Dr. Ashley, I thought to myself.)

"Just consider going to the video teleconference," Jody said. "And think about what I said."

"Yeah, yeah, yeah. Whatever."

I clicked over to the other line, and put on my friendliest and hopefully prettiest voice—just in case!—before saying hello.

"Sarah, it's Dad."

"Dad who?"

"Your dad."

I tried to mask my shock. Had Dad actually picked up the phone and used it? To call me?

"Oh, what's going on?" I said. "Where's Mom?"

"I have some bad news, Sarah," he said. "And I need to talk to you."

My knees gave out and I crumpled to the floor. In Dad's position he often got word of military-related accidents before they were released to the media, and I felt certain in that moment he was calling to tell me something about Dustin.

"What's happened, Dad? Is it bad?" I cried.

"I'm afraid it is, Sarah."

I went completely cold and put a hand to my chest. "Oh, God! Is it Dustin? Is he all right?"

"It's not about Dustin," Dad said. "Remember your friend John from high school?"

"John?"

"Yes, your mom said he sat behind you in Spanish, I think. And you sang together in drama class."

"John Tillman! Yeah, he was in Pensacola for flight school with us, too. Isn't he on deployment? What's happened to him?"

"He was involved in a midair collision this morning," Dad said gently. "You'll probably see it on the news soon, so I wanted to tell you first."

"What? But . . . but he's all right, isn't he, Dad?"

Dad cleared his throat. "They only found his helmet. He's presumed dead."

"But, Dad . . . not John! It couldn't be John. Are you sure? He was so young—" I could picture John's broad smile in my mind, and the way his personality instantly filled up a room. He was always so alive and young; how could he be dead?

"I'm sorry," Dad said. "I know how hard it is the first time it happens to someone you know."

Then I remembered that John had recently gotten married. I pictured his wife and knew she had woken up—probably in the middle of the night—to a knock at the door and men in uniform on her doorstep.

What is she doing now? I wondered. How will she go on? How will she get through this day?

Her husband is never coming home. Not ever.

My tongue seemed to catch in my throat and I nearly choked on the thought. Tears ran off my cheeks and disappeared into the cotton of my shirt.

"Oh, my gosh, Dad! I've gotta go. I have to go right now!"

"Sarah, I don't think you should drive," he said in a calm, steady voice.

"No, I have to," I yelled. "I've got to go, Dad. I'll explain later."

Ford and Owen were both asleep, so I ran outside, where Brent was mowing his grass. "Brent," I yelled. I was hopping on one foot, trying to tie my tennis shoe. "Brent!"

He looked up and released his hand from the mower. The blade wound down to a thumping whirl, and Brent walked over to the driveway.

"What's up?" he said. "What's going on?"

I could barely catch my breath, and one shoe was still untied. "Can you go inside and watch the boys? I've got to go to the base and see Dustin. We have this video teleconference, and I wasn't going to go, but my dad just called and—"

"Go!" he said, smiling. "I'm on my way inside right now." He walked up the sidewalk and waved over his shoulder.

I hopped into the Explorer and called out the window, "I'll finish your grass for you when I get back!"

It would take me thirty minutes to get to the base, and I'd be cutting it close, but if I hurried, I could make it in time to see Dustin.

Rows of pine trees flew past the window as I sped down the

highway. They were like a green blur out of the corner of my eye, but I hardly noticed. I was laughing and crying at the same time. In my mind, visions of our marriage spilled into my head like water filling a glass and splashing over. I thought about our military wedding and how my hands trembled during the vows, and how Dustin had squeezed them and smiled.

I thought about the night we rushed to the hospital when I was in labor with Ford, and how Dustin had laughed because I paced in front of the emergency room, waiting to be checked in, and the automatic sliding-glass doors kept opening and closing, and opening and closing.

I thought about the time I had the flu and Dustin went to the grocery store at midnight to get Popsicles.

I thought about how much Dustin loved Ford and Owen, and how Ford liked to call him "SuperDad."

There was no traffic coming into the base. Most of the cars were in the other lane, on their way out, as I pulled up to the guard shack in front. A man in camouflage and carrying a gun stepped forward, and I rolled down my window.

"Need to see some ID, ma'am," he said.

I riffled through my purse to find my wallet. My hands were shaking.

I handed him a laminated tan card with all my military information on it. He looked it over, checking my face against the picture, then handed it back and said, "Thanks, Mrs. Smiley."

Mrs. Smiley? I repeated it to myself. Mrs. Smiley?

I started to roll up the window, but the man put out his hand for me to stop. "Uh, is everything OK, ma'am?" he said. "You look a little upset."

"Thanks for calling me Mrs. Smiley," I said and drove away.

The parking lot of building number eight was full, so I parked alongside the curb and barely remembered to put the engine in park before jumping out the door.

It was three forty-eight.

I ran up the sidewalk that was discolored and cracking, and pushed through the glass doors of the cinder block building. There was an officer on duty at the front desk.

"I'm here . . . for a video teleconference . . . with . . . my husband," I said, out of breath.

"That way," the officer said, and pointed to the left. "Up the elevator, to the third floor, room number twenty-two."

I started running again. There was an elevator across the hall and a group was just then piling into it. "Wait!" I yelled. "Hold the door!"

I ran into the crowded elevator, still trying to catch my breath. Tears spilled over my cheeks, and the front of my shirt was damp from crying and from sweat.

When the doors slid open on the third floor, I slipped through other passengers, saying, "Excuse me, excuse me," and ran out into the hallway.

A group of sailors dressed in white bell-bottom pants was standing outside a door down the hall, so I ran in their direction, yelling, "Wait! I'm here! I'm here! Tell my husband I'm here for the conference."

One shoelace was still untied and it smacked against the floor and my shin as I ran. When I finally reached the group, I was panting and had to grab the wall.

"I'm here," I said again between breaths. "I'm here."

The men looked at one another, and then one of them, a tall, red-haired man with long arms and a boyish face, looked at me and bit his lip.

"Mrs. Smiley?" he said.

"Yes! That's me! Dustin's wife. We had a conference at three forty-five. But I'm running late and I had to rush to get here, and I'm—"

The man bit his lip again. The other men looked away or at

their feet. "I'm so sorry, ma'am," the sailor said. "You've missed it. Mr. Smiley waited until three fifty, but then we had to let the next couple go. They're real strict about keeping the schedule."

I stared at him. He was shrugging his shoulders and looking at me in a fearful sort of way.

"I missed it?" I said.

"I'm so sorry," he said again. "We have to stay on schedule, and the guys in charge tell us we can't wait for anyone."

I put my hands on either side of my head. "I missed it?"

Then I fell to my knees and cried. The sailor knelt down beside me and patted my back. "Do you need anything, ma'am? A glass of water? Some fresh air?"

"Just tell me," I said, "have they already shut down the e-mail and telephones on board?"

"I'm afraid so, ma'am. But hey, homecoming isn't that far away. It's going to be OK. You'll see Mr. Smiley again soon."

I drove home in silence. There were no more tears, or music, or memories. I was hollow and tired. My throat was coated and sore from crying. I imagined Dustin's face as I drove, and for the first time in months, it came to me as clearly as a picture. He was smiling, and then crying. I had never seen Dustin cry.

I stopped for a red light on Ninth Street, and was glad for the chance to stare out the window. My eyes were frozen in a trance, looking at the street sign—NINTH STREET—when suddenly I said to myself, "Ninth Street? Isn't that where Melanie's church is?" It was Wednesday. Melanie always went to church on Wednesday evenings.

Without thinking again, I flipped on the blinker and turned right.

Ninth Street was covered with a canopy of thick oak trees full of shade and leaves. The road looked cool and I was glad: The weather had been so hot, and it would only get worse.

I pulled into the rock-and-gravel parking lot of Saint Luke's

Church, and looked for Melanie's car. She was parked right up front—just where I'd expect her to be.

The church, which was all brick except for a white steeple with a cross at the top, seemed small on the outside, but the inside was cavernous. Or maybe it was just the tall ceilings and cool air that made it feel big. The air was damp and smelled like dark wood and old books. I walked across the thick red carpet and opened the heavy wood doors of the sanctuary. A couple dozen people sat with their heads bowed in red cushioned pews. The organ played "In the Garden," and the notes seemed to vibrate through the thick wood-paneled walls and stained glass.

I saw Melanie halfway up the center aisle. She had on a navy blue dress with a boatneck. Her silver necklace sparkled under the lights and I smiled. It was so like her: subtle blue dress and shiny silver jewelry.

I walked down the aisle and slid into the pew beside her. She looked up and raised her eyebrows with surprise, but then she smiled and grabbed my hand. I laid my head on her shoulder and cried.

After the service, Melanie and I stood on the front steps of the church. The weather was perfect. The sun was setting, and I could almost imagine the smell of hamburgers and corn cooking on a grill. Melanie's honeysuckle perfume floated with the wind and crickets chirped from the bushes beside us.

Melanie was radiant. I knew she wasn't wearing makeup, but her face was flushed and healthy, and though she wasn't exactly smiling, the crow's-feet coming from the corners of her eyes revealed some inner happiness.

She never asked why I had come, and she never asked why I was crying. So I didn't try to explain, because it would take too long, and maybe I didn't want Melanie to think badly of me.

But after a few minutes of talking about the comfortable weather, Melanie suddenly took my hand and said, "I want to tell you something, Sarah."

"OK. Is it good or bad?" I didn't think I could handle more bad news.

She smiled playfully. "Oh, it's good . . . very good!" Then she took a deep breath and said, "I'm pregnant . . . from my trip to France."

I covered my open mouth and screamed; then I jumped up and down, shaking her hand. "Oh! My! God—I mean, gosh!—Melanie!"

"I know, I know," she said. "I waited to say anything until I knew for sure. Because of the miscarriages and everything."

"Oh, of course," I said. "This is just so exciting, and so amazing! I just can't believe it!"

"I know," she said again, looking upward at the blue twilight. "It is amazing—almost like a miracle."

I felt a pain in my chest remembering the way I had yelled at her on Lynette's driveway. So I looked up at the twilight with her and said, "And it's also a blessing."

She looked at me and smiled. "Yes, exactly: a blessing."

16

THIS IS IT, LADIES

My knees shook as I sat in the cold exam room, waiting for Dr.
Ashley to come in. I had decided not to bring Owen, despite it being "his" appointment, because I didn't want his well-baby
checkup muddied by the soap opera that had become my life. This is
probably the reason doctors aren't supposed to be involved with their
patients: It's hard to talk about leaking breasts and bowel movements
when you can't stop looking at the doctor's biceps. Obviously, Dr.
Ashley and I had other things to discuss besides my infant son's
health, so I would reschedule his appointment for another day.

Dr. Ashley knocked on the door. "Hello?" he said, and peered
around the corner. He came into the room without his usual rush
of air and excitement. He almost seemed—could it be?—unsure
of himself. His shoulders were more stooped and rounded than I
had remembered, and he was smiling, but it seemed awkward.
When he sat down, it was like he didn't know where to look; his
eyes darted around my face and above my head, but when our
gazes finally locked, he quickly looked away and flipped through
some papers in Owen's chart.

"So you decided not to bring Owen," he said.

I scratched at my head, even though it didn't itch, and looked at the ground. "Yeah, it just seemed like you and I have other things to talk about, and I didn't want his appointment to lose focus."

"I understand," he said and put Owen's medical records aside.

"So I feel a little weird after that phone call," I said.

"Don't be embarrassed. I'm glad you told me what you were feeling. So have you decided—I mean, have you thought any more about, ah, what you want to do?"

"What are my options, Dr. Ash—or David or whatever? What am I supposed to do? You're the doctor. You tell me: Is this normal?"

"Well, 'normal' is such a broad term," he said. "Obviously your feelings are natural and you've been very honest about them. Much more honest than others might have been." He stopped and cleared his throat. "But in regards to your care, I can't be your doctor if there is something . . . um . . . romantic. . . ."

He looked at me and paused. I wondered if he wanted me to talk next, but I wasn't ready. So he rubbed at the back of his neck and said, "Now I can keep things professional, but you need to be comfortable with me as your doctor."

His voice was warm and smooth, and he was looking at me with that same thoughtful frown. I couldn't look at his eyes because I knew they would be deep and blue and concerned, and that they would suck me into that state of adrenaline and nerves. I could only look at his white coat and try to believe he was "just another doctor."

But I could feel his eyes nearly burning a hole in my face. Could he really keep things "professional"? I wondered. How could he do that? Could he just move on and pretend nothing had happened? Maybe he doesn't like me as much as I thought. Maybe it's all been in my head. The mere idea made me sick with disappointment. And all at once, I felt hurt and rejected by him.

But wait. I'm married and he's my doctor and—

I moaned aloud—"Arghh!"—and banged my fists on my knees. Then I stood up and paced across the room.

"Yes, I have feelings for you," I said. "And I don't know if I can just ignore them and keep things 'professional.' "

I was pulling at my hair and I felt like I was walking on sand.

"Because here's the thing, David: I know, without a doubt, if I had met you ten years ago, I would have fallen in love with you. I knew it the first time we met. We had 'chemistry'—whatever that is—and I could feel it like electricity right through this room."

Dr. Ashley stood up. "I know, Sarah. We've had a great relationship, and I probably enjoy you more than any other patient."

Tears came down my cheeks. "When I met you, you blew a hole right through my theory of there being 'one person for everyone.' I used to think Dustin and I were destined to be together, that fate had brought us into each other's lives. I never even questioned it! And then I met you, and I felt these things, like I had known you all my life—and suddenly I realized there is more than one person for me. There are probably hundreds of people I could have married. There are probably hundreds of men I could have felt this chemistry with."

"I know what you mean," he said. "Feelings can be so hard to understand."

I stopped pacing and looked him in the eyes. "There are hundreds of men I could have had this chemistry with, but I chose only one."

He nodded and looked at the ground.

"I probably could have loved you," I said. "These feelings are probably reciprocal. Although I'll never know because you can't say."

He nodded again.

"And maybe I'm making a big mistake here, but I need to give what Dustin and I have a shot. I need to give him a chance . . . because he was the first one I felt these things for."

I looked up at his gold-rimmed glasses and knew I was seeing them for the last time. He wasn't smiling.

"So what I'm saying is, I think I need to change doctors."

"I understand," he said, and then, "I'll give you a referral for whomever you'd like."

I gathered my purse off the blue plastic chair and put it on my shoulder. "Thank you. I'd appreciate that. And you know how I am, so pick someone patient and incredibly ugly, why don't you?"

He laughed and smiled, tilting his head to the side to look at me. Then he reached out his hand and I shook it. When I let go, he held on.

"Good-bye, Sarah Smiley," he said.

I smiled through tears and nodded, and walked out the door.

It was warm and muggy on the day of homecoming, and that meant disaster for my hair. I would need a good two hours to get ready and sufficiently goop up my hair so that it wouldn't fall flat before Dustin got off the plane. Danielle and Brent offered to watch the boys while I took a bath, shaved my legs, and basically enjoyed every minute of getting ready to see Dustin again.

I had decided to wear a gray skirt and red V-neck wrap shirt, with Dustin's favorite black beaded necklace, which fell to a point on my chest. He always liked to say the necklace "points to fun," and I knew he'd smile and laugh—in a knowing sort of way—when he saw me wearing it.

I was surprised when I looked in the mirror and saw my body for what felt like the first time in months. It was almost like seeing myself—my body—again, only I was rediscovering a "new" me somehow.

I walked outside to collect the boys from Brent's driveway. Ford and Blake were making a very serious attempt to get Owen to crawl on an exercise mat, but he just lay on his belly and cooed.

And I was glad he would wait for Dustin before changing and growing any more.

Brent and Danielle clapped and whistled when they saw me walking up the driveway. "Hot momma," Brent called out, and I felt a little like a high schooler on her way to the prom.

Their attention embarrassed me a little, but what the heck? I stood erect anyway and did a curtsy before smiling and saying, "I certainly feel hot today!"

Brent came over and leaned on my shoulder. "So do you think we could ask you to babysit Blake tonight? You know, since I took care of your lawn all these months and helped you with—"

I shoved him teasingly off my shoulder. "No way in hell!"

He laughed as he spun around from my push.

"No, really," Danielle said. "If you want us to watch the boys tonight while y'all . . . um . . . celebrate . . . just let us know."

I bent down to pick up Owen off the mat. "Thanks, guys. Thanks for everything."

Brent helped me load the boys in the car, and then he patted the hood with his palm. "Good luck," he said.

At the air terminal, I could see that Courtney and Kate and the other women on the homecoming committee had been busy decorating. There were balloons and streamers and red, white, and blue bunting hanging from anything that would sit still long enough for them to slap some tape on it. Large homemade banners hung from the ceiling with things like WELCOME HOME and WE MISSED YOU DADDY painted on them. Confetti was scattered across the floor and chairs, and although there was no music playing, there was a definite buzz in the room as women squealed with delight and excitement. Kids dressed in their finest Sunday clothes darted in between their mothers' legs, chasing other children.

"Looking good," Courtney said when she saw me come in with Owen on my hip and Ford at my side. She knelt down next to

Ford and fixed the collar of his red, white, and blue striped shirt, which was crinkled from the car seat strap. "Aren't you spiffy, little man!" she said. "Excited to see your dad?"

Ford nodded and twisted his fingers.

Courtney was wearing thigh-high boots with a sparkly tank top, and when she stood up again, she looked a good three to four inches taller than me.

"Wow, look at you!" I said. "You look fantastic."

She did a 360-degree turn to model her clothes, and then held out one arm to give me a hug. "Gosh, I wish Jody was here, don't you?" she whispered.

I patted her back and said, "I know. It just doesn't feel the same."

When she stood back away from me again, her eyes were puffy and red.

"Well, now, don't cry," I said. "You'll ruin your makeup!"

Kate, who was standing at the center of the room dressed in an empire-waist sheath dress, clapped her hands and then whistled to get everyone's attention. "Five-minute warning," she yelled. "The plane has landed on the runway and they are taxiing it around right now!"

The women and children in the room shouted together and turned to hug whoever was standing next to them.

"They're here! They're really here," Courtney said, jumping up and down. Then she grabbed my hand. "Come on, let's go out on the tarmac to watch the plane pull up."

"Wait. Where's Melanie?" I said. "And Hannah?"

"Paul flew in on one of the helicopters early this morning," Courtney said. "They should already be back home together now."

Often wives feel jealous of the other wives whose husbands get to fly in. Although our husbands are all pilots, only so many can fit in the helicopter at a time, so some have to ride the ship into port and then fly home in a transport jet instead. Coming in on the "jet" is considered a tad less romantic than the noisy and dramatic helicopters flying in formation and kicking up gusts of wind, but I couldn't be jealous of Melanie.

Courtney took Ford's pudgy hand and offered to help lead him out to the tarmac while I followed behind, struggling to walk in high heels with Owen in my arms. Groupings of families spilled out onto the black asphalt beyond the glass doors, and lined up behind yellow tape set up to keep us from getting too close to the runway.

The sun was hot as it beat down on the tops of our heads, and my hair had probably already turned flat, but I hardly noticed. We all had permanent smiles plastered on our faces, and we jumped up and down with chattering teeth, as if it were freezing outside. I guess we were just nervous.

Margo stood outside the door and handed each of us minia-ture American flags on wooden sticks. When we heard the faintest sound of a whistling jet coming closer, yet still too far away and behind a building for us to see, we all shouted and waved the flags until they whipped in the air and became a blur of red, white, and blue.

When we finally saw the nose of the giant gray jet taxiing around the corner, all hell broke loose. Women pushed at the yel-low caution tape, dying to get even an inch closer to the ap-proaching jet, and children squealed with delight and excitement. Some babies cried from the noise of the screeching jet engine, but most of them—including Owen—were simply stunned by all the commotion.

News reporters with bulky cameras and equipment ran among the crowd trying to get the perfect picture. "How are you feeling?" some of them asked. "What's the first thing you'll say to your hus-band?" But as the jet drew even closer and grew louder, all we could think was: Get your camera out of my face and give me room to see my husband! Most of the reporters were happy to oblige.

The whistle of the jet engine pierced my ears and I tried to cover Owen's with one hand. But he squirmed and dodged, too curious to care. His dark, round eyes seemed to grow between each long, deliberate blink as he took in the sights and sounds of the crowd. I bounced him on my hip and sang, "Daddy's here! Daddy's here!" He just stared at me, his mouth set open in a perfect O.

The tips of the jet's wings looked like they would clip the metal siding of the hangars on its right as it rumbled down the asphalt toward us. Soon, the whistle was all we could hear, and although Courtney tried to talk—or yell—in my direction, I only saw her lips move.

The jet rolled past the yellow tape, and everyone jumped and screamed to have it seemingly within arm's reach. Then the plane stopped and the whistling slowly wound down, but the wives were still screaming, and some were even crying.

Margo was off to the side, being interviewed by the news reporters, but when she saw the steps of the plane fold down and the first set of boots appear in the doorway, she ran to the yellow tape and said, "This is it, ladies!"

We jumped and screamed again.

One by one, men filed out of the airplane in their flight suits and heavy black boots, with bags slung across their backs. Leslie, the first to spot her husband, broke the yellow tape in front of her and ran onto the tarmac. Carrying their newborn baby, she ran and skipped toward her husband until finally they met and the baby's smooth white head disappeared in their embrace.

Sasha ran to her husband and leaped into his arms, making a big show of wrapping her legs around him. Courtney and I rolled our eyes at each other as he carried her that way toward the crowd.

Poor Margo had a throng of news reporters following as she went to hug her husband, and I knew Sasha was probably mad they hadn't filmed her instead.

The tarmac was by now covered with families hugging and kissing and twirling one another around.

Courtney spotted Derek and ran into the crowd toward the plane. I laughed as I watched her teeter in her high-heeled boots and try to keep her skirt from flying up.

I peered at the plane's door, looking for Dustin. More men in uniform came down the steps and met their families, and one by one, the clustered groups of husbands and wives and children were making their way back into the terminal, where a reception was waiting for us.

Courtney and Derek walked toward me, their arms wrapped around each other.

"Hey, Sarah," Derek said; then he looked back at the plane like he, too, was looking for Dustin. "Dustin should be coming out soon," he said. "He was kind of toward the back."

"Do you want us to wait?" Courtney asked.

"No, you guys go in and enjoy yourselves," I said. "He'll be here soon."

Courtney winked and gave me a thumbs-up as they walked away toward the building.

There were only a half dozen families on the tarmac now, and it was beginning to look like an "old party" with stepped-on banners and signs lying on the ground.

No more men were coming out of the plane, and my stomach began to sink. Margo and her husband walked past me, on their way inside. "Welcome home," I said and smiled, but a knot of emotion was rising in my throat, and I had to look away because I thought I might cry.

The pilot of the plane came out and mechanics drove their carts underneath the wings to begin inspecting. I looked around the empty tarmac and squeezed Ford's hand. "He'll be here soon," I said. "I know he will."

I was so dumb to have thought everything would magically be

OK. I had worked out my issues with the doctor, but had Dustin worked out his issues with me?

I looked back at the airplane and saw a figure in green coming down the steps and looking at the ground. I could tell by his walk, and by the way he hung his head slightly to the left, that it was Dustin. My breath caught in my chest.

"There's Daddy," I said to Ford.

"Where, Mommy?" he yelled. "Where?"

I pointed toward the plane and at Dustin gathering up his bags from the cement.

"Daddy!" Ford shouted and ran past the yellow tape.

Dustin looked up and saw Ford running toward him. He dropped his seabag on the asphalt and got down on his knees to catch Ford in his arms. Then he stood up and spun Ford around.

Owen cooed and clapped his hands.

"That's your daddy," I said. "There he is."

Dustin set Ford to stand on the ground again, and Ford was jumping and clapping with excitement. I watched with eyes full of tears. Then Dustin looked up and saw me there. He waved and smiled.

I started to walk forward, and so did Dustin. Then I started running, and he did, too. I was laughing and crying and trying to catch my breath, until finally we met, and Dustin wrapped his arms around Owen and me and buried his face in my shoulder.

"I didn't think you would come," he said.

"But I'm so glad I did," I cried. "I'm so glad I did."

He pulled back and put his hands on the sides of my face. We stood on the tarmac kissing while Ford skipped in circles around us.

Dustin laughed and squeezed me again. "I didn't think you would come! I didn't think you would come!" he said again and again.

"I'm so glad I did. I'm so glad I did."

And we clung to each other and cried like children.

Only neither of us was really a child anymore.

ACKNOWLEDGMENTS

Someone once told me, when you're having a baby, never invite anyone to your house who cannot (or will not) cook, fold laundry, or say that you look thin.

It's also been said that the process of writing is similar to giving birth. But whoever said that must have been a man.

In any case, I gratefully acknowledge the following people who made this "baby" possible. You are welcome to cook, fold laundry, and tell me I look thin anytime.

To my agent, Rick Broadhead, thank you for your patience, for sharing my excitement, and for always having the best way to give good news.

Thank you, Tracy Bernstein, my editor, for laughing at the perfect time, providing indispensable insights, and, ultimately, having patience (is that becoming a theme?).

To Miriam Gallet (JaxAirNews), Lesley Conn and Bob Bryan (*Pensacola News Journal*), and James McCarthy (*The Times Record*): You were my first very, um, *patient* editors. Thank you always for the opportunities you've given to me.

ACKNOWLEDGMENTS

Cheers to Darcy and Kristi—there is no story without you—and Sally, without whom there was no faith.

A big, grateful thumbs-up to my mom and dad, who always allowed me to make movies, write books, and pursue other lofty childhood aspirations, even if it meant making a mess of the living room or pulling out all the soup cans in the kitchen. I love you guys.

To Dustin—can we say "good sport"?—I cannot repay you for all the support and extra helping hands as I wrote this book, but I hope to make a start by doing my share now. Thank you for understanding and for allowing me to tell this story.

I also owe so much to the people of Saint Luke United Methodist Church, Leslie Thornton Stephens, Amy Spore Kalten, Justina Manero, Jennifer Richardson, Kelly Diamond (thank you for always asking to read more), and my brothers, Van and Will.

Last, to Ford and Owen: You may be in the background of this story, but you are the forefront of my life. Everything I've done has been for you.

ABOUT THE AUTHOR

Photo by Brad Walters

"A witty observer of her life and times!"
—*The Times-Record* (Brunswick, ME)

"An endless supply of funny stories."
—*Pensacola News Journal*

SARAH SMILEY is the author of "Shore Duty," a syndicated newspaper column that reaches more than two million weekly. She has been featured in *The New York Times* and *Newsweek,* and on ABC's *Nightline,* CNN, and MSNBC.

Sarah's life rights were optioned by Kelsey Grammer's company, Grammnet, and Paramount Television. A half hour sitcom based on her book and columns is now in development for CBS.

Besides "Shore Duty," Sarah's work has appeared in various

ABOUT THE AUTHOR

books, including two *Chicken Soup for the Soul* editions, and magazines (*USAA, U.25, Military Spouse* and *Military Money*).

Sarah is the daughter of Rear Admiral Lindell Rutherford (USN, Ret.). She has been a military dependent, in one way or another, for thirty years.

Find out more at www.SarahSmiley.com.

GOING
OVERBARD

*the misadventures of a
military wife*

Sarah Smiley

A CONVERSATION WITH SARAH SMILEY

Q. *What is your writing routine?*

A. My day begins like most people who are only creative at night, with my five-year-old son, Ford, standing next to my bed, saying, "Mommy, if you don't get up now I'll be late for school." I consider insomnia a hazard of my profession, and the fact that, besides being a columnist and author, I'm also a wife and mother of two doesn't help. I do my best writing after ten o'clock at night when the kids are finally asleep and the dog is lying at my feet. I've tried writing in the morning, but it's never very good. My brain simply doesn't start working until after dinner. So, in the meantime, while I'm driving the kids to school or shopping at the store, I generally have to scribble notes and ideas that pop into my head in a small notebook I keep in my purse.

Q. *What was the biggest difference between writing a weekly column and writing a book?*

A. For "Shore Duty," my weekly newspaper column, I'm only allowed eight hundred words, so I have to develop an idea fast, get to the point, and then finish with a clever ending all before

I hit the second page. I had a lot of fun with *Going Overboard* because I was able to go off on tangents and tell the story at my leisure. Column writing and book writing are definitely very different and I have to get into a different frame of mind for each. I usually think about my book ideas while I'm driving, and I think about columns in the shower. I don't know why this is, except that I feel more thoughtful and insightful in the car, and usually when I'm in the shower, there are two little boys banging on the door, screaming, "Are you done yet?" Basically, that's what keeps my columns so brief and wry.

Q. How difficult was it to juggle two kids and a husband while you wrote your book? Was Dustin home and able to help while you worked?

A. [Laughing] While I was writing *Going Overboard,* Dustin actually preferred being at work because revisiting that time in our lives brought up a lot of old memories, and generally I walked around being mad at him all the time. But he couldn't stay away forever, and when he was home, he was great about doing the kids' bath and dinner and bedtime routine so that I could concentrate on writing. While he's on deployment, I have to take on the role of "Dad," so it seems only fair that he became "Mom" now and then while I was writing my book.

Q. Was there any fallout—from your family or from the military—from the publication of Going Overboard?

A. My mom cried for two weeks after she read the book, mostly because of the doctor thing. Later, however, she confessed to having a crush on Benjamin Netanyahu while my dad was serving in the Gulf War, which is obviously a lot different from having a crush on someone you actually know and see . . . while you're naked! But telling me that was Mom's way of meeting me halfway and trying to understand my point of view. To me, it illustrates the notion that military wives of her generation and mine aren't really that different, except that they didn't talk about their problems and we are just beginning to.

My mother-in-law was a little hurt by my portrayal of her, especially the pecan pie story, but admitted that she read that part of the book while baking for a potluck meal she was invited to. She couldn't decide which "covered dish" to make, so she made three, and it was then that she realized I had pegged her pretty well in the book.

I'm sure the publication of my book and the ensuing publicity showed up as a blip on the military's "radar," but so far I haven't heard from them.

Q. *What's been the response from readers?*

A. Civilians in particular have written to say they enjoyed *Going Overboard* because my story gives them a glimpse into the lives of military families. But also, I think the things I went through in the book are universal to many marriages and friendships, not just military ones. The fact that *Going Overboard* takes place within the context of the military, which is an unfamiliar world to most, just gives the book an interesting backdrop, I suppose.

Q. *What was the most surprising part about publishing your first book?*

A. When Kelsey Grammer's company, Grammet, and Paramount Television bought the rights to *Going Overboard*, it was definitely an unexpected thrill. I was eating at Chick-fil-A with the kids when my agent called to tell me the news. "Do you have a bottle of French champagne ready?" he asked, and I said, "Well, I'm eating french fries, if that counts." Luckily, the boys and their world keep me grounded.

Q. *Which authors do you most enjoy or admire?*

A. My two favorite books of all time are Elie Wiesel's *Night* and Anne Tyler's *The Amateur Marriage*. Those are two very different books, I know, but I tend to go back and forth between genres. *Night* is so vivid and honest, I have never been able to forget it. It's the book that really piqued my interest in reading. My high school English teacher made us read it, and I was hooked. After a lifetime of avoiding school reading assignments, suddenly I was obsessed with reading.

Anne Tyler is one of my favorite contemporary writers, and *The Amateur Marriage* still makes me cry. I'll be walking through Wal-Mart and, bam, suddenly I'm crying about that book again. I love that Tyler's books are never really about anything except relationships.

Q. *Where is Dustin now? Will he stay in the military?*

A. Amazingly, Dustin is still here and we're still married. Right now he trains new pilots for the Navy. As a military family, however, we never can see much further than our current assignment. We try not to guess what will happen next or where we'll go. "Future plans" are abstract in the military.

Q. *What's next for you as a writer?*

A. I continue to pick up more newspapers to run my column, which I still enjoy writing on a weekly basis. Someday I'd like to publish a collection of all my columns. I'm also working on a new book. I'm going with fiction this time . . . so Mom doesn't have to cry again. Well, at least she won't be crying for *me*.

QUESTIONS FOR DISCUSSION

1. Do you think the Smileys' relationship is typical or atypical of a marriage? How is it the same or different from your own marriage?

2. In *Going Overboard,* Sarah reveals both positive and negative aspects of life in the military. Which of these surprised you the most?

3. In the book, we only get a glimpse of the Smileys' marriage as told by Sarah. How do you think the story might be different from Dustin's point of view?

4. It seems as though Sarah married young and found herself later, causing her to make certain changes in her relationships. What personal changes have affected your own relationships? Were they positive or negative changes?

5. How did Dustin's and Sarah's upbringings affect their marriage? How has your own upbringing affected your present-day relationships?

6. Is there a moral difference between an "emotional affair" and a physical one? Do you think Sarah actually had an emotional affair or just a fantasy? Was it all in her head or did the doctor "cross the line"?

7. Do you think military marriages are more susceptible to extramarital affairs then civilian ones? Why or why not?

8. Why do you think Sarah was drawn to the doctor in particular? How are he and Dustin alike and different?

9. Would this story be different if Dustin were not in the military? How so?

10. On page 177, Sarah asks, "Oh, so just because my husband is serving our country I'm supposed to excuse him for any bad behavior?" and "So why does everyone expect me to suddenly deem everything else in my life null and void just because my husband is in a war?" Do you think Sarah is right to feel this way? Should certain persons be given leeway in their behavior if they are considered heroic?

11. In the end, who do you think has changed the most, Dustin or Sarah?